CAROLI

The Piedmont

Erica Lineberry

Carolina Rocks: The Piedmont

Erica Lineberry

© 2015 Erica Lineberry

ISBN - 978-0-9915802-2-4

PUBLISHED BY:

Earthbound Sports, Inc.

Post Office Box 3312

Chapel Hill, NC 27515-3312

Printed and published in the United States of America

ABOUT THE AUTHOR:

Though life's adventures have taken her far and wide, Erica Lineberry has lived in NC (and specifically the Piedmont) all her life, making her uniquely suited to write this book. Like so many NC climbers, Erica's first forays onto real rock came from the areas featured in this book—first slinging topropes at Pilot, then following and eventually leading at Moore's and Stone. Crowders became her home crag in 2011 after a move to Charlotte. Although this is Erica's first book, she has been writing for years, most notably on her blog, Cragmama.com, which is a resource for families seeking to continue an active, outdoorsy lifestyle with kids in tow. Speaking of kids, Erica and her husband Steve have two—4 year old Canaan, and almost 1 year old Zoe. Both have already logged enough days at the crag and nights sleeping on the ground to be considered dirtbags in their own right. When she's not climbing (or writing about climbing), Erica can usually still be found outside somewhere with her family—whether it's hiking, mountain biking, or just stretched out in a hammock in the yard.

ABOUT THE BOOK'S DESIGNER:

During the development of this book, Garrett Davis worked as a Transportation Planner at the Town of Chapel Hill. This was the first book he ever worked on. Now he attends law school at UNC Chapel Hill. Like many potential users of this book, Davis enjoys nature, rocks and vertically exaggerated terrain features. However, instead of climbing up sheer rock faces with ropes attached, he opts for climbing up fireroads in Pisgah National Forest and "shredding" down technical singletrack on his YETI 575 mountain bike.

ACKNOWLEDGEMENTS

This project would never have gotten off the ground were it not for the help of numerous individuals. I would like to acknowledge the friends and family who helped keep this project afloat, many of whom went above and beyond the call of duty. Many were instrumental in providing detailed historical as well as anecdotal information about routes and development in each area. Several could be counted upon for invaluable personal help – both with research logistics as well as well-timed encouraging words. And there are a host of others who stepped forward to share their own stories and perspectives. A big thank you to each and every one of you!!!

Sean Barb, Chris Barlow, John Black, Sean Cobourn, Garrett Davis, Alison Domnas, Manuela Eilert, Tim Fisher, Rob Fogle, Scott Gilliam, Stephanie Gilliam, Gus Glitch, Mike Grimm, Bennett Harris, Porter Jarrard, Diane Joseph, Joe and Beth Lineberry, Steve Lineberry, Anthony Love, Wes Love, Tony McGee, Edward Medina, Gary Mims, Johnny O'Connell, Frank Orthel, Steve Orthel, Matt Paden, Brian Payst, Mark Pell, Paul "Thor" Pelot, John Provetero, Diab Rabie, Eduardo Ramirez, Lloyd Ramsey, Jae Sun Rhee, Bob Rotert, Sam and April Stephens, Bubba and Kathy Southern, Seth Tart, Bill Webster, Matt Westlake, Sarah Wolfe

If your name is not here and it should be, please know it was an unintentional oversight. Next time we cross paths I'll be happy to buy you a drink and let you give me a hard time.

SAFETY

There are many words that can be tossed around to describe the sport of rock climbing but "safe" is not one of them. Proper use of equipment and good judgment can mitigate, but not eliminate, the inherent risks involved. The bottom line is that rock climbing is a dangerous sport that can result in serious injury, paralysis, or even death.

This book is designed to be used as a reference for experienced climbers, not an instruction manual for beginners. For beginners wishing to learn how to climb safely, it is strongly recommended to employ the services of a professional guiding service.

Due to ever-changing natural and environmental factors, the author and publisher cannot guarantee the accuracy of the information listed in the book. Pitons and other gear mentioned in this guide may be gone on the day you decided to climb, and rock fall can change the difficulty of routes. The assessment of the difficulty level and associated risks of documented routes and trails found in this guide are based on a subjective consensus of opinions, and should never replace your own common sense. Seldom climbed routes tend to lack ratings developed through a consensus process. Do not climb above your ability, and always use good judgment.

DEDICATION

This book is dedicated to my favorite partners in climb as well as in life, Steve and Canaan Lineberry. Steve you are the best, and Canaan you are my sunshine!

INTRO

INTRODUCTION

The Piedmont Region of North Carolina could be summed up rather nicely in one word: central. Not only is it located geographically in the center of the state, but its landscape provides a key backdrop of adventure for hundreds of thousands of city-dwelling professionals looking to find a haven far away from the hustle and bustle of the work week. Though not nearly as mountainous as the western part of the state, what the Piedmont Region lacks in quantity is made up for in both quality and convenience. Both Moore's Wall and Stone Mountain offer world-class climbing that is as good as, if not better than, their counterparts on the west coast. Crowders Mountain and Pilot Mountain are ideal for both beginners and experienced climbers, many of whom flock to these cliffs on the weekends from the surrounding urban areas. The popularity of these cliffs are enhanced because they are both located within two hours from three of the biggest population centers in the state (Charlotte, the Triangle, and the Triad).

This guidebook is certainly not the first to document the climbing to be found at Pilot, Moore's, Crowders, and Stone, and it probably won't be the last. Routes have been documented in these areas as early as the 1960's, with an underground Moore's guide by Chapel Hill climbers George DeWolfe and Hugh Owens. In 1973 Art Williams wrote *A Climber's Guide to the Carolinas*, and in 1977 Buddy Price wrote the *Carolina Climbers Guide*. In 1983 Bill Webster wrote a small pocket guide to Stone Mountain titled *Dixie Crystals* under the pen name of Roid Waddle, and in 1981 Chris Hall included all Piedmont areas, except for Pilot, in *Southern Rock*. Most of Pilot Mountain's early history was passed on through oral tradition (which is why so much of it remains largely unknown now…). Nothing was officially published until the crag was included, along with the rest of the Piedmont, in Thomas Kelley's: *The Climber's Guide to North Carolina* which came out in 1988. In 2002 Yon Lambert and Harrison Shull took a different approach with *Selected Climbs in North Carolina*. This guide excluded many areas in exchange for providing more detailed information on certain popular cliffs. With the dawning of the technology age, even more route information is available from online climbing websites such as Mountain Project and Rockclimbing.com. This guidebook, *Carolina Rocks: The Piedmont*, is an attempt to consolidate the information from previous and current sources into one accurate crag resource, making it easier and less time consuming to research climbing options.

THE CONTROVERSY

Though I've poured my heart and soul into the makings of this book, I can't say that everyone I've interacted with has shared my sentiments, or been supportive of my endeavors. Some have presented legitimate concerns about problems that could arise with the publishing of a new guidebook for the Piedmont. I feel that those concerns deserve a voice; at the very least to remind us that climbing in state parks is a privilege, not a right. While it's my opinion that most rock climbers are cut from the same cloth, I'd go out on a limb to say that the North Carolina climbing community in particular is truly a rare breed. Many Piedmont climbers are bold traditionalists with staunch ethics, who pride themselves on the spirit of adventure found in their home crags. One of the pushbacks to this project has been the idea that a new, updated, full-color guidebook will attract the masses to areas that locals would rather not have advertised, as problems can sometimes arise with an influx of climbers to a given area. An increase in people equals an increase in environmental impact, and an increase in impact can definitely affect access. Another fear is that a detailed, comprehensive guide will take away from the "ask around, or figure it out yourself" type ethic running through many Tarheel climbers' veins.

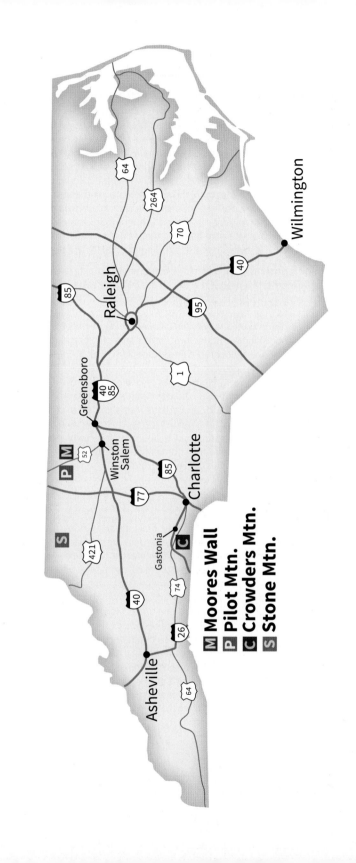

THE REBUTTAL

While I certainly do not take these concerns lightly, I think ultimately this new guide will do much more to preserve access than to thwart it. While there may be a rise in the number of climbers frequenting Piedmont crags, it is my belief that a more comprehensive guide will disperse crowds throughout the cliffs, rather than keep the masses hovering over just a few, select classic areas. As far as impact goes, climbers armed with up to date area knowledge create far less environmental damage than the uninformed. I believe that my friend and fellow climber Chris Barlow said it best – "I'd rather have 10 informed folks who know where they're going at the crag than 9 who don't have a clue." With regards to adventure, the wonderful thing about books is that they are not forced upon anyone. For those that prefer to wander around the crag and hop on whatever line speaks to them, no book can ever take that opportunity away. But for those that want to minimize their bushwhacking time and maximize their climbing time, a guidebook can most certainly help. A guidebook can also be a powerful educational tool to promote awareness of important access issues.

My vision for this book is that it will not only become an invaluable reference to have at the crag, but also an entertaining read that will not only educate, but also enlighten climbers, both young and old, with an appreciation for those that have gone before them. North Carolina has a colorful climbing history, and my hope is that I have captured that uniqueness throughout the pages of this book.

> *"What I love most about climbing is the adventure and excitement factor. The fact that it makes you extremely focused and present and you don't think about much else except what you are doing at that moment. I love both the physicality of climbing along with the cerebral aspects and mind control that is involved. I also love the way it connects you with who you are climbing with, being outside, and takes you to beautiful places and puts you in very exciting and sometimes even life threatening situations. I have the most respect for climbs that require you to rely on a combination of skill and mind control. One of the things I like about climbing in North Carolina is that it has a lot of climbing that contains both adventure, beauty, excitement, in addition to requiring focus, skill and commitment. Bolted sport climbing was not embraced early on in North Carolina and the folks I climbed with endorsed the trad ethic over bolting everything and making every climb "safe". I like that early ethic of climbing – ground-up, and as clean and bold as possible. I think it has been demonstrated and preserved pretty well in NC."*
>
> *-First Ascensionist Bob Rotert, on his love for NC climbing*

ETHICS

Though each of the four areas covered in this guide were established by different people with varying ethical standards, there are a few sweeping generalizations that can be made with very few exceptions.

RETRO-BOLTING: Although it is considered good stewardship to replace ratty soft goods, such as rap station slings and webbing, adding bolts or fixed gear of any kind to an existing route is considered highly offensive to both the first ascensionist and the Piedmont climbing community as a whole. If you happen to come across a piece of existing fixed hardware that is in need of replacing, please contact the Carolina Climbers Coalition.

CHIPPING, EPOXY, and ARTIFICIAL HOLDS: This is highly frowned upon throughout North Carolina. Just because you can't do a move doesn't mean that someone else can't. Don't water down projects for the next generation.

FOLLOW THE CROWD: It is common courtesy to continue to support the local ethics that previous developers have already established before attempting to leave your FA mark on an area. Do keep in mind that all four of the areas covered in this guide have already seen a substantial amount of development, and there is very little room for new routes.

For unique ethics-related eccentricities for each crag, please check out the introductions at the start of each chapter.

RULES AND CONSIDERATIONS FOR CLIMBING IN NORTH CAROLINA STATE PARKS
In general climbers have had good relations with the NC Park System. Don't be the one that ruins it for everyone else. The following regulations apply to climbing in any NC State Park, which includes all four areas documented in this book. Please see the "Access" sections at the beginning of each chapter for any rules specific to a particular area.

REGISTER AT THE KIOSK OR PARK OFFICE EACH TIME YOU VISIT - Not only is a permit required for every vehicle, but it's also the main method that park staff use to gather information on climbing usage. You will need your vehicle license plate number and emergency contact information. There is no fee for this permit. Take the yellow copy with you. Leave the white copy in the designated box.

> *You know that section on the Climber's Registration Permit for "emergency contact" numbers that you may be tempted to blow off and leave blank? Perhaps you should write down a number – and preferably one that works! Brandy Walters from Gastonia, SC sure was glad she did in the spring of 2012 – "After a nice warm-up in the Resurgence Area, we moved on to Red Wall…but no sooner did we get the ropes set up than all of our cell phones started ringing non-stop! The callers turned out to be the emergency contacts for everyone in our party – in my case, my mom. When she had seen Gastonia on the caller ID, she got pretty nervous. The ranger proceeded to tell her that our car had been hit very badly in the parking lot, leaving my poor mom hanging until the very end when he finally got to the part about our group being nowhere near the accident when it happened. Apparently an older woman's car had "malfunctioned," causing her to run over a curb into our SUV and our friend's brand new car (as well as causing their car to bump into a third car! Quite the debacle! Once we got back down to the parking lot (courtesy of a partial ride with the park rangers!), we were shocked to see that our car was missing its headlights, grill, and bumper! The worst part was that we had hiked so far only to have to pack up and leave, even though we still had food, water, 3 behaving children, and plenty of energy left to climb! But on the plus side we had extra time for margaritas and Mexican food!"*

RESPECT AREAS THAT ARE OFF LIMITS TO CLIMBING - There are some sections of cliffline where climbing is prohibited. Please obey all trail signs and respect all posted closures. There is plenty of rock to be had in legally climbable areas without venturing off into illegal territory that could endanger everyone else's access in the future.

NO GARDENING ALLOWED – All cliff dwelling plants, including lichens, are protected. Tread lightly on the soil at the top and base of the cliffs, as quite often the vegetation surrounding popular climbs has seen better days.

USED FIXED AND GEAR ANCHORS WHENEVER POSSIBLE - Avoid using trees as anchors. Repetitive use of trees can damage root systems and the living tissues just beneath the bark.

DON'T OVERSTAY YOUR WELCOME – Respect seasonal hours, and remember that closing time means you should be out of the park at that time, not topping out your last pitch of the day. Allow enough time to pack your gear and hike back out to your car before curfew.

LEAVE YOUR DRILL AT HOME – New anchors and bolt placements are prohibited without the park's consent. The Carolina Climbers Coaltion works closely with park staff to maintain/replace existing hardware.

DON'T TEMPT FATE – Any valuables that aren't kept on your person should be stowed out of sight in your LOCKED car.

ACCIDENTS – Any incident resulting in personal injury or damage to property should be reported to park staff.

USING THIS BOOK

The four areas documented in this book are divided into four chapters. Each chapter includes an introduction about the style of climbing found at that area and what makes it distinctive, along with detailed historical information and basic trip planning beta. Approach times (as well as other helpful information) are conveniently displayed in a table at the beginning of each chapter, and described in detail at the beginning of each area's sub-sections. The approach times are approximate and obviously depend on how fast you are walking. Those that prefer a forced march can expect to arrive sooner, and dawdlers can expect to arrive later. Routes are described from left to right, except in the case of a few cliffs at Crowder's. The buttresses at Crowder's are jumbled and sometimes overlap. Also scattered throughout the guide are anecdotal blurbs compiled from interviews, emails, phone calls, and casual conversations with the author. These stories are intended to add humor, character, and a bit of flavor to each area. While all of these anecdotes were most assuredly based on actual events, many were recounted in the spirit of story-telling around a campfire – some tales, especially the older ones, may have grown a little taller over the years. May they preserve memories and promote a sense of camara-derie for North Carolina climbers!

WHAT'S IN A NAME?

With the possible exception of Stone Mountain, North Carolina has a long history of parties not reporting their first ascents. Sometimes another party will climb the same route, think it's a first ascent, and give it a new name. This issue can occur anywhere, but is most prevalent at Moore's Wall. In addition, during the preparation of this book, several routes were given names to avoid routes in the guide identified only as NAME UNKNOWN. The author of this guide is dedicated to giving credit were credit is due. If you see incorrect route names and/or first ascent parties please contact me so I can correct it for the next edition.

ROUTE DESIGNATION AND RATINGS

Difficulty: Routes described in this book are rated using the Yosemite Decimal System for dif-ficulty.

Safety: In addition, some routes have an "R" after the difficulty rating. These "R"-rated routes all have some sort of characteristic that makes them more dangerous than the typical routes at the same crag. Often this means the route has one or more larger sections of unprotected climb-ing (known as a runout). A fall in the wrong place on an "R" rated route means that the climber could very likely be seriously injured or killed. Some routes have an "X" listed after the difficulty rating. These routes typically offer very little protection and are considered to be very danger-ous. A fall in the wrong place on an "X" route would almost certainly result in death or serious injury. Please note that the "R" and "X" ratings are only a guide. You can certainly be killed or se-riously injured on any route at any crag, but please take extreme caution on "R" and "X" routes. Be honest about your climbing ability, know your limits, and use good judgment.

Type of Route: This guide continues a recent trend set by other guides that easily differentiates between sport and trad routes. This guide expands the list even further to cover the unique-climbing found at Stone Mountain.

● **Red** indicates a traditional climb that requires gear. Red also denotes mixed routes that can be led with mostly quickdraws, but may need a piece or two of gear.

● **Blue** indicates a "pure" sport route that can be led with only quickdraws.

● **Green** routes are only found in the Stone Mountain section of the guide. They are bolted, but are far from being considered a sport route. Green routes may have 50 foot or longer runouts with no opportunity for supplemental protection. Routes at Stone that provide some supplement gear opportunities in between the sparsely placed bolts are still shown as a "green" route.

"SPORT" CLIMBING IN THE PIEDMONT

Spend any amount of time in the climbing community in North Carolina, and you'll quickly learn that it takes more than a few bolts to make a sport climb, and that quite often the addition of bolts moves a route to that vague and sometimes scary category of "sporty." True sport lines were really only developed by a handful of players in relatively recent history (John Black, Porter Jarrard, Doug Reed, Wes Love, Gus Glitch, and Diab Rabie to name a few). When the bolted sport craze took off around the country in the 1980's and 1990's, it was not well embraced by the NC climbing community as a whole. However, despite a few distinctive party lines being drawn, the Piedmont did end up with a handful of bolted gems that can be classified as "sport routes." So if clipping bolts is your game, check out this list of must-do clip-ups in the Piedmont, and work your way up through the ranks. More specific route descriptions can be found in that route's designated section in the guide – and be sure to read those, as a few of these might climb better with a stray cam here or there, this is North Carolina after all.

Pole Dancing (5.7) – Pilot Mountain
Chicken Bone (5.7) – Pilot Mountain
Black Rain (5.9) – Pilot Mountain
Opinionated (5.9+) – Crowders Mountain
Smooth Sailing (5.10a) – Pilot Mountain
Burn Signals (5.10c) – Crowders Mountain
Electra (5.10c) – Crowders Mountain
Devil in the White House (5.10d) – Pilot Mountain
Energy Czar (5.10d) – Crowders Mountain
Overhanging Hangover (5.11a) – Pilot Mountain
When Shrimp Learn to Whistle (5.11a) - Pilot Mtn.

The Whining (5.11d) – Crowders Mountain
Scimitar (5.12a) – Stone Mountain
Welcome to Crowders (5.12a) – Crowders Mountain
Slabster's Lament (5.12a) – Crowders Mountain
Blind Prophet (5.12b/c) – Pilot Mountain
The Carnivore (5.12c/d) – Crowders Mountain
Nicotine (5.13a) – Moore's Wall
Black and Blue Velvet (5.13a/b) – Pilot Mountain
Zeus (5.13b) – Moore's Wall
Season in Hell (5.13c) – Moore's Wall
Hercules (5.14a) – Moore's Wall

THE CAROLINA CLIMBERS COALITION

The Carolina Climber's Coalition (CCC) was established to preserve, protect and expand climbing opportunities in North and South Carolina. The Coalition was created as a result of a mistaken rumor that spread throughout North Carolina in 1994 that climbing would be banned in all state parks. State park officials and climbers met in Charlotte and determined that a park closure was not planned, but one result of that meeting was that a coalition would best serve the interests of both climbers and park officials. In January 1995 almost 100 area climbers voted unanimously to create the coalition to help preserve climbing access in the Carolinas.

Today the CCC is a 501(c)3 nonprofit corporation with over 200 members. Over the years the role and importance of the CCC has greatly expanded. The Coalition has several key roles including:

Advocacy: The CCC is the go to organization for climbing issues in North Carolina. Public and private land owners contact the CCC if there are issues that require attention in the state's many climbing areas. The CCC acts as the official voice of the climbing community.

Access: The CCC has been extremely successful in gaining access by direct purchase or lease of climbing areas. The CCC purchased Laurel Knob (one of the tallest cliffs in the east), 6 acres of the Rumbling Bald boulder field, and most recently the Hidden Valley cliff in Virginia. The organization also leases the Asheboro boulders and has worked out temporary access to Sauratown Mountain after a 6 year closure.

Rebolting Initiatives: The Carolina Climbers Coalition has stepped in more than once to replace aging hardware. Major rebolting efforts have resulted in the replacement of hundreds of old bolts at Stone, Moore's Wall, Crowder's, and Pilot Mountain.

The CCC also works with national organizations like the Access Fund and the American Alpine Club to influence policy on state and federal lands and maintains close relationships with public land managers across the Carolinas. In recognition of the hard work of CCC volunteers, the Access Fund recognized the CCC with a Land Conservation Award in 2011.

Members help fund stewardship of climbing areas, bolt replacement work and a variety of other projects that help to sustain the areas we all love. If you're not already a member, please consider joining by visiting http://carolinaclimbers.org and signing up!

Continued COLLABORATION with land owners, rangers, and other wilderness oriented organizations

Gained seasonal access to SAURATOWN

Worked with park officials to reignite climbing at ROCKY FACE

RUMBLING BALD: Purchased and own 6+ acres of prime bouldering. Currently working with Chimney Rock State Park to expand climbing access within the Park

TRAIL BUILDING and MAINTENANCE

CAROLINA CLIMBERS' COALITION

SUPPORT THE CCC
Join Today
Carolinaclimbers.org

BOLT REPLACEMENT

LAUREL KNOB: Purchased, own, and manage the biggest and baddest cliff east of the Mississippi

Great climbers' EDUCATION via carolinaclimbers.org

HANGING ROCK STATE PARK: Worked with rangers on peregrine closures and established climbers parking

LOOKING GLASS: Worked with PNF Rangers to achieve climber-friendly road closures

Worked with park officials to approve "hiking on rocks" in JOCASSEE GORGES

ASHEBORO BOULDERS: Secured a lease with landowners for access to superb bouldering

Worked with the Town of Lake Lure in support of bouldering at BUFFALO CREEK PARK

7

AN ODE TO PIEDMONT CLIMBING BY MATT PADEN

Growing up in a condo sucked. Obviously not like growing up in a 3rd world country sucks, but in a "my-parents-moved-into-a-soul-killing-dwelling-and-everything-feels-numb" kind of way. My parents moved to the Triangle from Asheville when I was about 4, so the mountains always felt like a promise of what could have been, and I pined for them like a 12-year-old girl drawing hearts and initials on her notebook.

Growing up in Chapel Hill, most everything seemed counter to what I felt was important. The emphasis seemed to be on achieving and owning, and though I hadn't quite discovered what my path in life should be, I felt like achieving much of anything sure seemed like a lot of work. I knew the outdoors made me feel great, and in a way provided a sense of salvation from my teenage angst. But other than occasionally hiking and backpacking, I didn't have a real window to the outdoors. I felt there was a missing element between me and the deeper connection I sensed was there with nature. I was just missing the spark.

Then one summer, at age 15, I discovered climbing on a trip to Alaska, and everything changed. I saw people toproping at a small roadside cliff and I saw all my pining for the mountains and my search for a way to get all cozied up with Mother Nature combined into one perfect package! I thought, "Matt, that is something you need to try, dude. That looks way cooler than rollerblading!" (This was the mid-90's after all).

I hate to admit I was a gym rat for the first year I climbed, but I didn't even have a driver's license. You try convincing your mom to drive her minivan to Moore's Wall for the weekend and see how it goes. Once my gym rat partners and I were legal drivers, we headed west on I-40 to the nearest crags around Winston-Salem. At first, we were bummed we didn't live in some of the amazing destinations out west that we had read about in all the magazines. But as it turns out, being off the map was pretty sweet. The rock in North Carolina proved to be everything we needed and more.

I could tell numerous tales of finding freedom in the hills, salvation in getting the crap scared out of me leading routes like Zoo View, and developing self-reliance while bouldering in the Zschiesche corridor before we knew what crash pads were. And all of it would be mostly true. I could also tell you about great moments with friends, like skipping school to work a project at Pilot, or stopping at Fazoli's Italian restaurant after 99.9% of our climbing trips to Moore's (free breadsticks. Need I say more?). I could perhaps even share the story of how I back clipped every 'biner on my first ever sport lead at Pilot (and even managed to Z clip), but I don't like to talk about that one much.

Instead, I'll just say that the rock of the Piedmont is an oasis in a landscape of achieving and owning. And it's an oasis seeped in an exciting history of bold route development that might make you feel like you're walking in the footsteps of some super strong and heady dudes. So if you find yourself living in a condo or a too-well-groomed cul-de-sac (and chances are you do) and life is missing something, you could do much worse than to immerse yourself in the boulders, cliffs and adventure that defines climbing in the Piedmont. Who knows, it might give you a spark that will change your life, as it did mine. And it just might even make you finally give up those rollerblades.

WHAT TO DO WHEN IT RAINS...

While some climbing destinations boast large amounts of wet weather climbing (the Red River Gorge comes to mind…), the Piedmont Region is NOT usually placed in that category. However, don't despair completely. For determined climbers in need of a real rock fix that can't afford to be picky, dry rock can usually be found. So if the forecast is looking a little less than ideal, check out the following ideas for sketchy weather scenarios.

IF IT IS GOING TO RAIN: Did you check the forecast for EVERY Piedmont destination? There could easily be an 80% chance of rain at Moore's and Pilot, but with only a 30% chance at Crowders or Stone. One of the nice things about Piedmont climbing is that the destinations are far enough away to have different weather systems, and close enough that day trips between each are quite reasonable.

If the weather is looking foul at multiple destinations, you're options become limited. Go ahead and cross Stone Mountain off of your list entirely, as the last place you want to be when the clouds let loose is on a hairball slab, 40 feet out from your last pro! (Not to mention that climbing wet rock is against park rules at Stone). Moore's, Pilot, and Crowders offer a meager selection of rainy routes, however, so if you've got nothing else to do, grab your rain gear and head outside!

IF IT JUST STARTED RAINING: Generally speaking, overhanging routes (the steeper the better) or walls that are capped by a large roof are your best bet.

Stone: Head up or down from wherever you're at, whichever provides the quickest and safest retreat. Air out your Mother Nature complaints (and your soggy socks) to each other over ice cream at the general store on the way out.

Pilot: Head to the Amphitheater area. OVERHANGING HANGOVER (5.11a), BLIND VELVET (5.11b), and BLACK AND BLUE VELVET (5.13b) will stay mostly dry in a heavy rain, and the slabs – CRACK-IN' UP (5.7+) through COW PATTY BINGO (5.9) - will remain dry for a couple of hours or so until water starts to seep out from under the roof. At the very least you'll have a large area below the massive roof in which to wait out the storm.

Moore's: The left side of the Amphitheater (Sun Wall) and many North End routes are steep enough to be climbable in a light rain. On opposite ends of the cliff, P1 of SHADOWDANCE (5.10c), and FIRST IN FLIGHT (5.12a) never see a drop of rain and are climbable in a downpour. Much of the massively steep Hanging Garden also stays dry, but the tops of many of the climbs will get wet pretty quickly. Also, the approach gully can be rather treacherous, so unless you happen to be up there already when the rain starts, it's an ill-advised rain plan.

Crowders: Some of the routes at Hidden Wall, such as THE WHINING (5.11d), and SLABSTER'S LAMENT (5.12a) stay relatively dry in a moderate rain, as well as the steeper routes on the Car Wall – BURN SIGNALS (5.10c) and SCORCHED EARTH DEFENSES (5.10d). Gumbies Roof provides dry rock and a good shelter for waiting out a storm, although the tops of the climbs may get wet.

IF IT FINALLY STOPPED RAINING: Areas that are exposed and out in the open will dry much faster than areas that are hidden beneath the trees. A little bit of sun can go a long way, and as a rule, walls facing south and/or east will dry faster than their shadier counterparts.

Stone: Although they are instantly wet in even the slightest drizzle, the large expanses of slab at Stone dry almost as quickly, making odds in your favor the day after a rain. Water grooves and cracks, however, not so much. Part of the reason why the slabs dry so fast is due to the water being funneled into the grooves, some of which can stay wet for long periods of time. In very cold weather, ice chutes can even form in these grooves, especially on the shady North Face. As the ice melts in subsequent warmer temperatures, the ensuing runoff can cause some routes to be unexpectedly wet.

Pilot: Most of the routes dry out reasonably quickly after a rain, and are generally climbable within 24 hours, especially with the help of sun and wind. One unique phenomenon however is the seepage effect on the previously mentioned slab routes in the middle of the Amphitheater. While they are sheltered initially from the rain by the massive capped roof, after a period of steady rain, water will begin to seep through the roof, making waterfalls that can last for days, sometimes even weeks.

Moore's: Though it doesn't have the sunny southeast-facing advantage that other Piedmont crags have, Moore's still dries out relatively quickly. A little breeze does wonders, especially for exposed areas such as the Circus Wall, Amphitheater, and North End. Cracks will tend to retain water for a little longer than the overhanging faces. Still, if it just stopped raining or if it's misty or foggy, head somewhere else. Misty conditions will mean that practically the entire cliff will be moist at best.

Crowders: Crowders takes the prize for fastest drying crag in the Piedmont, as the exposed perch on the cliff and mostly sunny walls add up to a perfect drying formula! Even if it rains all week long, Red Wall is guaranteed to be dry by the weekend, as long as the skies are clear on Saturday morning. Hidden Wall, David's Castle, and Practice Wall won't be too far behind.

PIEDMONT GEOLOGY BY ANTHONY LOVE

Crowders Mountain

Crowders Mountain is composed of the 650-700 million year old Battleground Formation (Horton, 1984). The Battleground Formation is composed of a type of meta-sedimentary rock (preexisting sedimentary rocks changed by heat and pressure) called schist. Schists are deformed rocks that contain minerals that have formed parallel to stress they encountered while under pressure. The Battleground Formation is one of the many units of rock in North Carolina that has experienced significant deformation due to the events that created the Appalachian Mountains. Battleground schists are composed of quartz, mica and elongate crystals of the aluminum-rich minerals, kyanite and sillimanite. The mineral alignment and elongate crystals in the rock at Crowders creates the spiny texture you feel while grabbing holds. The parallel alignment of minerals in the rock is also parallel to the layering within the rock unit. Geologists have mapped the exposures of rock containing the Battleground Formation and found the have been deformed and warped upward into a series of folds (see photo below). The crest of the ridge that contains the best cliffs at Crowders occurs in the hinge of one of these folds. Within this location, the layers of rock are oriented vertically.

The orientation of rock layering at Crowders is one of the features that creates the forms of flakes and cracks that make the cliffs of Crowders Mountain very unique. Perhaps one of the most unique features of the rock at Crowders is its origin in geologic time. The Battleground formation originally formed from silts, sands and gravels that were being eroded from the Grenville Mountains on the eastern edge of the continent. At this, point, South America and North America were being separated by a rift zone and the Appalachian Mountains, the Piedmont, the Blue Ridge and the Atlantic Ocean did not exist.

Moores Wall and Pilot Mountain

Moores Wall, Pilot Mountain and Sauratown Mountain are composed of quartzite (another metamorphic rock) exposed in an area geologists call the Sauratown Mountains Anticlinorium. An anticlinorium is a fancy word explaining a structure where the rocks are warped up into an upside-down-U-shape. Quartzite is a type of metamorphic rock composed almost entirely of quartz. In addition to the quartzite, we see beds of schist cropping out in between quartzite layers The protolith (precursor) of this rock was a quartz-dominated sandstone with lenses of mud (=schist). While at the cliff, you can see a number of features that help characterize this rock. In

parts of the cliff line along the ledge springs trail at Pilot, you can observe structures called crossbeds (see picture) that indicate these rocks were deposited by wave currents as beach sands in ocean basins. We can see features such as bedding and crossbedding highlighted by darker layers of heavy minerals that would have been deposited in sand layers.

We also see the tectonic effects that deformed and metamorphosed these rocks in the folded beds of quartzite (see picture). Within the quartzite, we commonly find very small crimps or blocky holds. The

ABOVE: Folds in quartzite on "Break on Through" on the Circus Wall at Moores Wall.

in the folded beds of quartzite (see picture). Within the quartzite, we commonly find very small crimps or blocky holds. The hardness of the rock and minimal fracturing make for sparse holds on sections of rock within beds (see picture). However, between beds or at the interface between schist layers, sharp jugs can be found. When placing protection in horizontals at Moores or other areas within the Sauratown Mountains area, be wary of placing gear at the sand/mud (=schist) interfaces, they are softer rock!

Stone Mountain

Stone Mountain is composed of a series of igneous rocks geologists call granodiorite and quartz diorite. Most people call them granite. The 330 million year old granite at Stone Mountain is an example of a structure known as a pluton. Plutons are large blobs of low density molten material that form in the subsurface. Their density relative to surrounding rocks makes these liquids buoyant and mobile. We see evidence of their travels through the subsurface in the rocks they pick up and incorporate along the way – xenoliths. Xenoliths (foreign rocks) are the dark-colored pieces of rock that occur occasionally form random jugs along the cliff face. Plutons represent the chamber of magma (molten rock) that feeds volcanoes on the surface. As volcanoes go extinct, the magma in the chamber, which feeds them cools forming a pluton.

Stone Mountain is part of a series of similar aged plutons (Whitesides, Mt Airy, and the Spruce Pine granites) that occur in a NE-SW trend within the Blue Ridge belt. These plutons help to constrain the timing of the second major pulse of mountain building that formed the Appalachians. In a few places at Stone Mountain, one can observe dikes of younger material that crosscut the granite. A series of sub-parallel dikes create the main features on Grand Funk Railroad. We also see the prominent effects that weathering has on these rocks. Weathering is responsible for the exfoliation (peeling off like layers of an onion) that creates small flakes and large features such as the flake of Bombay Groove and the Great Arch. Other features that result from weathering are of course the water grooves that make the brilliant climbs like Great White Way. Water grooves form when water takes the most preferred path down the cliff face.

Typically, the preferred path is dictated by some feature at the top of the dome or may be a weakness such as a crack. Once you have topped out you might see potholes while trying to find the walk off. Potholes are similar to water grooves in that weathering from rain water, takes physical and chemical advantage over a weakness in the rock. Over time as granules are separated, from the surface, they may mechanically erode and scour these depressions while caught in wind and water currents. While climbing at stone it is a bad idea to let weakness take advantage of you during a long runout as you may be dressing pot holes in your body from the long tumbling whip you may take!

INTRODUCTION

This southernmost Piedmont climbing area is conveniently located within an easy drive of many climbers in both North and South Carolina. Situated approximately 20 miles outside of Charlotte, North Carolina, Crowders Mountain is an important piece in the colorful puzzle that makes the Piedmont climbing community unique.

When it comes to reputations, Crowders is often lumped in the same category as Pilot – fiercely defended by newbies and snubbed by the more "hard-core." But, as with Pilot, most of this reputation comes from unfair expectations. Will you find world-class climbing at Crowders Mountain? Certainly not. But you will find something for just about everyone.

What the majority of walls lack in stature, they make up for in variety. From easy 5th class romps to noteworthy test pieces, there is something for timid newbies all the way up to aggros with superhuman tendon strength. For those who are either new to the sport or simply looking for a casual day of toprope moderates, David's Castle and the Practice Wall are both great options. More advanced climbers interested in leading harder, bolder lines will have their hands full at Red Wall and Hidden Wall.

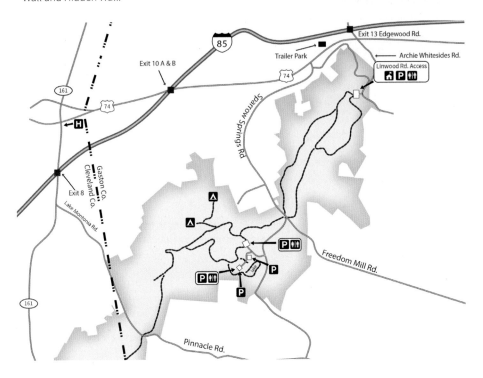

LOCATION

Crowder's Mountain is located a few miles off of I-85, just southwest of Gastonia. Head south on I-85 past Charlotte, taking exit number 13 (Edgewood Road). At the exit ramp make a left onto Edgewood Road. From here, it depends on which areas you want to climb in, as the parking lot for Hidden Wall is in a separate location than the parking for the Main Areas.

For Hidden Wall – From Edgewood Road, turn right at the first stoplight, which is Franklin Blvd/ Highway 74. Drive approximately 2 miles before reaching the next stoplight, Sparrow Springs Road. Turn left and drive for another 2 miles before making a right hand turn to stay on Sparrow Springs Road. The main entrance to the park will be in less than a mile on the right.

For the Main Area – From Edgewood Road, turn right at the first stoplight (Franklin Blvd/Highway 74). Drive approximately 2 miles before reaching the next stoplight, Sparrow Springs Road. Turn left and drive for .4 miles, then turn left onto Linwood Road. Continue on Linwood Road for 1.6 miles, then turn right into the park. There will be brown Crowders Mountain State Park signs along the way.

THE CLIMBING SEASON

Considering its southern latitude as well as exposure, it shouldn't be surprising that conditions are less than stellar during the summer months at Crowder's. Climbers who are lucky (stupid?) enough to survive drowning in a sea of perspiration on the approach will be rewarded with unre- lenting sun, broiling rock that is hot to the touch, and very little shade upon reaching the cliff top. If this brand of masochism sounds un-appealing, note that Hidden Wall, The Fortress, and the backside of the Middle Finger Wall get afternoon shade. No such relief for David's Castle, Practice Wall, and Red Wall, however.

The silver lining to this cloud, however, is that as hellish as that endless sun and low supply of shade may feel in the throes of summer, it makes for a positively delightful haven sometime around January.

For fans of less extreme conditions, the most pleasant seasons for Crowders climbing are of course the same as the majority of North Carolina crags – spring and fall.

GEAR

By and large, Crowders Mountain is considered a toproping crag, so rack up accordingly. The rock is very sharp and can take quite a toll on a rope if you're not careful, so be sure to pack several long pieces of webbing (30 feet) to prevent unnecessary abrasion. A pad of carpet can also come in handy. Bolt clippers can get by with about a dozen or so quickdraws, and various types of both active and passive gear up to 3 inches should be sufficient for most traditional lines.

ACCESS

In addition to the general rules and regulations about climbing in NC State Parks, please remem- ber the following access issues that are specific to Crowder's Mountain.

USE ESTABLISHED TRAILS ONLY – Access to climbs should be from the Backside, Tower, or Ridgetop trails only. Please do not bushwhack to the cliff base from sections of the Backside Trail – this will jeopardize access for everyone.

BRAIN BUCKETS RECOMMENDED – Because of the broken, jumbled nature of the cliff line, hikers and other climbers are often right above the climbing routes, sometimes inadvertently kicking off loose rock. Because of this as well as the sometimes uncontrollable redneck-type urge to hurl bottles off the cliff, helmets are not a bad idea.

CLOSED AREAS – At the time of this writing, those areas are Pyramid Wall, Unemployment Wall, and Meaty Okra Wall. There is plenty of rock to be had in legally climbable areas without ventur- ing off into illegal territory that could endanger everyone else's access in the future.

PARK FACTS
522 Park Office Lane, King's Mountain, NC, 28086
Office Phone: (704) 853-5375
Email: crowders.mountain@ncdenr.gov

The park opens year round at 8:00 am, but closing times vary depending upon the month.

HOURS
November, December, January, February – 6:00 pm
March, October – 7:00 pm
April, May, September – 8:00 pm
June, July, August – 9:00 pm
Closed Christmas Day

"I don't ever remember seeing Doug actually work out – he just climbed all the time! I was the one who was always doing pull-ups, lifting weights, or something (anything!), to try and keep up with him. Doug always had a smile and a drive, WITH NO EGO, and I was so lucky to tie up with him. Not only was he an unbelievable climber, his personality and friendship was beyond compare. Thanks to him we climbed with a standard of ethics I am proud of. Doug had the eye to see a new route that I would have just walked by. He was also my motivation - we took turns on leads and I knew if I didn't send it, then he would! Without teaming up with Doug I would have never climbed as hard as I did and wouldn't have had the opportunity to travel to so many amazing destinations and meet so many great people. I could never say enough good things about Doug Reed, but here's just one – on a week-long trip to the Gunks one time I'd forgotten my tent poles. Doug went and bought himself a new tent and gave me his – now that's a good dude! "

– Wes Love, on his partner in climb

"I started climbing while in the Reserve Officer Training Corp, back in 1970. That was mostly climbing on aid (pitons), rappelling, and doing a few of the old bolted routes the Army Corp of Engineers established in the 1960s. We climbed in hiking boots and tied Swiss Harnesses with 20 foot sections of webbing. By 1975 I was a member of South Point Lifesaving Crew, and we practiced wilderness rescue on Crowders and Kings Mountains. Some of us also climbed - usually the CATERPILLAR, GASTONIA CRACK, or the west face of Kings Pinnacle. In those days it was fine to use any method you wanted to get to the top of a wall, and aiding up easily climbable routes was common practice, even when on top-rope. There was always a lot of hammering, and you often saw people at places like Burn Crack hanging on placements. It wasn't until the later 1970s that free climbing on top-rope or lead became the primary climbing activity at Crowders.

The late, long-time local Gary Mims, reflecting on the early days of Crowder's climbing

EMERGENCY SERVICES

If someone in your party is in need of a rescue, call the park office (704-853-5375) or Gaston County 911. The closest full-service hospital is Gaston Memorial (704-866-2000), and there is also a hospital in the town of at King's Mountain (704) 739-3601.

GEAR SHOPS

REI Charlotte 9755 Northlake Centre Pkwy, Charlotte, NC 28216 (704) 921-0320

REI Pineville 11067 Carolina Place Parkway, Pineville, NC 28134 (704) 341-7405

Jesse Brown's Outdoors 4732 Sharon Road, Charlotte, NC 28210 (704) 556-0020

Great Outdoor Provision Company 4341 Park Road, Charlotte, NC 28209 (704) 523-1089

CLIMBING GYMS

Inner Peaks Climbing Center (indoor climbing gym) 9535 Monroe Rd., Ste 170 Charlotte, NC 28270 (704) 844-6677

US National Whitewater Center (partially covered outdoor artificial climbing wall) 5000 Whitewater Center Parkway Charlotte, NC 28214 (704) 391-3900

CAMPING

Primitive backpack camping is available at Crowder's Mountain State Park, for both individuals as well as groups. All sites are located about a mile hike from the Visitor's Center Parking Area (follow directions for Hidden Wall parking on pg 26). Follow the Pinnacle Trail and turn right at the Campground Junction. Individual sites can accommodate up to 6, are equipped with a large tent pad, grill, and picnic table, and group sites can accommodate up to 15, and have a fire circle for cooking and post-climbing tales. Both types of sites have nearby pit toilets and fresh drinking water. Reservations, which are required for group sites and strongly recommended for individual sites, can be made by calling (704) 853-5375. Pricing is $13 per site per night. Don't forget that once the gates close, no cars will be able to get in or out, so make sure you are in the parking lot in time.

BOULDERING

There is quite a bit of good bouldering to be had at the Dixon School Road Boulders, which is also owned by Crowders Mountain State Park, although it is located in a different area from both the Main Area and Linwood Road Entrances of the Park. To get there, take exit 5 from Interstate 85 (Dixon School Rd). Turn left off the exit ramp and drive 1.5 miles to an intersection with a flashing yellow light (Bethlehem Rd). Take a left onto Bethlehem Rd, and continue 1.2 miles, then fork right onto Vandyke Rd. Turn right into the Boulders Access area. Just as for roped climbing, be sure to fill out a permit at the ranger's station!

The Dixon School Road Boulders began to see development in the early 1980's, although access was not secured until 2009, when a land purchase was made by a collaborative effort by the Carolina Climbers Coaltion and the State Park. Just like any other climbing area, it is a privilege to climb at Dixon – please treat it as such!

There are well over 200 problems to be climbed at Dixon,

April Stephens at the crux of BACKSPLIN-TERS (V1)

75 of which are highlighted in a Selected Guide by Matt Beliejeski, published in 2011. Books can be purchased directly from Matt at firesnakestudios@gmail.com.

The rock at Dixon is sharp, gritty, and fun to climb on. Although there are plenty of hard lines to be found (even a few classics in the V8-V10 range), the majority of problems at Dixon are v4 and under. Most of the topouts are pretty straightforward, which is convenient since a good percentage of the problems there are highballs. In fact, many of the harder lines were originally rehearsed on toprope numerous times. Toproping is no longer allowed at Dixon, so don't forget to bring a pad and spotters you trust.

HISTORY

Crowder's became a protected state park in 1974, the same year in which the first known ascent was recorded (Middle Finger, on the aptly named Middle Finger Wall, by Kip Connor and Derek Brown). Also in that year, Gil Connor climbed a David's Castle route they named Peaches and Cream (5.6, A1). It was later renamed INSTANT KARMA, after being freed by Cal Swoager and Wes Love 8 years later.

Although a few of the obvious, easier lines went up in the 1970's, most of the major development at Crowder's was pioneered by locals several years later during the age of big hair and neon lycra. Doug Reed and Wes Love led the way early on, establishing numerous lines in the early 1980's. Other key individuals who bagged dozens of FA's included Shane and Sean Cobourn, Gus Glitch, Diab Rabie, Mark Pell, Rodney Lanier, and Alvino Pon, to name a few.

Unlike other North Carolina climbing areas, ethics at Crowders could best be described as "situational." Ground-up style ascents ruled in the 1980's as most of the natural lines went up, but after that, many climbers took an "ends justifies the means" approach, and rap-bolting became the norm for routes with dubious rock quality. First Ascensionist Gus Glitch often jokes, "The French were NOT the first to rap bolt – we started that at Crowders in 1985!" Some routes, including neighboring classics such as ELECTRA and ENERGY CZAR, were initially aided, then later free climbed on gear and fixed protection. A few lines, such as AERIAL ACT (FA Shane Cobourn), were put up by free-soloing during a moment of boldness.

In 1985, climbers began exploring sections of the park other than the Main Walls. With an initial flurry of development with TOP THAT, TOP THAT DIRECT, and TOXIC SHOCK, the ascent of DIXIE FURY sparked an onslaught of hard ascents at Hidden Wall, with notable classics such as THE

THE PIEDMONT BOULDER TOADS

"The first person to coin the term "Boulder Toads" had to have been my roommate and one of Charlotte's best climbers, Shane Cobourn. In the early 1980's every night of the week the Toads came together at Buzzard's (aka Poplar Tent Boulders). If you missed a night, then you were given no spot the next day! The rules were tough, but there was no better camaraderie between climbers than what the Toads shared. Scrappy Cloggins, Eddie N. Pain, Killer Bill, Crisp N. Wobbly, Alvino Pon, D. Slab, and Mr. Reed…a collection of personalities that inspired cohesive bonding, and no ill will. Everyone helped everyone. The Toads turned Crowders Mountain into more than just a choss pile, and I'm proud to have been a part of it."

-Gus Glitch, one of the main developers at Crowders

WHINING, SLABSTER'S LAMENT, and the SNAG going up one right after the other.

Routes began going up left and right on the northern side of the park in 1987. The Unemployment Wall and Lover's Lane areas saw a lot of action throughout the late 1980's and early 1990's,but are unfortunately no longer open for climbing, due to nesting vultures as well as the presence of an endangered plant species, Ground Juniper.

With the 1990's came a lot of activity on the southeastern side of the park, on many of the smaller buttresses now collectively known as the Resurgence (or Renaissance) Walls. Many of the routes here were established under the "3-Bolt Rule." (aka The New Policy.) This unwritten, situational ethic adopted by the main developers of the area called for no more than 3 bolts to be used on any given route. Sean Cobourn summed up the rationale as follows – "Make it good. Make it safe as far as loose rock goes, but since rap-bolting and cleaning are technically cheating, at least keep it bold. Any more than 3 bolts were not allowed."

In 1998 the Carolina Climbers Coalition took on a rebolting initiative throughout the park, replacing not only old pitons and bolts, but also installing new fixed anchors along the top. Although this upkeep was well-intentioned, a few controversies sprung from this effort, as some routes were retro-bolted without permission from the first ascensionists, and a few newer lines crept too close for comfort beside older, traditionally established lines. There have been several other grassroots efforts over the years by local climbers who have taken it upon themselves to provide the necessary TLC and maintenance to keep bolts and anchors safe. At this point, most of the hardware at the Main Area is less than 13 years old.

"The ethics of climbing at Crowder's have changed a good bit since the 1970's. When free climbing first caught on it was considered poor form (cheating) to pre-place protection on rappel, severely limiting FAs on Crowders. By gentlemen's agreement (there weren't many female climbers then) most NC climbing areas were declared trad-only. But, over time pre-placing bolts on single-pitch top-rope problems became accepted at Crowders, a practice later to be known as "sport climbing," which took off everywhere. The ground-up-only traditionalists did not like this change and there were some vicious arguments in the newsletters. I personally never put up a route using pre-placed protection, but I admit I've rapped down on some to get the beta before attempting a FA. However, there is something to be said for pre-bolting. Pre-placed bolts have tremendously expanded Crowders' climbing opportunities. For instance, there would be very little climbing at the Red Wall or Hidden Wall if sport climbing had not become part of the Crowders' culture. By later in the 1980s, the unwritten rule was that pre-placing bolts or fixed pins to establish a new route was okay, but you should never add fixed pro to an existing route."

Long time local Gary Mims, on ethics

"The only pure climbing style is to go naked, chalkless, and free solo and I've done that too, but who cares?"

-Crowders First Ascensionist Eddie N. Pain, on ethics

THE CLIMBING

Despite the bad rap Crowder's often gets for rock quality (the term "choss pile" has been tossed around on more than one occasion), most of the rock on popular routes is pretty good. On some of the less travelled routes, one will of course find more instances of bad rock. Be especially careful on the upper portions of certain routes, as the rock quality tends to diminish towards the top. While there are plenty of leadable bolted routes to keep the sport monkeys happy, as well as several solid gear lines, the majority of ascents at Crowders are via topropes, which in many areas are very easy to set up. The cliffline, however, is not as easy to read as other Piedmont climbing areas. Rather than a continuous line of quartzite, Crowders is a series of broken cliff bands strewn haphazardly along a mountainside – expect to lose your bearings a time or two on your first few visits.

Three year old kidcrusher Canaan Lineberry on RAZOR'S EDGE (5.6)

HIDDEN WALL APPROACH

From the parking lot at the Visitor's Center, hike along the Crowders Trail for one mile until you exit the woods at the intersection of Sparrow Springs Rd. and Freedom Mill Rd. Cross Sparrow Springs Rd (don't forget what your mama said about looking both ways), where you will see two trails. Take the right most trail (Rocktop Trail) for just a couple of minutes, but instead of heading up the ridge, veer right onto an indistinct climbers trail that will take you to the base of the cliff. As sport climbers are not known for their ability to carry heavy loads over long distances, dropping packs at the Rocktop Trailhead on the way in is common practice. A word of warning: Should you choose this option, make sure your pack is stashed well out of view of the road. At least one climber has arrived at the intersection early on a Sunday morning, only to discover that his entire pack had fallen victim to a drive-by theft in the 20 minutes it took to drive to the parking lot and hike back up to the road.

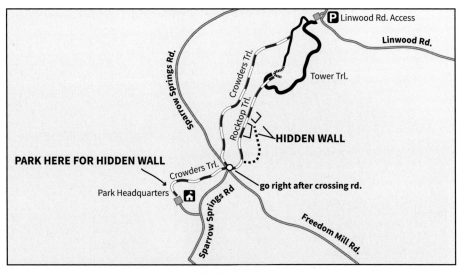

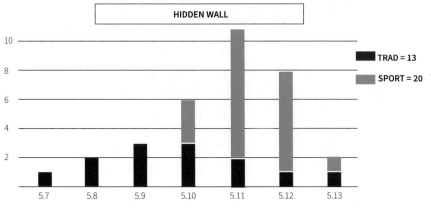

① BELLY CRAWL 5.9

This line is found on the first section of climbable rock. Worm your way up the squeeze chimney, angling up and right. (30 ft.)

② THE BOLTER PROBLEM 5.10c

It's debatable whether one lone bolt qualifies this route as a sport climb, or just a well-protected boulder problem. You be the judge, but you'd better be solid at the grade before attempting to lead it. The route is located on the right side of a fourth class gully, at an arête. Follow the arête to a bolt under the roof, and then surmount the roof with a long move to sharp, juggy flakes. 1 bolt and chain anchors. (30 ft.)

③ PERPLEXUS 5.11c

Work your way up through incut crimpers on the face just right of BOLTER PROBLEM to gain a stance at the roof. Traverse right through a series of perplexing moves, then angle up

and left towards the anchors. 2 bolts, bolted anchors. (30 ft.)

④ WASPAFARIAN 5.11a

The "wasp" is actually an acronym – White Anglo-Saxon Protestant-afarian. About 10 feet right of PERPLEXUS, negotiate a few tricky moves down low, passing a bolt and an old pin. A couple of long pulls get you through the roof. Finish by running for the anchors. 2 bolts and 1 pin to anchors. (30 ft.)

⑤ TOP THAT 5.9

This is one of the first lines established at Hidden Wall, though ironically seldom climbed nowadays. Start 10 feet right of WASP. Follow the broken crack system on the face through very sharp rock, then traverse right and pull up and over the roof. (50 ft.)

TOP THAT DIRECT 5.10b ★

This harder direct variation really only shares terrain with TOP THAT for the last few feet. It provides a good warm-up for the rest of the wall. Boulder up a shallow dihedral, then navigate through the pocketed face above to the TOP THAT finish. 4 bolts to anchors. (50 ft.).

LINK-UPS: The close proximity of all of the routes at Hidden Wall lends itself well to link-ups, in particular the section of rock between KOMA'S ARETE and THE WHINING. With ELASTIC REBOUND THEORY and THE WHINING as starting options, climbers have the unique ability to choose their own adventure, combining sequences from those routes and/or the PAGAN ROOF, with whatever happy ending (KOMA'S ARETE, ANTHRAX, ELASTIC, THE WHINING) tickles your fancy. Most of the FA's of these link-ups were well-documented and recorded in the back of this book, but most options are not described on the topo, for the sake of readability. Here's a quick and dirty list of what's been done before, however bear in mind that some of these variations have seen only a handful of ascents, therefore many don't have much of a grade consensus. As always, treat grades as a subjective guideline, and climb within your abilities. Happy linking!

THE ELASTIC SHAMAN 5.13 = ELASTIC + PAGAN + KOMA'S ARETE

PAGAN ROOF 5.13 = ELASTIC + PAGAN + ANTHRAX

WHINING AGAIN 5.12 = WHINING + ANTHRAX

THE WHINING PAGAN 5.13 = WHINING + PAGAN + ELASTIC

THE WHINING VERMIN 5.12 = WHINING + ANTHRAX

 KOMA'S ARETE 5.11d ★★

Start on ELASTIC, and cut left at the fourth bolt towards some junky-looking, pocketed rock, and head up the sharp arête. 7 bolts to shared anchors with ANTHRAX. (65 ft.)

⑧ ANTHRAX 5.12a ★★★

Also shares a start with ELASTIC. At the fourth bolt, trend up and left towards a bulging arête with a shallow dihedral. Pull the bulge and enjoy the exposure! 7 bolts to anchors. (65 ft.)

⑨ ELASTIC REBOUND 5.11d ★★ THEORY

Mixed. Climb the sloping jug rails to a bulging roof that was originally protected with slings threaded through pockets. Blast through the roof, then traverse a few feet to the right, aiming for a moderate, right-facing overhanging corner. Unless you want to test the theory, be

> **ELASTIC REBOUND THEORY -**
> *"Although it's since been retrobolted by others to facilitate access to nearby routes, fixed threaded slings were initially the only protection on that hard roof crux. I went up first and took one long swinging fall reaching out from under the roof, then lowered the few remaining feet to the ground. We bounce-tested the slings and they still seemed good so we pulled the rope and Alvino Pon tied in and went up next. He bombed out of there too but got turned upside down by the rope, and when the rope went taut, he actually bounced back up again (hence the name of the route). He swung so close to the ground that he sliced his forehead and eyebrow on a sharp edge on the slab below the route. If he had fallen another inch it probably would've been very serious or even deadly. I bandaged him up, we drank a couple beers and had a smoke, and after a little while he felt okay to belay. I sent the route cleanly on my second try, cheered on by my fellow Boulder Toads. Alvino followed without falls and it was a done deal. That was my last new route at Crowder's before moving out west."*
>
> *- Eddie N. Pain, First Ascensionist*

careful on the upper section, especially if you are not supplementing with gear. The rock quality is poor in spots, but a ½ inch piece can bring some peace of mind. 4 bolts to anchors. (70 ft.)

10 THE WHINING 5.11d ★★★

A classic line with a distinct crux that will have shorter folk whining for sure! Start right of ELASTIC, beneath the obvious large hole in the middle of the wall. Work up through steep flakes and launch to the good spot in the sloping hole (crux). Finish on steep but straightforward terrain as your pump management skills are put to the test. 4 bolts to anchors. (40 ft.)

11 STARK WHINING 5.11d

This variation clips all 4 bolts on THE WHINING, then steps right to another bolt and finishes straight up to bolted anchors. (70 ft.)

12 DIXIE FURY 5.12a ★★

Mixed. Scamper up easy ledges to the first bolt, then make a few committing moves up into the alcove. Bring a 3 inch piece of gear for the roof. Sink a few bomber jams and storm out the roof, following a juggy flake system to the STARK WHINING anchors. 5 bolts, bolted anchors. (70 ft.)

> **DIXIE FURY** - *This grunt fest was the first hard line established on the wall. The original line finished at a fixed hex just after the roof. However, rodents chewed through the ratty slings long ago and the line sat idle and untouched for years. When Matt Stark bolted the extension to THE WHINING in the mid-1990's, the real estate above the DIXIE FURY roof became protectable. Local climber Sam Stephens brought new life to the old fury in the spring of 2012. Though it's not possible to know for certain, it's highly likely that his onsight ascent was the first to link the original line into the STARK WHINING finish.*

13 MUDBONE 5.12

Climb SLABSTER'S for the first two bolts. Instead of continuing right, head straight up over the roof past 2 more bolts to a set of double hangers without rings. 4 bolts. (25 ft.).

14 SLABSTER'S LAMENT 5.12a ★★★

One of the best lines on the wall. Start on the slabby face near two holes low to the ground. Follow the line of weakness up and right past interesting pockets, then check your daintiness at the door. As the name implies there is nothing delicate or intricate about the crux of this classic line. Battle the wide crack and sloping undercling, pulling yourself onto the steep face for an exciting finish. 4 bolts to anchors. (40 ft.)

THE LAMENT IS OVER

My first experience with this line was in the summer of 2011, and I was anything but a worthy opponent. I marched in to the crag filled with excitement and optimism, and left feeling (and looking) like I'd been in a bar fight. Not to make sweeping generalizations about gender, but I'm a girl…and I climb like one. Like the name may imply, SLABSTER'S LAMENT is anything but a "girly" route. The climbing is scrappy, burly, and a far cry from the thin, delicate, technical faces I was accustomed to. My first time on the route was an outright flail fest. I wasn't anywhere close to doing all the moves without some major toprope assistance. The next few times I made it out to Hidden Wall I avoided Slabster's like the plague, but on a stray weekday 8 months later, the rope was already up, so I decided to give it a few whirls. Definitely not clean, but decidedly less thrashy – still needed a lot of refining, but was well within my range to lead it. So a couple of weeks later I headed back to work on it. My first time leading the route was a heartbreaker. I reached up to grab the final hold and literally missed by about half an inch. I took a nice, long (clean) fall. Surprised I'd come so close, I felt confident that I'd send it later on in the day. Unfortunately for me, (as well as my poor belayer that had to carry me out across his back), my next attempt ended with a fall at the exact same spot – but this time my foot clipped the belayer's side of the rope on the way down. I helicoptered around and bashed my left foot into the wall, fracturing my talus bone in two places, along with a decent sprain.

The next 6 weeks were a blur of hangboard workouts, pull-ups, and one really sweaty foot inside a boot. I can't tell you how many times I relived that last move, wondering if I somehow could have summoned an ounce more of strength to latch that last hold, and then I wouldn't have ended up in this mess. Although I can say that it was a learning experience that did have some positives, I definitely came away feeling like I had some unfinished business with Slabster's Lament.

Ten weeks after the injury, I'd been out of the boot for a month, my ankle was holding up quite well, and my lead head was coming back, so I decided to try again – but it was painfully obvious that I wasn't ready yet. Despite top-roping it clean, I wasn't able to rally much of an attempt on lead – I was timid and hesitating on every move so by the time I got to the crux I was completely gassed every time. It was pretty disappointing to drag up all of that emotion from the injury and still walk away empty-handed – but at least that time I walked away on my own two feet. The saga continued.

A few days later I wound up with a break in my schedule mid-week and a willing partner, so it was the perfect opportunity for one more shot at redemption, before the heat and humidity settled in and rendered the sloping crux unmanageably manky. I was cautiously optimistic, but afraid to get my hopes up too high. I'm not really sure what happened in only a matter of five days, but something must have switched in my head. This time around I felt calm, focused, and not at all hesitant – to be honest it went so well it was almost anti-climactic. But regardless of how it went down…SLABSTER'S LAMENT is officially checked off the tick list, and I feel like I'm free to move on, hopefully to better and brighter things.

Erica Lineberry, on SLABSTER'S LAMENT

Erica Lineberry preparing for the steeps on
SLABSTERS LAMENT (5.12a)

15 SLABSTER'S DIRECT 5.12c/d ★★

This direct variation lets the slabsters test their mettle before beginning their lament, and will likely feel significantly harder when it's hot. Start below a bolt on the face just a few feet right of SLABSTER'S LAMENT. Long reaches on very small holds will deposit you at the crux for SLABSTER'S. Finish on SLABSTER'S. 4 bolts to anchors. (40 ft.)

16 THE TERRORIST 5.13a ★★

This line shares the same start as SLABSTER'S DIRECT. However, instead of angling up and left into the sloping bulge, climb straight up and pull the bouldery roof. Hijack the technical face above, finishing at bolted anchors. 5 bolts to anchors. (50 ft.)

17 THE SNAG 5.12b ★★

A hard boulder problem right off the deck leads to a moderate, but pumpy finish. 4 bolts to bolted anchors. (50 ft.)

MORE LINK-UPS: As with the left side of the cliff, there are a opportunities for link-ups here as well. If you get bored and want to add a few more lines to your training circuit, here are some link-up options put up by the original first ascensionists back in the day.

- FELON 5.13 = SLABSTER'S DIRECT + TERRORIST bulge + SNAG finish
- SNAGGING TERRORISTAS 5.13 = SNAG + TERRORIST
- BLACK SAND BITCHES 5.11d R/X = TOXIC SHOCK + SNAG

THE TERRORIST – *This controversial line was the recipient of two drilled pockets – courtesy of Gus Glitch and Diab Rabie in 1989. After all the local hardmen got tired of getting shut down on the blank face towards the top, Gus and Diab broke out the drill and performed the unthinkable. Several more valiant attempts by all of Crowder's major players followed, until the line finally fell to Diab. He called it THE TERRORIST, partly as a sarcastic response to those that opposed his actions, and partly as a good-natured salute to his Palestinian heritage.*

Doug Reed, Shane Cobourn, and Gus Glitch worked THE SNAG repeatedly on toprope. Shane was first to climb it clean on toprope, while the others hadn't come close. Seeing how Gus bolted this line, Shane's toprope ascent lit a fire under him, and the FA hungry Gus immediately pulled the rope and "snagged" the FA, protected by nothing more than one bolt and a fixed pin. A week after the FA, part of the namesake crimper that is "snagged" during the crux broke off, leaving a remnant that was even sharper (but just as tiny). For years this route was known as Crowder's' first 5.13, however the retro-bolting job in 1993 took all the sting out of the tenuous gear stances at the crux, rendering the line far easier.

18 TOXIC SHOCK 5.11c ★

A bouldery, beta-intensive sequence to the ledge above the overhang (stick clip recommended) makes for a difficult onsight. Catch your breath on the ledge, and then cruise through moderate terrain up and left to a crack with a small bulge. 4 bolts to anchors. (50 ft.)

Variation: A slightly easier alternate start, called BLACK SAND BEACHES, utilizes all of the same bolts, but begins below a left-facing corner a few feet left of the original start. Stay left of the bolt line until it is possible to traverse right at the second bolt.

19 PTERANODON 5.11a

Start right of TOXIC SHOCK, on top of the ledge at the right end of the main Hidden Wall face. Climb past a weakness in the coral-like huecos and pockets to a roof. Pull up, scout for holds, then crank up and over the roof (crux). Finish by climbing the left side of the dihedral past a small tree through moderate (5.8) but runout territory. 4 bolts to anchors. (50 ft.)

20 PATH TO EXTINCTION 5.10a

This link-up takes the path of least resistance up this side of the wall. It's a bit contrived, but makes for a decent warm-up. Start same as PTERANODON, but at the second bolt traverse left to finish on the upper half of TOXIC SHOCK. Clip the second bolt of TOXIC SHOCK at your feet to protect the traverse. 4 bolts to TOXIC SHOCK anchors. (50 ft.)

21 FREUHLEIN 5.11a

This line was named in honor of the "girl-power" that put it up – women made the first two ascents, which was a rare occurrence for the area at that time. Start the same as PTERANODON through the crux roof. Next traverse right across the dihedral and then finish straight up. 4 bolts, bolted anchors. (50 ft.)

22 NOT SEE 5.11b

Start the same as PTERANODON, but after the second bolt traverse right, pulling the roof at a different bolt a few feet right of the PTERANODON crux. Finish same as FREUHLEIN. 3 bolts, bolted anchors. (50 ft.)

23 SPITTER 5.12b

Starts 10 feet right of PTERANODON, just right of a large, left-facing flake. Climb up to a bolt, and then angle up and slightly left. (Gear can provide some peace of mind between the first and second bolt, but is not necessary.) Pull the roof, and continue climbing past two more bolts, where a dirty, lichenous crux will be waiting to spit you off at the top. 3 bolts, bolted anchors. (40 ft.)

24 DOUG'S DIHEDRAL 5.11c R

Mixed. Climb past the first bolt of SPIT-TER, but then work directly up and into the leaning, left-facing dihedral. 1 bolt, bolted anchors. (40 ft.)

25 THE CARNIVORE 5.12d

The meat of the matter awaits just off the deck. Small holds and a scary second clip make for a predatory crux sequence. A couple of long pulls on jugs will get you through the roof, where you can then breathe easier through moderate terrain towards the top. 5 bolts, bolted anchors. (55 ft.)

26 THRATCHER 5.13a

This is the right most line on the wall. Claw, scrap, and scratch your way past a low crux, climbing past three bolts until it is possible to step left and join up with CARNIVORE. 6 bolts to anchors. (55 ft.)

The following routes are located well right of the main section, and rarely see any traffic. Although not worth a special trip to Hidden Wall, a few of the lines are decent and worth doing if you find yourself in the area. Topropes may be set up by scrambling up the gully on the far right side of the cliff.

The next four routes start from a vegetated ledge.

27 LAKE VIEW SLAB 5.7

Start about 50 feet right of THRATCHER. Follow a flake system, trending up and right to a small roof at the top of the cliff. Bolted anchors. (50 ft.)

28 AIR VIEW SLAB 5.8

This slightly harder variation takes a direct line from the ledge to the same anchors as LAKE VIEW. It's not as well-protected as it's neighbor to the left and is probably a better option for toproping. (50 ft.)

29 DR. JECKYL'S HIDE 5.9

Ascend the large crack/chimney feature. Bolted anchors. (50 ft.)

30 DR. JECKYL'S RIDE 5.10a

Take the path of least resistance, up the face to the right of the chimney, to the same anchors as DR. JECKYL'S HIDE. (50 ft.)

The next three traditional routes all share a start at the extreme right end of Hidden Wall, about 150 feet right of THRATCHER. All have natural anchors using gear and rock horns at the narrow, jagged summit. Bring long webbing and small gear. To descend, walk off and scramble down and right along the gully.

31 ABSENT FROM THE BODY 5.9+

Start at the right-most end of the wall. Begin at an arête that is located just before the gully. Clamber up the arête until it is possible to move left into a broken, vertical crack system. Follow the crack to a right-facing corner and the top of the cliff. Natural anchors. (50 ft.)

32 MANDATORY REACTION 5.10

Scramble up the gully to the north-facing side of the wall. Start at the arête on the left side of the wall and climb past one bolt and a series of thin, vertical cracks on a technical face with tricky gear. 1 bolt, natural anchors. (25 ft.)

33 MANDATORY ACTION 5.10

This is a link-up of the previous two routes. Climb ABSENT FROM THE BODY until you reach an overlap/undercling feature. Traverse right and around the corner onto the north-facing wall. Finish on the upper section of MANDATORY REACTION. Natural anchors. (50 ft.)

32

GUS GLITCH

A stark contrast to many other Piedmont pioneers, Gus Glitch's mantra could very well be summed up with, "If you bolt it, they will come." A master at finding the hardest, most direct lines (a few of which remain unrepeated), Gus's contributions to the climbing community have at times been called into question because of his love for the drill.

Gus's climbing career began in 1984 (before the age of the V boulder scale, or even pads for that matter), and in a span of two years, Gus was sending 5.13 boulder problems. Famed first ascensionist Doug Reed took notice, telling Gus, "You should lead." Gus got his first taste of FA at Crowder's in 1986 (RAWLHIDE, 5.10b, ground-up), and after that he was hooked! In addition to leading the charge of development at Hidden Wall, Glitch went on to leave his mark at several crags throughout North Carolina, Virginia, West Virginia, and Colorado.

Of his more than 600 FA's, it was without hesitation that Gus remembered his favorite line – "It'd have to be NEBULA out at the (Hidden) Valley..." Checking in somewhere around the neighborhood of 14a, Gus worked this route 35 times before sending. His other 14's (one being the somewhat controversial SUPER WHINY BUGS at the New River Gorge) only took a fraction of that time.

Gus's fun-loving but raucous personality, combined with a desire for thrill-seeking has gotten him into trouble more than once over the years. Never one to turn down a dare, and a self-proclaimed cocky young gun back in the day, Gus somehow managed to make it through his aggro, testosterone-driven years more or less unscathed. With bold, ropeless ascents of countless lines, to a number of larger than life tales (most involving trash talking and too much booze), Gus has acquired more than a few broken bones and a handful of enemies. But for those that have stuck with him and are willing to give him the benefit of the doubt at times, Gus is a light-hearted, jovial character who, though perhaps a bit rough around the edges, is a guy you'd want to have your back in a bar fight.

Although he can still crank on a lot of his old routes whenever he gets the notion, much of his time these days are spent in his "barn," an 800 square foot climbing haven containing over 3,000 holds. So much more than the typical home gym however, this place could be described as a museum. The walls are littered with pictures of old school, lycra-clad heroes, as well as old bolts, pitons, and pieces of broken holds kept as souvenirs. A TV in the corner on top of the mini-fridge is constantly at the ready to replay the glory days of old ascents caught on VHS tapes. In between project burns, there are plenty of photo albums and detailed history records from areas where Gus had a hand in developing. The flooring is made from old mattresses and covered in a psychedelic carpet that would be right at home in a 1970's bowling alley.

No tape is used for marking new problems – there is an infinite amount of unique lines to be had, with a laser pointer dangling from a hook at the entrance to point out the next challenge. Many an up and coming hardman has gotten plenty strong in Gus's barn over the years.

Gus Glitch remains a permanent fixture in the Charlotte climbing scene, both past and present. His contributions to the writing of this guide were not only extensive, but also riddled with laughs, rants, and many tall tales.

MAIN WALLS

The character of climbing at Crowder's Main Walls couldn't be any more different than the vibe at Hidden Wall. Whereas Hidden Wall gets so little traffic it can sometimes feel like a personal crag for bolt-clippers looking to push their limits, the Main Area offers more of just about everything except solitude. There are a host of moderate routes, most of which can be easily top-roped. Unlike many climbing areas that consist of a long cliff band that is more or less intact, the buttresses at the Main Area are jumbled and strewn haphazardly along the ridge, sometimes making for a confusing and disorienting initial experience. For a bird's eye visual of the entire cliff layout, please see the next page. Routes in the Main Area are described in this order – Practice Wall, Wrestling Wall, David's Castle, Nuke the Whales, Fortress Area, Two-Pitch Wall, Car Wall, Red Wall, and Resurgence Areas.

APPROACH

From the parking lot at the Linwood Road Access, hike along the Backside Trail up a very steep but wide gravel road, bearing right at the fork. You won't have to feel guilty about missing your buns of steel workout video, because this hike is more than an adequate substitute. After about a mile, negotiate the at times oddly-spaced wooden stairs that will lead you to the top of the Practice Wall. To reach the base of Practice Wall, David's Castle, and Red Wall, continue on a trail to the right that will take you down to the cliff base. For toprope setups as well as walls in the Fortress areas, head left along the ridge top trail. Note that some anchors require a bit of scrambling to access, so please take care in setting up topropes.

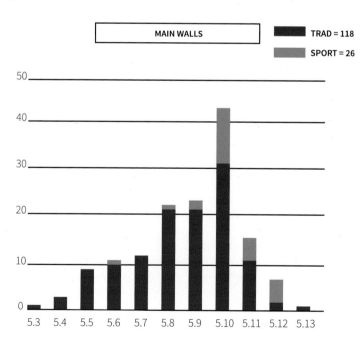

MAIN WALLS

TRAD = 118
SPORT = 26

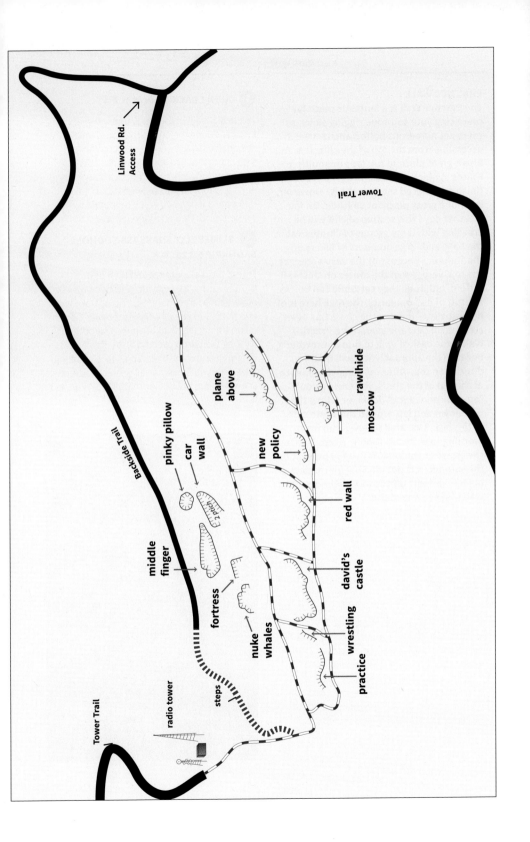

Linwood Rd. Access

Tower Trail

Backside Trail

Tower Trail

radio tower

steps

middle finger

pinky pillow

car wall

2 pitch

fortress

nuke whales

new policy

plane above

rawhide

moscow

red wall

david's castle

wrestling practice

PRACTICE WALL

The Practice Wall is a fantastic place for practicing your top-rope rigging skills, as there are numerous bolted anchors easily accessible from the top of the cliff. It is also a great place to run laps up multiple routes in quick succession, as many routes finish at a shared set of anchors. However, it is not a great place for solitude. On fair weather days this section of cliff will be crawling with large groups of climbers at the base and large numbers of hikers on the summit. Because of the easy access at the top, very few of the routes on this wall are led, although they certainly can be. As a result of its popularity, the rock here is of high-quality – most of the choss has been cleaned up over the years. The Practice Wall is the easiest wall to find at Crowder's, because the approach trail will land you directly on top. After catching your breath at the top of the steps, you can rig your top-rope and rappel down, or follow the trail down and left around the south side of the cliff. This area receives sun from morning to early afternoon. Note: Due to the crowds of onlookers usually present on the summit, it is not unusual for random objects to "fall" off the top – helmets and a watchful eye are advised.

> *"He worked on that problem nearly all of one summer, and when he finally pulled it off it was the hardest thing to date on the mountain. None of us knew what a 5.12 was supposed to feel like at the time, so we called it a hard 5.11. It was probably Crowder's first 5.12." Gary Mims, on Shane Cobourn's SKUNKPIE efforts*

1 BURN CRACK 5.10c/d ★★★

The first 30 feet of this burly line will give your forearms quite the burn. This route follows the obvious, overhanging crack on the left side of the Practice Wall. Powerful opening moves on smooth, polished rock lead to hand jams and long moves between good flakes. Pull onto a ledge and enjoy moderate terrain to the top. Bolted anchors. (80 ft.)

2 SLIMEBELLY SNAKEASS SODHOLE SKUNKPIE 5.12a ★★

Mixed. Start a couple of feet right of BURN CRACK. Grunt your way up polished laybacks, aiming for a large rounded, sloping flake with two bolts that are very close together. Continue up then traverse right along a smooth rail, fighting the pump over the last bulge before commencing with some casual face climbing. If leading, you'll need small gear to 1". 2 bolts, shared bolted anchors with BURN CRACK. (80 ft.)

The next three routes all share the same set of bolted anchors.

3 KLINGON TRAVERSE 5.12 ★★

Mixed. Start on SKUNKPIE. Climb up to the horizontal crack with two rusty pitons. Next, traverse right and finish on BLACK FLAG DIRECT. Rarely done. 2 pins, 1 bolt. (80 ft.)

4 BLACK FLAG DIRECT 5.13a ★

Mixed. So you wanna climb 5.13a? Here's a rare chance to try one on toprope. Locate a hangerless bolt about 30 feet right of BURN CRACK. Make for a horizontal crack, then trend up and right, aiming for another bolt. Pass the bolt and jug haul your way through steep terrain to the top. 1 bolt. (80 ft.)

5 BLACK FLAG 5.10d ★

This much easier (and therefore more commonly done) variation begins on the arête that forms the left side of GASTONIA CRACK. Climb the arête until it is possible to step left along the horizontal crack to a good stance at a bolt. From the bolt climb directly up steep terrain, same as for BLACK FLAG DIRECT. If toproping, be mindful of the swing at the start of the route. 1 bolt. (80 ft.)

The next three routes also finish at a shared set of bolted anchors.

Jennifer Kane in a winter wonderland on GASTONIA CRACK (5.4)

6 HEADY ARETEDDY 5.9

Although this line may have been previously climbed, local climber Eddy Ramirez popularized this harder variation to GASTONIA CRACK in 2011. Follow the arête left of the chimney, avoiding all holds right of the arête. For a full-value finish, top out via the boulder to the left of the ledge at the top of the cliff. (80 ft.)

7 GASTONIA CRACK 5.4 ★★★

This route is not only a perfect first outdoor climb, but according to famed first ascensionist Wes Love, it's the best line on the mountain. It includes interesting position and big, beginner-friendly holds. Climb the obvious corner/chimney system in the middle of the Practice Wall. Leaders should take big gear and be prepared for some runouts. (80 ft.)

8 PLAYGROUND 5.9+

This is a great "recess" option for trad students looking for a place to play. Start in the left-facing flake system just a few feet right of GASTONIA CRACK and follow this weakness all the way to the top. A few different variations are possible. (80 ft.)

9 THE WALL 5.10a R ★★

Start in the thin, right-angling laybacks five feet right of GASTONIA CRACK. Trend up and right towards a horizontal crack, then gain the incipient seam above via a long move to a sidepull (crux). Follow blocky edges to a notch on the left side of a large ledge, then scramble another 10 feet to the bolted anchors. (80 ft.)

The next two routes were originally considered a single line, called RIGHT SIDE OF THE WALL. At some point Doug Reed led two distinctive lines on this section of rock, although more than one source has confirmed that the "lead" was more or less a free-solo. Over the years a number of crimps and foot jibs have broken off, making the boundaries between the two lines a bit muddled. The two most obvious remaining paths are described in this guide, but since these routes are almost always

toproped from a shared anchor, there are endless link-up variations possible – have fun!

BURN CRACK was one of the first lines established on Practice Wall and it may be the best line in the whole park. In the 1980's, this line was the token route on which to run laps. Climbers would rotate through, each taking a dozen or so burns at the end of the day, until their forearms all felt like they were on fire (hence the name). But it wasn't enough to climb it the "normal" way. BURN CRACK quickly became the scene for some of the most interesting and creative ascents at Crowder's. Local climbers tell numerous tales of how they've tackled BURN CRACK barefooted and blind-folded. Rumor has it there's been at least one nude ascent.

🔟 BRICK IN THE WALL 5.10d ★★★

No dark sarcasm here, just technical face climbing at its finest! Start 10-15 feet right of THE WALL. Follow the line of sharp crimpers up to a funky undercling move at the second horizontal (crux). Trend up and left, aiming for a small left-facing corner. Work up the corner to gain the ledge, and then follow juggy flakes to the top. Bolted anchors (shared with either THE WALL or ANOTHER BRICK IN THE WALL. (80 ft.)

⓫ ANOTHER BRICK 5.10a ★ IN THE WALL

All in all it's just another fun face climb on the Practice Wall. This line starts a few feet left of MIKE'S CRACK. Crimp your way directly up the face to a large ledge. Bolted anchors. (80 ft.)

⓬ MIKE'S CRACK 5.6 ★

Named in honor of local hero Mike Smith, this route follows the obvious left-facing corner on the right side of the Practice Wall, just before the trail starts heading uphill. Climb the corner and top out at a large tree on a ledge. Leaders bring a wide variety of gear, as the

crack gets smaller towards the top. Shared bolted anchors with ANOTHER BRICK. (60 ft.)

⓭ SO IT GOES 5.8+

This line does indeed go, despite all the dirt. Follow the series of shallow cracks on the face just right of MIKE'S CRACK to the top. If leading, bring small gear. Bolted anchors (60 ft.)

WRESTLING WALL

Though the trail right beside this wall sees constant traffic, the 3 routes in this section are often overlooked. From Practice Wall, hike down to the lower tier of rock, heading towards David's Castle. After a couple of minutes and a lot of lichenous rock on your left, look up to see a large, looming, blocky roof. This landmark is also the start of the first two routes on the wall.

Long time local and first ascensionist Gary Mims recalls a time in the late 1960's when climbers would set up a Tyrolean Traverse between the top of the west side of David's Castle wall and the Summit Ridge Trail. This chasm provided a nice clean line across the gully. However the pine trees in the gully are much taller now – a similar set-up today would not be quite as open, and would probably require excellent tree-dodging skills! Climbers would set up the lines in the morning and take them down at the end of the day, using a Z-line pulley to get the main line as tight as possible. The bolts have long since been chopped, but the remnants can be found on a table-top shaped rock about waist high just up from THE DISH.

1 IN THIS CORNER 5.5

Locate the obvious blocky roof on the left side of the Wrestling Wall. Climb the left-facing corner to the roof, and then move left around the roof and up to the top. Natural anchors. (50 ft.)

2 CHAMPIONSHIP WRESTLING 5.9

Climb IN THIS CORNER to the roof, then skirt right around the roof and continue to the top. Natural anchors. (50 ft.)

3 MAIN EVENT 5.9

Mixed. This route is located at the right end of the Wrestling Wall. Look for a line of bolts just before arriving at the David's Castle area. Follow the left facing flake system up to a roof. Pull the roof and follow the shallow cracks up the face to the top. Take a couple of small pieces of gear. 3 bolts to anchors. (50 ft.)

DAVID'S CASTLE

This sunny stretch of cliff is home to a number of fine, classic lines, and can be reached via several different options. From the summit ridge follow the trail; dodging in and out of a few rocky outcroppings until the shady, west-facing side of the buttress known as the Backside comes into view. To access the top of the cliff keep walking along the cliff top trail. To access the base, scramble down the gully. This gully can be a bit precarious, so for those with small children and/or dogs, it is easier to reach the cliff base via the trail from the Practice Wall. Hike down to the lower tier of rock and follow the trail past the Wrestling Wall and the gully. A number of routes are found on the Backside, including the classic hand crack OOGA CHOCKA – these routes don't see sun until the afternoon, and therefore make a decent summer option. The routes on the main section of wall are not as toprope friendly. Many of the bolted anchors are found in the middle of the cliff, due to questionable rock quality towards the top. Routes on David's Castle proper bake in the morning sun, and are a wonderful option on bright, clear winter days.

Eric Dudley on his way to onsighting ENERGY CZAR (5.10d)

① NUCLEAR COTTAGE CHEESE 5.9+ ★★

This line packs quite a pump for the grade, but the gear is bomber. Start on the left side of the wall. Follow the vertical crack system that leads to a two foot roof, 30 feet up. Blast over this roof and then continue up the broken crack system to another overhang. Crank up and over to the anchors. (80 ft.)

② OVERHANG DIRECT 5.8 ★

A little easier than its cheesy neighbor to the left. Climb the broken flake system past a ledge. Trend left and up, keeping right of the NUCLEAR roofs. Keep right of the roof and continue to the shared anchors with COTTAGE CHEESE. (80 ft.)

③ THE DISH 5.9 ★

Climb the pillar in the middle of the wall to a ledge. Climb straight up to reach an undercling/overlap feature. Step left and finish straight up on the smooth face. Bolted anchors. (70 ft.)

Variation: Hang a right at the undercling, then straight up for an easier variation. (5.7)

④ OOGA CHOCKA 5.8 ★★★

One of the Piedmont's best cracks, a must-do at the grade! Start in the corner at an obvious hand crack. Jam and stem your way up the corner to a small roof, then pull the roof and continue up the crack to the top. Bolted anchors. (70 ft.)

⑤ THE NOSE 5.6 ★

A good option for beginning climbers. Take the path of least resistance up the blocky ledges on the face right of OOGA CHOCKA. Shared bolted anchors with OOGA. (70 ft.)

⑥ STUPID ROOF 5.10

This line could be considered a divider between the backside of David's Castle and David's Castle proper. Locate the obvious roof

down and right from OOGA CHOCKA. Climb the sharp, friable face and pull the roof on its left side. There are boulders at the top that can be slung for natural anchors. (70 ft.)

7 REDISCOVERY 5.8

Climb the crack just left of ROCKY's ROOF, and continue up the right-facing corner onto the orange face. Stay right of STUPID ROOF, then romp up and left to the top on jugs. Use a 60m rope or longer. There are plenty of pillars to sling for natural anchors. (90 ft.)

8 ROCKY'S ROOF 5.10

One of the earliest 5.10's at Crowder's. Just around the corner from STUPID ROOF is a low roof with some interesting pockets. Follow the weakness and angle up and right to the roof, then crank up and over. Continue to the top of the cliff, or traverse right to the anchors shared by the next three routes. (70 ft.)

The next three routes all end at a set of rap rings 25 feet off the deck, above an obvious bulging overlap

9 PSYCHOTIC REACTION 5.11a

This route can be protected quite well. However, nowadays most people tackle this techy highball line by toproping it after climbing TWO STEP. Climb the shallow, right-facing dihedral beneath the left side of the bulging overlap and then battle the bulge. (25 ft.)

> *"Several years ago I remember a bat that had taken up residence behind the undercling flake on NUCLEAR COTTAGE CHEESE. Anytime a climber would approach his perch, he would chitter furiously to ward off the intruder. I'd often peek into his lair to catch a better glimpse at what was causing all the ruckus, but all I could ever see was a pair of beady eyes and a gaping mouth – kind of intimidating since the very next move involved sticking your hand in there…" -Edward Medina (Charlotte, NC)*

10 TWO STEP 5.10b

A bit easier than its neighbor to the left, this short but enjoyable romp packs a lot of variety into just a little bit of real estate. Follow the thin seam and crank over the bulge via a juggy weakness in the middle of the overlap. 2 bolts. (25 ft.)

11 BETWEEN THE BETWIXT 5.10b

Unlock the boulder sequence on the face right of TWO STEP, then trend left to join up with TWO STEP's second bolt at the center of the overlap. 2 bolts. (25 ft.)

12 GOLDEN SHOWER 5.9+

Mixed. This route shares a start with ELECTRA. After the second bolt, trend left to follow the left most of two thin vertical seams. There are two finishing options – head right to the ELECTRA anchor 2/3 of the way up the cliff (popular), or continue up into friable rock to the top of the cliff (original line). (80 ft.)

Variation: For a 5.10 option, start directly below the low overhang 5 feet right of the parallel seams. Pull the bulge, and then merge onto GOLDEN SHOWER.

13 ELECTRA 5.10c ★★★

Start just to the left of the obvious chimney. This full-value line utilizes long reaches and good footwork to gain a juggy flake system. Decipher one last tricky section before cruising to the anchors. 5 bolts, bolted anchors. (50 ft.)

14 CATERPILLAR 5.7 ★★★

This very distinctive chimney feature offers an excellent experience with a wide variety of climbing techniques and exposure. The gear is adequate, but not abundant. Despite the low level of difficulty, the ricochet fall potential leaves other routes as better choices for beginning trad leaders. Most topropers bail to the left and top out the cliff via the steep, juggy face, whereas leaders often continue tunneling their way to the very top of the feature. (80 ft.

> *"My favorite line at Crowder's is actually....CATERPILLAR! I love that thing, and make a point not to go too long without getting back on it. Fun moves, good gear, big line – and not too many suitors. Chimneys aren't all that cool I guess...Try it without cams sometimes!"*
>
> Sean Cobourn, early developer at Crowder's

Javier Licon on the pumpy classic, ELECTRA (5.10c)

Jennifer Kane inching her way up the
CATERPILLAR (5.7)

15 ENERGY CZAR 5.10d ★★★

A Crowder's must-do. A few tricksy opening moves on a thin slab lead to aesthetic climbing up a gorgeous orange left-facing dihedral and a few heady moves towards the top. Some parties choose to supplement the bolts with small stoppers. Many onsight attempts end with bail biners before reaching the recessed fourth bolt - keep climbing, it's there! 4 bolts, bolted anchors. (60 ft.)

ENERGY CZAR and INSTANT KARMA originally topped out in two pitches – one to the ledge, and then a short, chossy romp to the top. When Mark Pell (aka Eddie N. Pain) did the FA of TEMPORARY TRADITION in 1988, he added a bolted anchor station on the ledge halfway up that could serve all three routes. This caused an immediate leap in the popularity of the original two lines, although ironically TEMPORARY TRADITION hasn't seen nearly the same amount of action. These anchors are still there, but at the time of this writing are in very poor condition. Until they are replaced, it is strongly recommended to bring very long runners for the next four routes, and use the rusty anchors as a directional only; instead traverse up and left to use the anchors on the ENERGY CZAR ledge, which were added by another party much later.

16 BUTCHER OF BAGHDAD 5.11d

This much harder variation splits off from ENERGY CZAR after the third bolt. Trend up and right past three more bolts and some razor sharp crimps to the ENERGY CZAR anchors (bring long runners). Be careful, as "The Butcher" isn't afraid to cut! 6 bolts, bolted anchors. (60 ft.)

17 INSTANT KARMA DIRECT 5.10d ★★

Make sure you're up for the challenge or INSTANT KARMA's "gonna knock you off your feet." This stout line will certainly shine on as a Crowder's classic. Stem your way up the obvious corner and thin upper crack. Bolted anchors. (60 ft.)

18 INSTANT KARMA 5.10b ★

Start same as KARMA DIRECT, but move right along pockets and small huecos to the arête. Shares bolted anchors with INSTANT KARMA DIRECT. (60 ft.)

19 TEMPORARY TRADITION 5.11a

Mixed. Locate a low first bolt just right of the KARMA dihedral. Decipher the hard boulder problem off the deck, powering through a few long reaches past a bolt and a rather untrustworthy fixed pin. Finish on easy terrain with dubious gear options. Mostly toproped. 1 bolt, bolted anchors. (60 ft.)

20 PINK FLAMINGOES 5.11a ★

Steep, sustained, with sequential movement. Walk around the arête and climb the wall that faces the chimney/gully type feature. If leading, bring some micronuts for the crux, and be prepared for some tricky placements. (90 ft.)

"I flashed the FA of PINK FLAMINGOES on preplaced gear (pinkpoint). Rodney Lanier did the second ascent in the same style immediately after that. Our climb started about 20 feet up the gully. Doug Reed led it a few weeks later from the ground level and placed all gear on lead for the route's first redpoint ascent. For most people this route was (and is) done as a toprope climb, as it had a dangerous reputation. Rodney named this route well in advance and it had nothing to do with our style of ascent, which was a spur of the moment decision, partly because of the extreme heat that summer which made the route quite slippery at the crux. I believe he had targeted this as a project in the early 1980's when he climbed frequently with Wes Love and Benny Fowler and he had already given it the name then. Protection at the crux (micronuts) is very difficult to place – you wouldn't want to fall on these, and we didn't! We considered placing a bolt on the crux and I had the kit with me but Rodney was dead set against it and it wasn't worth arguing about. I would be surprised if this route has been led 10 times in 25 years " - Eddie N. Pain, First Ascensionist.*

Variation: Bailing out onto the arête offers excellent exposure as well as significantly easier climbing, although the rock quality is suspect in some places. (5.10a)

The routes on the right side of David's Castle don't see a lot of action, therefore may house more loose rock than your average Crowder's climb. It is likely that increased traffic would clean up these routes pretty well – so don't stay away, just be careful and use good judgment!

21 WHAT ELSE IS THERE TO DO 5.7+ ★

This fun little romp lies 25 feet right of PINK FLAMINGOES and has two starting options. Climb either the left (easier) or the right (harder) crack for 20 feet to a ledge. From the ledge, negotiate the slabby dihedral ramping up and right to the top. Natural anchors (70 ft.)

22 SADISTIC RHYTHM 5.9 ★★

This route begins just right of WHAT ELSE in a wide, striking crack angling up and right. Climb the crack to the face, and then continue up. Natural anchors. (80 ft.)

23 FOUR PLAY 5.4

This aptly named route begins beneath a triangular alcove shaped like the number "4," approximately 20 feet right of SADISTIC RHYTHM. Take the easiest line up a blocky ledge system, past the "4" and to the top. Natural anchors. (80 ft.)

Variation: A direct start offers harder climbing (5.7), but great protection

24 RESPIRATOR 5.8 R

Tricky crux gear sandwiched in between fairly mellow climbing. Follow a seam to an overhanging, right-facing flake 50 feet off the deck. Climb past the flake (crux) and follow easier terrain to the top

25 HANDLE WITH CARE 5.6

This route starts at a small, left-facing dihedral on the extreme right side of David's Castle. Climb the corner to a large, left-facing flake system that leads to a ledge, and eventually, the top.

On one particular day at the crag (during the pre-bolt era of ENERGY CZAR), local pioneer Gus Glitch was 11 weeks out from a broken heel bone, and feeling particularly cocky. After watching his friend take a lap (who was only climbing in the 5.10 range at the time), Gus nodded towards ENERGY CZAR and sneered, "If he can do it, so can I!" Reminded by Doug Reed to back up the fixed pin just before the crux, Gus set off with a little bit of gear and a lot of testosterone. He couldn't finagle the opposing RP placements just right to back up the pin, so he gave up and kept climbing, without even bothering to clip the fixed pin. Feeling pumped at the crux, he told his belayer to take, expecting to drop about 30 feet onto his last Friend placement. However, as he went whizzing past his gear, the cam managed to wiggle its way out, grounding Gus at the base of the cliff amidst a pile of greenbrier and small rocks, with legs and arms twisted behind him in a disturbingly unnatural state. Gus was knocked unconscious briefly, and as he came to, he recalls hearing fellow climber Rodney Lanier shouting from atop INSTANT KARMA, "What was that thud? Did somebody throw a pack off the cliff?!?" Belayer Tony Ledford responded back, "Nope, not a pack – that was Gus! He grounded!" The crowd that gathered around urged Gus not to move until help arrived, certain that he had broken his back and probably several other bones. Not known for his compliance however, Gus methodically unwound his limbs out to a normal position one by one, and gave each a test shake, muttering, "This one ain't broken," after each one. Amazingly enough, it turns out that he was mostly right. After hobbling back up to the summit and hitching a ride with some of the construction workers over by the towers, his numerous X-rays showed only one fracture – ironically on the same foot he had broken 11 weeks prior.

Eddy Ramirez finishing THE DISH (5.9)

Wade Parker in the midst of a REDISCOVERY (5.8)

Tom Caldwell on OOGA CHOCKA (5.8)

NUKE THE WHALES WALL

If you're looking for a secluded, shady mid-summer haven, head over to this small area. It won't see the sun until mid-afternoon. Due to a fair amount of sharp rock, take care when setting up natural toprope anchors, and be sure to bring a beefy rope. Despite the chossy looking exterior, most of the rock in this area is quite good and accepts plenty of gear, making it a wonderful option for newer trad leaders. All routes utilize natural and/or gear anchors. To reach this area, hike along the summit trail, past Practice Wall and David's Castle, and then take a narrow but well-defined trail down and left. The trail will weave through rhododendrons for a bit and curve back to the right, where eventually the obvious ORANGE CORNER will come into view. The first route listed, DIRT-HEDRAL, lies 25 feet left of the big dihedral.

1 **DIRT-HEDRAL 5.6**

This route shares a start with LICHEN. Upon reaching the ledge, step left into the vegetated dihedral, and continue to the top. (60 ft.)

2 **I'M LICHEN THE CLIMB 5.7**

Take the path of least resistance to gain the sharp arête on the left side of the wall. Follow the arête to the top. (60 ft.)

3 **NUKE THE WHALES 5.6** ★

Scramble up well-featured and juggy terrain (with a bit of vegetation here and there), aiming for a dihedral that forms the left side of a short chimney. Follow the dihedral to the top of the cliff. (60 ft.)

4 **SAVE THE WAILS 5.7** ★

Follow the thin seam that leads to the short chimney right of NUKE and then shimmy up a left-facing corner to the top of the cliff. (60 ft.)

5 **LOYAL ORDER OF THE TOAD 5.7**

This line follows a broken crack system that lies halfway between the NUKE/SAVE chimney and ORANGE CORNER. (60 ft.)

6 **A FINE LINE 5.7**

Start beneath the orange dihedral. Follow the arête that leads out to a flake system just left of the dihedral. Follow it up and slightly left, exiting through a cleft just right of an anvil-shaped overhang. (60 ft.)

Variation: For a harder version (5.10a) try PLAYING AN ELIMINATE. Stay on the narrow face of the dihedral, keeping right of FINE LINE, and left of ORANGE CORNER.

7 **ORANGE CORNER 5.5** ★★★

This aesthetic line follows the obvious, large, right-facing dihedral on orange-colored rock. Rope management is easier with a few extended runners. (60 ft.)

8 **WHALE OF A TALE 5.5**

Great for beginners, this line follows the thin crack system right of ORANGE CORNER. Climb the crack to a ledge, then continue past friable rock to the top, or traverse left to join up with ORANGE CORNER. Natural anchor. (60 ft.)

Jennifer Kane sampling A FINE LINE (5.7)

FORTRESS AREA

This area can be reached by taking a left at the top of the steps. Continue past the top of Practice Wall and David's Castle along the summit ridge trail, then head down and left when the walls come in to view. You can also scramble up the hillside to the summit trail via the gully separating David's Castle and Red Wall, or keep hiking past the base of Nuke the Whales Wall. This is a popular section of the park, so the rock here is pretty well-travelled. For the most part, it is now devoid of obvious choss. Sub-areas of the Fortress include Fortress Wall, Gumbies Roof, and Middle Finger Wall, and due to the layout of the walls, you could easily chase sun or shade (whichever is more desirous, depending on the season) without travelling very far.

Fortress Wall

If hiking from the summit ridge, the Fortress Wall will be on your left, beyond both Practice Wall and David's Castle. This wall sees shade most of the day so it's a good option on warm, sunny days. Many climbs share bolted anchor stations, allowing for convenient top-roping.

1 BIG CRACK 5.5

This one starts on the left side of the Fortress Wall, and is pretty self-explanatory. Follow the big crack to the top. Be sure to bring bigger gear if leading. Bolted anchors. (50 ft.)

2 DIRECT 5.9+ X

Maneuvering through a thin, low crux will put you in a "direct" line for the fun pocket-pulling above. There are few options for gear after the second horizontal crack; therefore most parties choose to toprope this from the anchors of BIG CRACK or FORTRESS FINGERS. (50 ft.)

3 FORTRESS FINGERS 5.10a/b ★★★

A nice technical line that is unfortunately as short as it is sweet. Start at the small cave on the right side of the Fortress Wall, and head up a diagonal crack. Traverse left into the thin, horizontal finger crack and then continue straight up to the top via small pockets and edges. Bolted anchors. (50 ft.)

Variation. A popular toprope variation climbs the arête on the left side of the cave and heads straight up to the anchors.

4 FINGER CRACK 5.8 ★★★

This is a nice line that travels up the right side of the wall. Start same as FORTRESS FINGERS. Follow the right angling crack, then continue up the juggy, slightly vegetated flake system to the top. Shared bolted anchors with FORTRESS FINGERS. (50 ft.)

The next three climbs are found in a cave known as Gumbies Roof. A key feature to get your bearings is a large hueco containing two bolts in the middle of the wall. If style points are what you're after, there are a few opportunities to practice your bat-hangs. All routes share the same bolted anchor at the top, so this area makes for a great training session. Many enjoy running laps on steep, pocketed terrain reminiscent of the Red River Gorge. If top-roping, be sure to bring several long runners and/or cordelette, and be mindful of the swing. Your rope would also probably appreciate a carpet to minimize contact with sharp rock.

5 AERIAL ACT 5.10d ★

A casual start leads to a pumpy high-wire act. Start just around the corner from FINGER CRACK, beneath the large and imposing roof. Move casually up the face, aiming for an obvious crack heading out the left side of the roof. Gorilla swing your way out the roof via big jugs. Follow pockets to the top. (60 ft.)

6 EYE SOCKETS 5.10b ★

This route shares a start with AERIAL ACT, but instead of trending up and left to the roof crack, aim for the double bolts inside the large hueco. Fight the pump as you pull over the lip and continue up the pocketed face to the top. (60 ft.)

7 GUMBIES GO HOME 5.10d ★★★

Start at a right facing flake a few feet right of EYE SOCKETS. Follow the flake up and to the right, passing the bolted hueco on the left. (60 ft.)

Kelly Weinel crankin' through the roof of GUMBIES GO HOME (5.10d)

MIDDLE FINGER WALL

This buttress contains routes on both sides of the wall, although the ones along the backside see a lot more action. The namesake feature is best viewed from the left end of the western (proper) side. The Middle Finger Wall proper remains in the shade until late afternoon. With the exception of the bolted anchors on THE BALCONY, there is no fixed protection on this side of the wall, so make sure you are comfortable with both placing gear and building gear anchors before attempting these routes. This area lies 50 feet beyond Nuke the Whales Area, and can be reached via that same trail, or by scrambling around the Middle Finger Backside.

1 MIDDLE FINGER 5.7 ★★

This line starts on the left side of the wall, at an obvious left-facing off-width crack. A couple of 3-4 inch pieces are useful. Follow the crack system past an archaic looking fixed pin that should NOT be trusted. A short, overhanging section of rock leads to easy, but exposed scrambling on chossy, brittle rock. (90 ft.)

2 POCKET OF LIKE'N 5.7

About 25 feet right of MIDDLE FINGER is a somewhat indistinct "Z" feature, formed by two uneven roofs. This route starts at a weakness below the middle of the "Z." Climb up to the left side of the lower roof and then follow the middle of the "Z" up and right to the face. Take the easiest path to the top. (90 ft.)

3 FLEXIBLE FLYER 5.9+ R

This route starts in the short, ramping corner 15 feet right of POCKET OF LIKE'N. Head up to the right side of the lower roof, and continue directly to the top. (90 ft.)

4 CONNECT THE CRACKS 5.5

Start at a broken vertical crack system about 15 right of FLEXIBLE FLYER. Head directly up the center of the Middle Finger Wall, passing a ledge with a small tree about halfway up. (90 ft.)

5 THE BALCONY 5.5 ★★

Start in a right-facing corner by a large tree, about 15 feet right of CONNECT THE CRACKS. Follow the flake system and aim for a crescent feature just below a large ledge known as "The Balcony." (Some parties choose to belay here and break the route into two pitches. Bolted anchors. (90 ft.)

6 **THE BIG DIHEDRAL 5.6**

This line climbs the large, obvious, left-facing dihedral on the right side of the Middle Finger Wall. (90 ft.)

7 **IRON CURTAIN 5.7**

Begin on the right side of the wall, about 50 feet right of BALCONY. Locate a small roof on the face with some orange rock beneath it. Negotiate the face, pull the roof, and follow the crack to the top. Note: There are a couple of different variations that skirt the roof on the right and left sides. Gear anchor. (90 ft.)

MIDDLE FINGER BACKSIDE
If you are facing the Fortress Wall, the backside of the Middle Finger Wall will be on your right. These lines are much shorter than their counterparts on the other side, and see morning sun. Topropes can be rigged by scrambling up the narrow ridge on the right side of the wall. Please take care, as the summit is narrow and very exposed.

8 **PICK-A-DILLY PROW 5.11b ★★**

Mixed. This powerful line on the left side of the wall is by far the best line on the wall and should not be missed! After the "business" (getting past the first bolt), step left to the overhanging arête, doing battle with a holly tree along the way. This line protects well with small to medium –sized gear, although few parties nowadays can resist the easy toprope setup. 1 bolt, bolted anchors. (60 ft.)
Variation: An easier (5.10b) variation starts the same as the original line, but heads up and right out the roof, aiming for an obvious rectangular slot about 20 feet off the deck. Finish up by moving back left towards the arête, following jugs to the top.

9 PRICK-A-DIGI-OW! 5.11b/c ★

Yet another variation to the original PICK-A-DILLY line, this one starts the same as the easier 5.10b variation. Upon reaching the rectangular slot, head straight up the face via some vicious crimpers. (60 ft.)

10 PLEASANT DREAMS 5.8+ ★

Mixed. This one is located in the middle of the wall, beneath an obvious right-facing flake system. A few hard overhanging moves at the start might prove more of a nightmare to beginners, but the determined ones will find nothing but pleasantries awaiting in the flake and thin ledges that follow. 1 bolt and bolted anchors. (50 ft.)

11 THE BEAR 5.7

Begin in the chossy flake system just right of PLEASANT DREAMS. Lumber up and right along the flake, then head straight to the anchors using good face holds. Bolted anchors. (50 ft.)

PINKY PILLAR

This very small detached buttress lies directly across from Two-Pitch Wall. One set of bolted anchors serves several possible lines of varying difficulty, the most common of which are listed below.

12 ESCAPING LEFT 5.8

This variation to ESCAPE FROM THE GUMBIE climbs the face left of the arête

13 ESCAPE FROM THE GUMBIES 5.9

Locate a bolt on the face opposite Two-Pitch. Climb straight up, passing an old rusty pin and a bolt along the way. (30 ft.)

14 ESCAPING RIGHT 5.5

This variation offers an easy option for setting up a toprope for the original line. Scramble up easy ground on the right side of the pillar. (30 ft.)

TWO-PITCH WALL

This tall wall offers a handful of two-pitch climbs. Iffy rock quality and gear options keep this area from seeing more traffic; nevertheless, this area provides a great opportunity to exchange crowds and blistering sun for solitude and a shady respite. The right side of the wall can be accessed by scrambling down the gully that separates this wall from the Middle Finger Wall. The left side of the wall can be reached by hiking past the base of the Middle Finger Wall proper. The best descent option for these routes is to walk straight off the top to meet up with the Summit Ridge Trail.

"This was a favorite climb of mine, and while it's more of an undertaking to lead than a lot of Crowder's climbs I thought it was a great little adventure and worth the trouble. The exposure on the roof is fantastic. The first ascent was via rope solo using direct aid on a 101 degree weekday evening in August when I was absolutely alone in the park. That was really the only way to bolt it without being detected. Four days later I returned with Danny Caldwell for the first free ascent, which we flashed. Diab Rabie bagged the second ascent later the same day. Recommended rack is a standard set of wires, small-medium Tricams with doubles in pink and red, and SLCDs to 2.5". Carry a variety of slings and some extra biners. A longer sling is recommended for the middle bolt to avoid rope drag crossing the roof. This is a bolted route but it's a trad lead-and-follow line that happens to have some bolted protection. It is NOT a sport climb so select a partner who is not likely to pump out and fall off the roof or you may have to lower that person all the way to the ground. Prussiks are not a bad idea for the second if there is any doubt" - Eddie N. Pain, on SECRET SERVICE

① CAMBODIAN HOLIDAY 5.9

Start a few feet left of TWO-PITCH, at a crack system near a holly tree. Climb to a big ledge, where you can build a natural belay if you so choose. From the ledge angle up and left, skirting an overhang on its right side (crux) and continue up the face to the top. (90 ft.)

The next six routes all share the same first pitch.

② TWO-PITCH 5.4 ★

P1: Scramble up the blocky flake system to a large ledge. Gear belay. (5.4, 80 ft.)

P2: From the left side of the ledge, angle up and left along a juggy, pocketed face to the top. (5.4, 50 ft.)

Variation: PITCHES AND SCREAM (5.6)
From the belay ledge, follow the seam more or less straight up to the top of the cliff.

Variation: DITCH TWO PITCH (5.5)
Traverse left as for TWO PITCH, but then stem up and right along a ramp. Finish just right of a roof at the top of the cliff.

③ EAT A PEACH 5.7 ★

Though not quite as good as the Allman Brothers album of the same name, this line offers a slightly harder variation to the regular TWO-PITCH finish, and can provide a good introduction to multi-pitch climbing for newbies.

P1: Same as TWO-PITCH.

P2: Traverse right on the ledge to reach an arching finger crack that heads up and right. Follow the crack to a roof with juggy flakes. (5.7, 50 feet).

④ EAT A PITCH 5.5

This variation traverses left as for TWO PITCH, but then stems up and right along a ramp. Finish just right of a roof at the top of the cliff.

5 TWO PEACH 5.6

Variation: From the belay ledge of TWO PITCH, follow the seam more or less straight up to the top of the cliff.

6 PREDESTINATION 5.8

P1: Same as TWO-PITCH.

P2: From the P1 belay traverse to the far right end of the ledge. Climb up a funky vertical crack system that finishes at a series of ledges. (5.8, 50 feet).

7 DESTINATION 5.8+

This slightly harder variation to PREDESTINA-TION starts further to the right and climbs the open book dihedral. (60 ft.)

8 SECRET SERVICE 5.10c/d

Mixed. Begin in the middle of the wall, halfway up the trail, below and 15 feet right of the PREDESTINATION crack. Climb up and right over a slight bulge to a left-facing flake. Layback the flake up steep rock to a ledge, then traverse right to an arête below the blocky roof. Pull past three bolts along the upper section, crank over the roof, and continue up moderate, vertical terrain to the top. 3 bolts and bolted anchors. (90 ft.)

9 DOUBLE NAUGHT SPY 5.9 R

Start right of SECRET SERVICE. Angle up and right through a broken flake system, aiming for a triangular overlap near the top. Negotiate past the pod and continue to the top. Gear is sparse. (80 ft.)

10 THE INTIMIDATOR 5.8

Start at a small tree a few feet right of DOUBLE NAUGHT. Head toward a right-facing flake. Follow the flake system as it opens up to an off-width up high that will see you to the top. (70 ft.)

11 TRASH COMPACTOR 5.5

This dirty little number is compressed on the right side of the wall, at the top of the gully. Follow the crack system to the top. (40 ft.)

BELAY

CAR WALL

This short but sweet section of cliff boasts some of the steepest rock in the area. It stays in the shade the majority of the day and is located well off the beaten path. This wall lies slightly up and left from the Middle Finger and Two Pitch walls. From the left side of the Middle Finger proper (or alternately, after scrambling down the steep, rocky gully between Two-Pitch and Middle Finger Backside), take a faint trail up and around the corner to the right. All routes, except the last three, have natural anchors.

1 ENTERTAINMENT FOR MEN 5.9

Scamper up the Car Wall gully until you reach the extreme left side of the wall. Follow the widest, left-most crack. (50 ft.)

Variation: For a full value link-up, begin on DRIVE ON and traverse left into the crack system.

2 PASSING LANE 5.9 ★

This link-up variation pulls the boulder start of DRIVE ON, and then traverses left into FLAT TIRE. Instead of stepping right at the end of the flake as for FLAT TIRE, take the well-protected crack all the way to the top. (50 ft.)

3 FLAT TIRE 5.10

This line starts at a right-facing flake about halfway up the gully on the left side of the wall. Climb the flake, then traverse right and finish on DRIVE ON. Due to less-than-stellar rock quality, this is highly recommended for toproping only. (50 ft.)

4 DRIVE ON 5.8 ★★

This excellent crack climb would certainly see more traffic if it were parked in a more accessible locale. Start at the thin crack in the center of the wall, just before the gully gets steep. A boulder start leads to a V-shaped alcove. Shift into overdrive and continue up the crack. The gear down low can be pumpy to

place, although the rest of the climb is easily protected. (50 ft.)

5 FIRESTONE 5.10

Start as for DRIVE ON. Trend up and right, aiming for a right-facing flake/seam. Follow the thinning flake to the top. (60 ft.)

The next three routes share a set of beefy chain anchors.

6 BURN SIGNALS 5.10c ★★★

If it smells like something's burning, it's probably your forearms! The only bolted line on the Car Wall, this hidden gem rivals ELECTRA and ENERGY CZAR for Crowder's best 5.10. Start

out with a few bouldery moves to a ledge, then traverse up and right utilizing juggy flakes and high feet. 4 bolts. (50 ft.)

7 DIESEL 5.11a ★★

Climb straight up the overhanging face in between BURN SIGNALS and SCORCHED EARTH. (50 ft.)

8 SCORCHED EARTH 5.10d ★★★ DEFENSES

Mixed. This steep line offers excellent position and dizzying exposure. Start beneath the arête and fire up the prow, passing two fixed pins that some choose to back up with gear. (50 ft.)

Groove is in the "Heart"

Those of you on the other side of 30 may remember a TV show called Captain Planet. The heroes of this kid's series were 5 environmental good guys, known as "planeteers," each possessing a magic ring that controlled an element of nature (earth, wind, water, fire) that they would use in their valiant battle against pollution. Then there was the fifth guy – his magic ring supposedly gave him the power of "Heart." As kids we always thought this guy was dorky – the other planeteers were all much more suave and cool. In fact I was never really quite sure what "powers" the fifth guy ever really possessed – it seemed like his purpose was more or less to hang around and say cheesy, supportive one-liners to the other (cooler) heroes. But now that I am older and wiser, I'm realizing that the "Heart Guy" might have been on to something. When it comes to any athletic endeavor – be it climbing or another sport, this power of heart may just be the most valuable resource of all.

When I think back to my proudest sends, the ones that stick with me the most are the ones that, if I'm being honest with myself, somewhere in the back of my mind I think may have happened by accident. Sure, its fun to send something hard, but many of my hardest projects ended with a redpoint run that was so well-rehearsed it almost felt like cheating. In those instances, the journey itself was where the grunt work took place, and the actual send attempt was just the culminating reward. In my opinion, the most prized sends are not the ones where every move is executed perfectly, but the ones where you have to fight tooth and nail every step of the way – the ones that cause you to involuntarily hold your breath as you replay the climb in your mind because you still think there's an outside chance you might fall.

I think one of the major differences between these rehearsed versus ad-lib type sends lies in this mysterious power of "heart". Some days I have it, and some days I don't. When I'm feeling strong I don't necessarily need it – I can rely on my strength and technique to get me through to the anchors. These are perfect times to work hard routes that push my physical and mental limits, because I've got confidence in my ability to make the moves. But at the end of a climbing trip, when I'm exhausted and my body is rebelling, sometimes "heart" is about the only thing I have going for me on my very last chance to pull a send out from my you-know-where before we pack up and go home.

Can I summon it at will? I wish. It only comes in fleeting flashes of determination, where an overcooked body is able to latch that dyno, fight that barn door, or lock off on that nasty crimper against all odds. I guess if it were able to be summoned at any given point everyone would have it. And if everyone could have it, we'd all take it for granted, which would in effect cause it to lose all of its mystery and much of its power. Though I do wish I could tap into it more, it makes those magical moments where I nab a send by the skin of my teeth that much more special. And it gives me all the more reason to whoop and holler for my climbing partners when they eek out a crux sequence and I can tell by the look on their face that they're just as surprised as everyone else that they're still hanging on. –Erica Lineberry

RISING SUN WALL

When hiking along the base of David's Castle, this shorter section of rock is located on the extreme left end of Red Wall, a good 75 feet before reaching the first routes listed under Red Wall. The routes are short, bouldery, and feature sketchy protection in places. Originally the lines stopped atop a 25 foot ledge, utilizing a fixed pin anchor for the descent. The hardware is long gone, so nowadays it's best to top out the cliff and build natural anchors. To descend, scramble off the top and head down and left along the sloping gully. These routes are listed primarily for historical purposes, but if you've exhausted the rest of the mountain, it's possible to get a cheap thrill here.

1 BUDDHA BULGE 5.10a

This line probably deserves more action than it gets. Start just right of a bulge at some graffiti and climb up and left. Pull the second bulge and continue up and left past yet another bulge. Bail out left or continue up and right to a gear anchor just above the crack system. (60 ft.)

2 60 SECONDS OVER TOKYO 5.10a

This early line was initially sent as a highball boulder problem to the ledge. This short little number packs quite a punch. Start about 15 feet right of BUDDHA, and climb straight up to the ledge. There is no longer fixed protection at the ledge, so continue to the top via the dihedral (5.8+) If leading, be sure to bring micro gear. (60 ft.)

3 YOKOHAMA MAMA 5.11a

Begin 10 feet right of 60 SECONDS, and surmount the steep face and bulge via an incipient seam. Once atop the sloping ledge, angle up and left towards the top. (60 ft.)

> "The routes on the Rising Sun Wall are not for everyone but they each have their moments for folks who enjoy semi-dangerous, bouldery leads. The upper half of these routes follow more of a path of least resistance rather than a direct line. Anyone walking up to them just needs to know their order and approximate position then wander up like I did and climb with a soft touch and a long neck. Be on the lookout for unobvious or unorthodox gear placements. Some of these may be mostly just to improve your odds but others are bomber if you rig 'em right. For example, I always carried a hook, a blade piton, an angle piton, a Lost Arrow or Long Dong, and a couple of different-sized looped jam knots on my rack at Crowder's on new or unfamiliar leads." Eddie N. Pain, First Ascensionist

RED WALL

One of the longer walls at Crowder's, Red Wall boasts several harder sport lines scattered intermittently among beginner trad/toprope lines. High traffic has cleared most of the choss from the popular sport routes, but be very careful on the natural lines, particularly if you choose to tackle them on the sharp end, as the rock quality is not ideal. To access Red Wall, hike downhill and right from the base of David's Castle until the left side of the wall comes into view. If you are having trouble getting your bearings at Red Wall, locate RED WALL CHIMNEY, the obvious wide cleft splitting the middle of the wall, and work left and right from there.

A focused Joe Virtanen stands tall to make the clip of OPINIONATED (5.9)

1 ASK MR. SCIENCE 5.9+

This was the original line on the wall, and its more recent neighbor to the right might be considered too close for comfort by some. Clamber up the short dihedral to gain a no hands rest atop a pedestal. Take the most sensible line to the top, ignoring the bolts on your right.

2 TOM WAITS FOR NO ONE 5.10b ★★

This is the left most bolted line on the ledge. Climb the thin face to gain steep, juggy rails and flakes above. 6 bolts. (60 ft.)

Variation: A slightly easier alternate start stems up the dihedral of MR. SCIENCE before merging into the bolt line (5.10a). It was christened as THE FLYBY due its close proximity to MR SCIENCE.

3 NO ADDED WEIGHT 5.10b ★★

Fight the pump through sharp, juggy flakes past two bolts, then trend up and left into TOM WAITS FOR NO ONE. 6 bolts. (60 ft.)

4 THE ARBORIST 5.10c ★

Mixed. This is the first bolted line that starts from the base, about 40 feet right of the three previous routes. A bouldery start leads to a ledge. Bring a couple of pieces of gear (.5" – 1") to supplement the terrain between the bolts. Be careful of loose rock in the upper section. 4 bolts, bolted anchors. (60 ft.) Variation: Stay left of the first bolt to avoid the crux, keeping the route at 5.10a.

The next three routes share a set of anchors.

5 SILENCE THE CRITICS 5.12b

This is a very unique route when compared to other Crowder's climbs. This is an in-your-face, sequential, core-intensive, line with barely there feet and a heads-up clip at the last bolt. 3 bolts. (40 ft.)

6 DESPERATELY SEEKING 5.11b ★ JUGGAGE

Seek all you want, but there aren't many jugs to be found here – only technical face climbing and sharp crimps! This route lies just right of the SILENCE flake system. Use small but very positive crimpers to delicately move up the face, angling slightly left at the top. 3 bolts. (40 ft.)

7 JUMPING JUNIPERS 5.9-

Start five feet right of JUGGAGE, in the middle of a short, detached pillar. Make for a pine tree at the top of the pillar, then wander up and left to the SILENCE anchors. (50 ft.)

First ascensionist Shane Cobourn gave SILENCE THE CRITICS its name as a cheeky jab at another party who rap-bolted his project while he was laid up with a bum knee. On his comeback day post-surgery, he tied in and flashed the FA on the first go, finding that the addition of bolts took all the fear and mental challenge out of the equation.

Climber crushing NO ADDED WEIGHT (5.10b)

Garrett Debruin committing to the crux on SILENCE THE CRITICS (5.12b)

Steve Lineberry on WELCOME TO CROWDERS (5.12a)

8 **MELLOW FELLOW 5.8**

This chossy route is anything but mellow on the sharp end. Beware of loose rock! Start 10 feet right of the JUMPING JUNIPERS pillar. Take the path of least resistance up the vertical crack and face to a large ledge. Build a natural anchor here or continue to the top. (80 ft.)

9 **TARGET PRACTICE 5.8**

Start about 10 feet right of MELLOW FELLOW at a crack system just left of OPINIONATED. Follow this crack as it briefly disappears (crux), then reappears again. The original line topped out, but nowadays most traverse right to the OPINIONATED anchors. (60 ft.)

10 **OPINIONATED 5.9** ★★★

Popular opinion ranks this as one of the best lines at Crowder's. It's definitely worth the hike to Red Wall. This bolted line climbs up an obvious arête/pedestal feature. Work your way up the pedestal via juggy flakes. A

.3 camalot can be placed from the top of the pedestal to protect the moves high above the second bolt. If you don't have gear, be extremely careful, as this section has been the cause of many ankle injuries over the years. The gently overhanging finish is airy and exciting, so make sure to save some juice for the top! 6 bolts to bolted anchors. (60 ft.)

Variation: Traversing in from the left makes for an easier start (5.7).

11 **SPRING FLING 5.8**

Start at a small, right-facing flake system about eight feet right of OPINIONATED. Meander up and left through the corner system, following a series of blocky steps. Traverse left to shared anchors with OPINIONATED. Bring very small gear for the start, or be prepared for a runout. (60 ft.)

12 **SPRING SWING 5.8**

This variation starts the same as SPRING FLING, but swings off course about halfway

up. When you reach the horizontal crack at 40 feet, head up and right to a bulge. Next traverse back left to join up with the SPRING FLING finish. If toproping from OPINIONATED, be sure to place some directionals, or you could be taking quite a swing. (60 ft.)

The next three routes end more or less in the same place, so it is reasonable to use the same set of natural anchors for each.

13 BEER WOLF 5.9+

Start 15 feet right of OPINIONATED at a group of three vertical cracks. Climb the cracks to a bulge, then power over the bulge to easier terrain. Continue up another set of vertical cracks until it is possible to step right at the top of the steep gully. Natural anchors. (60 ft.)

14 SPRING FEVER 5.7

Follow the crack that leads to a blocky roof system approximately 15 feet right of BEER WOLF. Pull over the left side of the roof and onto a ledge. Continue to the top. Natural

anchors. (60 ft.)

15 SPRING BREAK 5.8

Climb the seam to the SPRING FEVER ledge, passing just right of the roof system. Trend up and left to the top. Natural anchors. (60 ft.)

16 RED WALL CHIMNEY 5.3

Start at the obvious chimney in the middle of the wall. Stem your way past a series of blocky ledges on the inside of the chimney. Continue to the top (original line) or step right to KITTY LITTER anchors. (60 ft.)

17 KITTY LITTER 5.9+

Start 10 feet right of RED WALL CHIMNEY. Follow the thin, right–angling seam/crack to a small blocky roof. Crank over the bulge, then step left to some bolted anchors atop a ledge. (60 ft.)

**18 WELCOME TO 5.12a ★★★
CROWDER'S**

This relentless line stays in your face from start to finish. This is the next bolted line after OPINIONATED. Start on a small ledge a few feet off the ground. Crank through a tricky, right-angling seam, then power up the right-facing flake system. At the top of the flake step right to the shared anchors with TKO. 3 bolts. (40 ft.)

Note: The original finish continued straight up, angling left through chossy rock to the KITTY LITTER anchors. Should you choose this option, bring small gear for the top.

19 T.K.O. 5.12a ★★★

A balancy techfest with just a touch of burly – flexibility is a plus! Start in a jagged flake system a few feet right of WELCOME TO CROWDER'S. Delicately traverse up and right to the high first bolt. Go big, then punch up and left through the beta-intensive crux. 3 bolts, bolted anchors. (40 ft.)

20 RED RED WINE 5.11b

Start at a right-facing flake 15 feet right of TKO. Follow the flake, then at the second bolt roll right onto the arête at the base of the SCRAMBLE dihedral. Make a few funky and committing moves and then pull back onto the left face via sharp holds. 3 bolts, bolted anchors. (50 ft.)

21 SCRAMBLE MY FEEDBACK 5.10a ★★

This line scrambles its way up a distinctive dihedral on the right side of Red Wall. Work your way up a thin face with relatively sparse gear to gain the orange dihedral. Follow the corner past one bolt to the top. 1 bolt. Natural anchors. (50 ft.)

22 911 5.8

This route starts directly in front of a tombstone-shaped rock jutting up from the ground. Climb the face between SCRAMBLE and MASTER BETA, trending up and slightly left on pointed, zig-zagging flakes. Natural anchors. (60 ft.)

23 MASTER BETA ★★ 5.10c

This popular line is the next sport route after RED RED WINE. Technical moves through a series of thin (and sometimes flexing) flakes combined with generously spaced bolts make for an exciting line with a spicy finish. Despite the questionable rock quality towards the top, this route makes for a great warm-up option for harder routes on the wall. 6 bolts to anchors. (70 ft.)

24 AXIS (BOLD AS LOVE) 5.11c/d ★★★

Mixed. Are you bold enough for this route? Just ask the AXIS. Start on MASTER BETA, but follow the crack out right, aiming toward a fixed pin in an obvious seam. From here climb directly up, finishing at the MASTER BETA anchors (70 ft.) You can also top out right of the flake (original line, 90 ft.).
1 bolt, 1 fixed pin.

Erica Lineberry getting a taste of RED RED WINE (5.11b)

25 FASHION 5.12b ★★

So you didn't onsight this one? Don't feel bad, rumor has it that Lynn Hill didn't either. Start at the seam to the left of the bolt (original line and slightly easier), or directly under the bolt (a.k.a. FASHION DIRECT, and slightly harder). Angle up and right to a rather stylish crux sequence. Bring your fancy footwork and be ready to commit. 5 bolts to bolted anchors. (80 ft.)

26 FASHION SUPER 5.12b/c ★★★ DIRECT

This line takes the most direct path (via the most heinous crimpers). The desperate start combined with the technical crux of the original line makes for a full-value send, well-deserving of a few turns on the catwalk. Clip the bolt at the bulge before joining up with the original line at the second bolt. 5 bolts, (80 ft.)

27 THE GIMP 5.10c ★★

This newer addition to Red Wall is just right of FASHION and features fun moves up an arête and a technical traverse up high. 6 bolts, shared anchors with FASHION. (80 ft.)

28 TOM TOM CLUB 5.9 R ★

This bold, exposed lead has unfortunately become somewhat outdated due to the addition of THE GIMP. Follow the arête just right of THE GIMP bolt line, continuing up and slightly left toward the top, finishing on a right-facing flake. Natural anchors or traverse left to FASHION anchors. (80 ft.)

29 RAZOR'S EDGE 5.6 ★ (a.k.a. BUTTER KNIFE)

This beginner line follows a line of bolts up an arête on the extreme right side of Red Wall, and is a great option for new leaders. Climb the pocketed face or layback the arête to the top. 4 bolts, bolted anchors. (50 ft.)

RIGHT: Johanna Nevins getting serious on THE GIMP (5.10c)

RESURGENCE WALLS (A.K.A. RENAISSANCE AREA)

The collection of small, broken buttresses on the eastern side of the park are known as the Resurgence Walls. They are named for the burst of new development that occurred there in the late 1980's and early 1990's. This area is home to several high quality lines that could benefit greatly from more traffic. The Resurgence is a great option if you desire to avoid the throngs of curious observers and other climbers over at Practice Wall and David's Castle. Approach this area by hiking along the cliff base trail that angles down and right just past Red Wall. After a couple of minutes, the New Policy Wall will come into view. Keep walking to arrive at the Plane Above Your Head Wall, then the Trundlesauras Buttress. The Rawlhide Buttress sits below Plane Above Your Head, and the Moscow Wall lies left of Rawlhide.

Eddy Ramirez's ARBORCIDE (5.9) beta is not for the inflexible

NEW POLICY WALL

There is a trail branching off directly behind FASHION that angles down and right from Red Wall. Follow this trail for about 100 feet until you reach a small buttress. This wall offers a handful of decent lines that don't get very much traffic. The first three routes all share the set of bolted anchors atop NEW POLICY.

1 THIS AIN'T NO PLACE 5.7 FOR YOU ALGEBRA

Climb the flake system on the left side of the wall. (50 ft.)

2 ONE TO THE FIRST POWER 5.8

Step a few feet right of ALGEBRA, and follow the path of least resistance to the top. (50 ft.)

3 NEW POLICY 5.10d ★★

A few tricky moves past the first bolt lead to some tufa-pinching fun up high. 3 bolts. (50 ft.)

4 ORANGE PRICKADILLY 5.11b

This aptly named route often bites back, whether from the briars at the base or on the razor sharp pockets encountered throughout. Start on the right side of the New Policy Wall, in a small gully. Follow the line of three bolts through some interesting layback moves and an ever-increasing pump to bolted anchors at the top. (50 ft.)

PLANE ABOVE YOUR HEAD WALL

This small buttress is a good landmark to use for finding all of the other walls in the Resurgence Area. It offers two bolted routes and a bold traditional line. It is located in between New Policy and Trundlesauras, and just above Rawlhide. To reach this area from New Policy Wall, continue along the vague trail that travels across the ridge for another 200 feet or so. The Plane Above Your Head Wall will be up and left.

5 THE PLANE TRUTH 5.10d

This line climbs the bolt line on the left side of the wall. Climb up to the overhang, then power up the arête. 3 bolts to bolted anchors. (50 ft.)

Variation: A harder 5.11 variation climbs directly up past the third bolt, avoiding stepping around the arête.

6 PLANE ABOVE YOUR HEAD 5.10a ★

This line follows the bolt line on the right side of the wall. Climb the juggy flakes to an overhang. A long move cranks over the bulge (crux) and finishes on steep rock and big jugs. 4 bolts to bolted anchors. (50 ft.)

7 SPIKE 5.10 X

Not recommended for leading. Once you're above the roof, the only gear you'll get are slung rock horns that offer only marginal protection. Boulder up the low roof just right of PLANE and continue up the outside of the arête. (50 ft.)

TRUNDLESAURAS BUTTRESS
From Plane Above Your Head Buttress, follow the trail up and right for another 50 feet.

8 CHRISTMAS PRESENT 5.8

Though there might be other lines that you'd rather find under the tree, this moderate line can make good use of your rack as well as offer a chance to escape the crowds. Follow the obvious crack in the middle of the wall all the way to the top. Natural anchors.

The following four routes share a recessed bolted anchor atop a ledge in the middle of the buttress.

9 BUSCHMAN 5.11b

This route climbs the bolt line 20 feet right of CHRISTMAS PRESENT, just right of a rotten looking fissure. Scramble up to the ledge, then follow four bolts to the top. Don't get tangled up in the bush. 4 bolts to bolted anchors. (50 ft.)

10 TRUNDLESAURAS 5.10d ★★

Mixed. Start on the same ledge as BUS-CHMAN, Climb past a bolt to a small overlap. Pull past the overlap on its left side, clip another bolt, and then continue straight up to the top. 2 bolts. Bolted anchors. (50 ft.)

11 TYRANNOSAURAS ROX 5.10b ★★

Mixed. Climb TRUNDLESAURAS to the second bolt. Trend up and right, heading for another bolt, and continue to the top. 3 bolts. Bolted anchors. (50 ft.)

12 FUGUSI 5.10

Mixed. This line is basically a link-up of WOLF TICKETS and T-ROX. Start with the left crack option for WOLF TICKETS and climb to the ledge. Climb straight up the arête, clipping 3 bolts along the way (the last of which is shared with T ROX). 3 bolts. Bolted anchors. (60 ft.)

FUGUSI was originally a 5.11+ eliminate variation established by Gus Glitch. He'll be the first to admit that this hardest path up the wall is rather contrived. In fact, most onsighters would probably down-grade it immediately by using holds that were originally "off," which is why this guide listed it at 5.10 and described the most obvious path. But if you're looking for a crimpy challenge, stay focused on the micro-holds, and try really hard to ignore the jugs to your right and left.

13 PASSING OUT 5.10a ★★★
WOLF TICKETS

This route starts at one of two vertical cracks in the middle of the buttress, just left of a large boulder at the base of the cliff. Choose either crack and climb to the ledge. Then follow the shallow dihedral past a lone bolt up high. Continue to the top. 1 bolt, bolted anchors. (60 ft.)

14 OVERLOOKED AND UNDERRATED 5.9 ★★

Scramble up the large boulder and step onto the wall. Trend up and slightly left past a line of bolts, savoring the exposure. A TCU might come in handy between the last bolt and the anchor. 5 bolts to shared bolted anchors with WOLF TICKETS. (50 ft.)

The next routes are found on the other side of a narrow tunnel formed by the base of the cliff and a large boulder.

15 NO EXPERIENCE NECESSARY 5.6

A pocketed face leads to a right facing flake. Climb up the flake, then step right to PROS-ELYTIZER anchors or continue to the top. (50 ft.)

16 THE PROSELYTIZER 5.10d ★

Start at the arête just before the gully, just right of the NO EXPERIENCE crack. Climb up and traverse right at the ledge to gain the bulging undercling flake. Paste your feet, layback the flake, and grunt your way to the top as the undercling turns into a sidepull, al-lowing you to reach down to clip the anchors. 3 bolts to anchors. (30 ft.)

Variation: Start directly under the first bolt and power straight up the bolt line. Avoiding the flake makes for a harder line. (5.11b).

This climber's looking for good news on THE PROS-ELYTIZER (5.10d)

THE PROSELYTIZER - *This route was originally named IDIOT SAVANT, intended as a snarky jab revolving around some accusations over some drilled pockets. There was a lot of finger pointing and blame slinging, until years later the matter was cleared up as a misunderstanding. As a gesture of good will, the first ascensionist decided to change the name to something less controversial.*

17 JUST LIKE OLD TIMES 5.8

Start around the corner from THE PROSELYTIZER, a little way up the small gully. Climb the face to a right-facing flake. Follow this flake along the pocketed face to the top.

18 DEWEY USED TO LOVE IT 5.10a ★

Sean Cobourn named this route in honor of famed Crowder's local Wes Love, who had taken a hiatus from climbing (Dewey was his real first name) at the time of the first ascent. Located on the right side of Trundlesauras Buttress, on a thin overhanging face that juts out from the gully. Work your way up the steep, sharp pockets (taking extra care at the runout between the first and second bolts) past three bolts to anchors. Some supplement with gear. (50 ft.)

19 HOLY GUACAMOLE 5.8 ★★★

This fun slab route ascends the face just right of DEWEY, and is a great option for a beginner sport lead. 5 bolts to bolted anchors. (50 ft.)

MOSCOW WALL
This narrow buttress lies below Plane Above Your Head, and left of Rawlhide. It has largely been forgotten – even the first ascensionists themselves have very little recollection of the area. It has been included in this guide because of its proximity to the Rawlhide Wall. Happy exploring!

20 MOSCOW CIRCUS 5.10

Follow the right-facing flake system to the top. (50 ft.)

RAWLHIDE WALL
This buttress is located 100 ft. down and slightly right of Plane Above Your Head Wall and to the right of Moscow Wall.

21 CRO-MAGNON CRACK 5.6 ★★

Find this short, well-protected crack on the left side of the Rawlhide Wall, as the base of the trail starts to cut uphill. Named after the cave that was once an old mining tunnel down and to the right of the wall. (The cave is an interesting side trip while you are in the area.) This line does NOT utilize the bolts on its perilously close neighbor to the right. Natural anchors or traverse right at the top to the bolted anchors of ROCKY. (40 ft.)

22 ROCKY AND BULLWINKLE 5.10c

Climb straight up the bolt line via some vicious crimpers to the right of CRO-MAGNON. The business is over after the first bolt. 3 bolts to bolted anchors. (40 ft.)

Garrett Debruin feeling DISGUSTIPATED (5.11d)

Variation: Moving in from the left to clip the first bolt makes the line significantly easier (5.8).

23 RAWLHIDE 5.10b ★★

This fun, wandering route starts in the middle of the face, below a bolt inside an obvious white "circle." Climb to the circle, make a big move, and then work your way up the face clipping the rest of the Rawl brand bolts as you go. A nice mantle move at the top ensures you're still awake. 3 bolts to anchors. (40 ft.)

24 DISGUSTIPATED 5.11d ★★

Finally one for the shorties! Technical, powerful, and very beta intensive with insanely high feet, this line packs a memorable crux sequence! Start slightly left of the bolt line, and negotiate crimpers to gain a long horizontal shelf. Get your feet up and launch up (crux). Finish up and left.

Note: The original line was harder and more direct using barely there micro-crimps and

The Chromagnon Cave, just down from Rawlhide Wall, provides shelter in heavy rain (so long as you don't mind sharing it with cave crickets)

bad feet directly under the first bolt to gain the shelf. 4 bolts to anchors. (40 ft.)

25 ARBORCIDE 5.9

Start on the right side of the wall at a sacrificial stump (may it's memory live on in the route's name), where the trail begins to cut upward. Make for a left-facing, left-angling flake system. Follow the flake for a few feet, then bust straight up along the seam. (40 ft.)

Variation: A harder 5.11 option climbs a bit right of the line of least resistance.

26 OVERHUNG AND UNDERSTATED 5.11

This highball boulder problem has rarely, if ever, been repeated, due to the horrible landing. It climbs the steep prow in the gully, around the corner from ARBORCIDE. (20 ft.)

PILOT MOUNTAIN

Pilot Mountain is one of the most prominent landmarks in the State of North Carolina. This striking hill, which rises out of the relatively flat piedmont, can be seen for many miles. Its crown is a beautiful band of quartzite that completely encircles the top of the mountain. However, don't get too excited because this gorgeous feature, called the Big Pinnacle, is off limits to climbing.

If you are looking at the mountain as you approach from the south on NC 52, drag your eyes reluctantly away from the beautiful Big Pinnacle. Look down and to the west and you will see a smaller cliff below the crest of the hill. This one-mile long, south-facing, quartzite band is the climbing area, and is the home to over 80 routes. It's also one of the easiest cliffs in the State to access.

Pilot Mountain might very well be the most misunderstood climbing area in the state. Take the following quiz to see if your knowledge of the area is accurate or based on rumors heard around the community chalk pot in one of the local climbing gyms.

Pilot Mountain is:

A.   North Carolina's most popular climbing area.
B.   Often swarmed by hordes of novices who stake all-day claims on certain routes.
C.   An important climbing asset a short distance from North Carolina's major population centers.
D.   A vital winter destination.
E.   A climbing area with questionable rock.
F.   A cliff with many excellent routes.
G.   All of the above.

Contradictory as it may seem, the correct answer is of course G. Despite the existence of numerous other areas across the state that might be perceived as more destination-worthy by many, this small, unassuming cliff line has remained without a doubt the most popular climbing area in the State. On fair weather days you'll likely find it overrun with large groups of beginners on their first rock climbing adventure. Top-ropes drape across the cliff while wilderness sounds are drowned out by the sounds of exuberant newcomers to the sport. The rock quality is questionable in some places and the routes are often short. So why is all of this activity happening on a cliff that many serious climbers snub their noses at in disdain?

Despite the chossy reputation Pilot has earned in some circles, it also has plenty of wonderful qualities that are far too often unsung.

1. The crag is only minutes from Winston-Salem and an easy day trip from the Triangle and Charlotte.

2. Because much of the rock is just shy of vertical with big holds, there are many really nice easy to moderate routes; making Pilot a perfect place for an experienced climber to get his/her newbie friends hooked on climbing!

3. Almost all of the routes can be easily accessed from the top – if you can't finish a route, it's usually pretty easy to get all of your gear back. Also, most of the routes now have bolted anchors.

4. Pilot offers a decent collection of sport routes from 5.7 to 5.12.

5. It's one of the few places in the state that can boast pleasant climbing in the dead of winter (so long as the sun is out).

6. The choss is mostly gone on popular routes. Years of climbing have resulted in clean, solid trade routes. However, if you like to climb obscure routes it's wise to be careful and mindful of loose rock.

In the author's opinion, the majority of complaints against this important asset for the climbing community stem from unfair expectations. Don't go to Pilot hoping for long, bold, aesthetic leads on bullet hard quartzite – if you want that, head down the road to Moore's. Don't go to Pilot hoping for remote solitude in a wilderness setting – if that's what you're after, keep on driving to Linville Gorge.

LOCATION

Pilot Mountain State Park is located about 21 miles north of Winston Salem, North Carolina, less than half a mile off the highway. From Winston-Salem, take US Highway 52 North to exit 131 (Pilot Mountain State Park exit). Follow signs to the park. From points north, follow I-77 South to US Highway 52 South, and take the same exit mentioned above.

Continue up the steep and winding access road for about 2.3 miles to the parking lot on top of the mountain. If the parking lot is full (as is common during peak fall color season) you can carpool to the top from the park office lot near the entrance. On occasion the road to the summit closes due to icy conditions in the winter. If in doubt, check http://www.ncparks.gov/Visit/parks/pimo/conditions.php. If you happen to discover the road closure after already making the drive, don't lose heart. Though a much longer hike, the Grindstone Trail from the park office will lead you directly to the western-most loop of the Ledge Springs Trail. (Bear right and you will be at the Pool Hall Area. Bear left and you will be on the cliff top trail.)

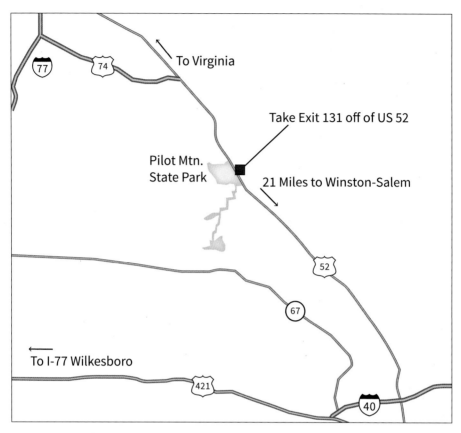

To Virginia

Take Exit 131 off of US 52

Pilot Mtn.
State Park

21 Miles to Winston-Salem

To I-77 Wilkesboro

ACCESS

One of the primary missions of Pilot Mountain State Park is the preservation of rare and endangered plants and animals. This mission is complicated by the facts that the park is heavily used (over 480,000 visitors in 2010), but also that the majority of these visitors congregate near the top of the mountain, which also happens to be the most biologically significant area.

Of the aforementioned 480,000 park visitors in 2010, park staff estimated that 7,000 of those visitors were climbers. Because there are so many climbers at Pilot the potential environmental impact is greater than just about any other climbing area in North Carolina. Thankfully most climbers have tendencies towards environmentalism, and therefore have been very good about working with park staff to protect the environment as a whole. However, despite good intentions there is still an impact. Please remember the following access issues that are specific to Pilot Mountain.

1.   CLOSED AREAS - The Big Pinnacle is designated as a National Natural Landmark and a Registered Natural Heritage Area due to the presence of rare plant species and its status as an isolated high quality natural area. The importance of the Pinnacle as a natural area has resulted in the climbing closure. The area below the parking lot is also closed, primarily as a safety and visitor management strategy. Several routes are closed for various reasons. In addition, the majority of the gullies in between cliff sections are closed to access.

2. ANCHORS – The park staff has taken great strides to preserve cliff top tree species by working closely with the Carolina Climber's Coalition and local climbers to provide bolted anchors at the tops of routes where trees were previously used. If bolted anchors are available do not use the vegetation.

3. NO TOPOUTS - The Park staff have asked that climbers adopt a "no topout" standard of use in order to protect vegetation at the top of the cliff. In other words, there should be no more than two visits to the top of the route - once to set up the toprope, and another to take it down. If a route is bolted try to lead it and lower from the anchors rather than setting up a top rope. The reason for this policy is to protect roots of trees and other vegetation.

4. HIKING TRAILS – Only access the cliff via the main hiking trail (Ledge Springs Trail), the 3 Bears Gully, and the Pool Hall Gully. No matter how convenient or tempting, do not use any of the other gullies. The Three Bears Gully was selected as the official descent because it is the most stable and is less prone to erosion, and the Pool Hall Gully was recently approved by the park staff because it is the only reasonable way to access the cliff top in the western end of the crag.

5. CURFEW - The parking lot on the top of the mountain closes 15 minutes before the rest of the park. Make sure your group allows plenty of time to clear the summit before it closes. It is extremely important that everyone respect the closing time. So far climbers and park staff have managed to maintain a positive relationship - don't be the jerk that messes it up for the rest of us!

6. DON'T BLOCK TRAILS – Don't take over the hiking trail with gear. Don't belay from the middle of the trail. Please share the trails. Every weekend casual hikers are forced off the trails in order to walk around belayers and piles of packs and gear.

7. BE CONSIDERATE OF OTHERS – Leave boom boxes, obnoxious egos, and dogs that don't play well with others at home. (Please see http://www.ncparks.gov/Visit/parks/pimo/rules. php for the park's rules regarding dogs). Please share the trails. If you see trash on the ground, assume it was left by an accidental oversight and gain some good karma by packing it out when you leave.

8. CUT NON-CLIMBERS SOME SLACK - Climbers do not comprise the majority of visitors to the park. Don't forget that most of us were non-climbers at some point in our lives. A typical climbing day will likely include encounters with hikers, picnickers, and other such outdoorsy folk that enjoy watching (and sometimes ogling) climbers from below as well as above. While it admittedly can get annoying, try to be good-natured about well-intended but often ridiculous comments from non-climbers about gear, technique, and safety precautions. My personal favorite was what I overheard a small boy ask his mother (rather loudly) while I was trying to make the roof clip on DEVIL IN THE WHITE HOUSE a few years ago – "Mommy is that lady going to die?" Evidently my body language was not inspiring much confidence…

THE CLIMBING
The cliff band is formed from a metamorphic quartzite that ranges from less than vertical to severely overhanging. The routes range in height from short, 30 footers in the Pool Hall and Three Bears areas, to taller routes approaching 90 feet on the eastern end below the parking lot. The style of climbing is mostly face climbing, often with at least one small roof to pull at some point.

Although CRACKING UP in the Amphitheater is the closest you'll get to a true crack climb, short, broken crack sequences can be found on several routes.

Pilot Mountain is in some ways a work in progress, or perhaps an example of geologic evolution. When the first climbers started developing the cliff in the 1960s, it truly was a choss pile. Loose rock was everywhere, and climbers simply had to be prepared to pull off chunks from just about every climb, even the ones that are now considered classic. Since those days thousands of feet and hands have smeared, pulled and cranked on every hold on the popular routes. As a result, most of the bad rock has been pulled off the cliff and now lies on the ground, though certain routes still have sections of questionable quality. However, while all of this climber-generated cleaning has made the cliff a much, much better place than in the past, it's still a far cry from the stellar quartzite of Moore's Wall and the granite of western North Carolina.

Because of this Pilot Mountain has remained a predominantly top-roping area – almost all of the routes have easy access to bolted top rope anchors. Keep in mind that while top-rope climbing is generally considered to be the safest method of climbing, setting up top-ropes can be hazardous. Exercise extreme caution when rigging top-ropes, as some of the anchors require down climbing near the edge of the cliff. It is wise to always anchor yourself anytime you work near the cliff's edge.

CLIMBING SEASON
Though many dedicated climbers in the Triad and Triangle areas avoid Pilot like the plague in favor of areas with less crowds and better rock, these same folks will descend upon it like a moth to a flame as soon as the weather turns cold, since Pilot is one of the only reasonable day trip options for many during the winter months. Whether you consider Pilot to be a three or four season climbing destination is largely dependent upon your tolerance level of heat and humidity. Keep in mind that since Pilot is a low-elevation, south-facing cliff situated in the heart of the Southeastern United States, it will be stricken with oppressive temperatures and almost tangible humidity levels throughout the summer. While many gluttons for punishment will still be cranking out there during July and August, for those that prefer less extreme conditions, I'd suggest September through May as the prime season.

If it feels like the arctic in the parking lot, don't panic. It's well worth the short hike down to the cliff to assess conditions before heading home. The parking lot is exposed to the wind and is almost always much colder than the cliff. On more than one occasion the author has gotten out of the car to 40 mph + winds and below freezing temps, only to be pleasantly surprised after hiking down to find sun-drenched rock protected from the howling winds up above.

GEAR
Since top roping is the norm rather than the exception at Pilot, you can easily climb there safely without signing your bank account over to your local outfitter. All of the best routes are equipped with bolted anchors, so a selection of standard slings, locking carabiners, and quickdraws will suffice. For those bolted anchors that are set further away from the cliff's edge, bring some webbing, as well as a scrap of carpet to pad any sharp edges. In instances where there is no fixed hardware present at the top of a climb, a full rack, a spare section of rope or some long slings may be needed to safely rig a top-rope anchor. Park rangers have pointed out that one of their top priorities is the preservation of natural features – which of course includes the park's trees. The park staff has authorized the placement of bolted anchors in order to preserve trees. Most routes have been equipped, but in the case of those that haven't, please DO NOT SLING TREES FOR ANCHORS.

Unless otherwise noted, routes at Pilot Mountain are considered top-rope routes. Lead routes are labeled as Sport or Trad. If you want to lead one of the trad or mixed routes bring a selection of draws and a light rack. Route descriptions should help with gear decisions. Although caution is recommended if you intend to lead many routes on traditional gear due to rock quality, a few routes make for great trad leads, and are noted as such in the route description. These routes will likely require a full rack. Be very careful placing your own protection, and carefully inspect any and all fixed protection before trusting your life to it.

PARK FACTS
Pilot Mountain State Park

1792 Pilot Knob Park Road, Pinnacle, NC 27043

Office Phone: (336) 325-2355

Email: pilot.mountain@ncmail.net

Hours

November - February, 8:00 a.m. – 6:00 p.m.
March, April, September, and October, 8:00 a.m. – 8:00 p.m.
May - August, 8:00 a.m. – 9:00 p.m.
The park is closed Christmas day.

Do not use trees as top rope anchors unless there are no alternatives. Most routes have bolted anchors.

CAMPING

There is a family camping area about 1 mile inside the park. The campground has 49 campsites suitable for either tents or trailers, each equipped with a tent pad, picnic table, and a grill. There are two bathhouses with hot water, and although there are no hook-ups, there is fresh drinking water available throughout the campground. There is a maximum of 6 people per site. Reservations are not required, although strongly advised. Unreserved sites are available on a first-come, first-serve basis.

As with all North Carolina State Parks the park gate is locked every night when the park closes. This means you have to be in before the gate closes and must wait until morning to leave.

GEAR SHOPS

Great Outdoor Provision Company – (336) 727-0906
402 Stratford Rd, Winston-Salem, NC 27103

Village Outdoor Shop – (336) 768-2267
3456 Robinhood Rd, Winston-Salem, NC 27106

CLIMBING GYMS

The Ultimate Climbing Gym (at Tumblebees)
6904 Downwind Rd, Greensboro, NC (336) 665-0662

GROCERIES/RESTAURANTS

Food, Groceries, Gas and ATMs are available at several exits along Highway 52 between Winston Salem and Pilot Mountain State Park. If you are looking for all of the above, a good exit to stop at is 115 (University Parkway).

EMERGENCY SERVICES

Unfortunately accidents are a relatively common occurrence at Pilot Mountain, due in part to climbers with limited experience getting in over their heads. Always use good judgment and remember that if a rescue is warranted, it will take time and effort for emergency personnel to reach the base of the cliff, and even longer to evacuate the victim.

If you witness or are involved in an accident, first call 911, and then call the park office at (336) 325-2355 to report the incident.

The nearest hospital is Northern Hospital – Surry County 12 miles north in Mount Airy, NC (336-719-7000). The nearest large medical center is Wake Forest University Baptist Medical Center in Winston Salem, NC (336-716-2255).

BOULDERING

Though not destination worthy by any means, the boulders at Pilot Mountain are of decent quality and worth an afternoon visit for locals. There are two main areas – the Trail Side Boulders and the Feel Good Boulders.

Trail Side Boulders – This area is located along the upper portion of the Ledge Springs Trail, less than 15 minutes from the parking lot. Hike along the trail as you would for roped climbing, and continue past the Three Bears Gully for about 5 minutes. The large Trailside Boulder is impossible to miss, and offers several taller, overhanging lines in the V0-V3 range. After warming up here, head to the Cave Boulder, located 150 feet (further up the ridge) from the Trailside boulder to try out a few harder lines.

Feel Good Boulders - These boulders are located downhill from the Pool Hall area. Problems are in the V0-V4 range. Until 2014 the boulders were accessed via the Ledge Springs Trail. In 2014 the trails were rearranged to prevent hikers from accidentally walking to the bottom of the mountain. If you want to access these boulders check with the park staff to see what the best trail is for access.

One of the Feel Good boulders

HISTORY

The name "Pilot" comes from the Cherokee word Jomeokee, which means, "Guide," or "Pilot." The mountain was used by the Cherokee for initiation rituals, as well as a navigational aid by the nomadic Saura tribe.

In 1968, Pilot Mountain became North Carolina's 14th state park. Prior to that time, the mountain was a commercial tourist attraction. Plans were underway to build an amusement park on the privately owned property – complete with a swimming pool, Ferris wheel, and a roller coaster zooming all around the pinnacle, but the Pilot Mountain Preservation and Park Committee stepped in. They proposed the establishment of Pilot Mountain as a state park in order to protect it and the surrounding area from further commercial development. Working with the conservation-minded owner of the property, Mrs. J.W. Beasley, the group secured options on the land and raised matching funds that made it possible to purchase the land with federal grants. In further support of the park, the committee

Most of the historical fixed gear from the Golden Age of Pilot Mountain development has recently been replaced.

acquired more than 1,000 acres of land along the Yadkin River that was added to the park in 1970. Additional acreage was later acquired, bringing the park to its present size. In 1976 Pilot Mountain was designated a National Natural Landmark switch National and Natural largely due to the large stands of Chestnut Oaks and Pitch Pines in the area.

Many climbers visited the park over the years, but for some reason most of the first ascent information has been lost. Lee Munson did a few routes including MAJOR DUDES and BLIND PROPHET. However, when it comes to climbing, the most well known character in the development of the area was the notorious John Black, who was responsible for literally all of the bolted lines at Pilot. Most were his first ascents. Some he bolted for others to have the glory. Black's passion for bolting could be described by some as overzealous, and most certainly didn't line up with the strong traditional ethics held by other first ascensionists in the State. Many of the popular toprope lines, however, were more than likely climbed well before Black brought his drill to the cliff. For this reason many of the original route names are uncertain, and a handful were made up by the author for ease of use.

THE GREAT HAWK MIGRATION

While climbers have been scaling the cliffs of Pilot Mountain for decades, avid bird watchers have been scouring the skies for almost just as long. The Little Pinnacle Overlook has played a very key role in monitoring the annual raptor migration since 1973, when Ramona Snavely, along with several others from the Forsyth County chapter of the Audubon Society, happened to observe a group of Broad-winged Hawks drifting southwest along the mountain. These birds rely on thermal updrafts to carry them high above the earth as they travel from as far north as Ontario and Quebec all the way to Central and South America. Effortlessly gliding across the air currents, the raptors can cover a lot of ground in a short amount of time – up to 800 miles per day. The Little Pinnacle Overlook is one of 200 official observation sites for the Hawk Migration Association of North America.

The overwhelming majority of the migrants are Broad-winged Hawks, but a large variety of North American raptors also funnel through the area - Sharp-shinned Hawks, Red-tails, Red-shoulders, Osprey, Cooper's Hawks, Kestrels, Turkey Vultures, Black Vultures, and even Bald Eagles. On an average year, volunteers usually observe around 4,000 Broad-wings during migration season. They usually fly by in groups (called kettles) of 5-30, and occasionally in the hundreds, or even thousands. But every now and then the raptor reporters are in for a special treat – on September 22, 1993, four hawk watchers calculated an astonishing 10,385 birds in nine hours, and in 2006, observers recorded a single kettle of 1,800 birds.

No one really knows why the raptors choose to make a side trip to Pilot Mountain – it's actually 20 miles out of the way from their path along the Appalachians. But regardless of the reason, many birdwatchers look forward to these annual fly-bys. Most of the migration happens from mid-September through mid-October, with the peak Broad Wing season usually occurring between September 20-30. For more observation tips and details on how you can become involved in the Hawk Watch, check out the Forsyth Audubon Society's website – www.forsythaudubon.org.

JOHN BLACK

It's impossible to talk about the history of climbing at Pilot Mountain without mentioning the name John Black, over and over again. Without John (and his drill), Pilot Mountain would not be the place it is today. Though admittedly he was "in bad boy mode" back then, John showed his unique love for Pilot, as well as his vision for climbing, by bringing to life numerous classic lines that have seen thousands of ascents over the years.

Born in Germany to parents from Great Britain, John Black grew up in typical military brat fashion, hopping from place to place. He first moved to the United States (Clovis, New Mexico) in 1972, and spent his formative years on the east coast, first in Alabama, then in Florida, before finally arriving in North Carolina in 1985. John first entered the climbing scene via a then little-known boulderfield called Horse Pens 40 in the early 1980's, where he "just went mad at it." Like many young climbers, John was obsessed with pushing himself as hard as he could, as often as he could. Nothing could stop him from climbing, not even the flatlands of Florida. Whether in the form of late night "buildering" sessions on local buildings, or pulling on self-collected rocks epoxied to a sheet of plywood in his backyard, John was always climbing something.

John first laid eyes on Pilot Mountain in 1988, and not long after that he showed up with power drill in hand and his faithful cat "Cragger" at his side. Prior to John's arrival, the only established climbing routes were the many moderate toprope lines near and around the Three Bears Gully, CRACKIN' UP, and Lee Munson's lines (ANY MAJOR DUDE and the first half of BLIND PROPHET). As John walked along the base of the cliff, he was shocked at all the potential that was lying beneath layers of choss, dirt, and other debris.

A lover of hard, steep lines, John found himself right at home in the Amphitheater. The first bolted lines he put up were (in order) WHEN SHRIMPS LEARN TO WHISTLE, OVERHANGING HANG-OVER, BLIND PROPHET (extended from Lee's midway anchors), MR. HENAR, and ARMS CONTROL. John originally took all of these routes to the top of the cliff, although he eventually established several intermediate anchors beneath the roof. He referred to these midway anchors as "rainy day routes," citing, "This way my buddies and I could get a full day of climbing in during a down-pour."

The rangers at the time, whom John affectionately refers to now as "Barney Fife and Andy Griffith" type characters, had a soft spot in their hearts for him, despite John's tendency to bend (and sometimes break) the rules. John fondly recalls the usual end of day ritual the rangers would go through at closing time. According to him, "They'd stand out there on the observation deck with a bullhorn and shout – 'John Black it's time to get out of here!'"

John Black devoted many years to the development of climbing at Pilot Mountain, commuting from wherever he could find a parking spot for his van. But reports kept coming in from other climbers on a newly discovered crag just north of Fayetteville, West Virginia. John couldn't resist, so in 1996 he and his drill headed north to the New River Gorge and beyond.

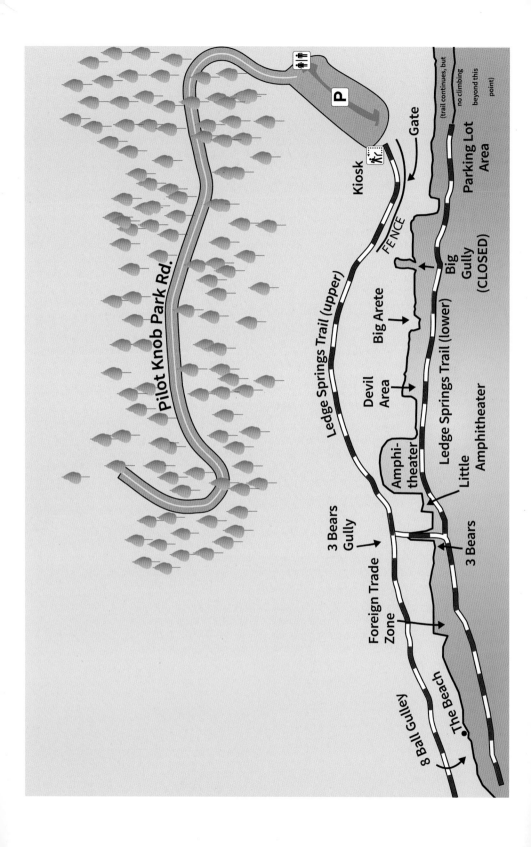

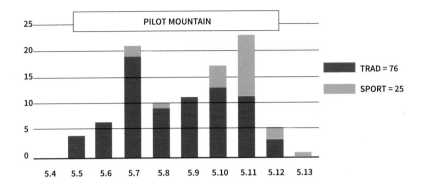

WARNING – PILOT HAS BEEN UNDERGO-
ING A BOLTING INITIATIVE FOR SEVERAL
YEARS. AT THE TIME THIS BOOK WAS
PRINTED THE FUTURE OF THE WORK WAS
NOT YET DETERMINED. BE AWARE THAT
NEW ROUTES OR OTHER CHANGES MAY
HAVE OCCURRED.

APPROACH (ALL AREAS)

All climbs are located west of the Big Pinnacle, and accessed via the Ledge Springs
Trail, which starts at the southwest corner
of the parking lot near the climber's kiosk
and permit box.

Hike along the Ledge Springs Trail for
about 10 minutes until you see a sign to
your left marking the Three Bears Gully. Be
aware that the first 10 feet of the gully are
very steep. It shouldn't pose any problems
for experienced climbers, but children and
dogs might need a helping hand. When

you reach the bottom of the gully, you will
be standing in front of ANY MAJOR DUDE.

Pilot Mountain routes are described and
numbered in this book as either left or
right of the Three Bears Gully. There are
numerous sub-sections starting at the far
left (west) end of the cliff line:

POOL HALL AREA

These are the first routes on the far western end (climber's left) of the cliff line. This
area can be accessed via a 15-minute hike
from the bottom of the Three Bears Gully.

Be ready to channel your inner pebble-
wrestler for the first three routes, as they
are basically boulder problems that lead to
easy face climbing.

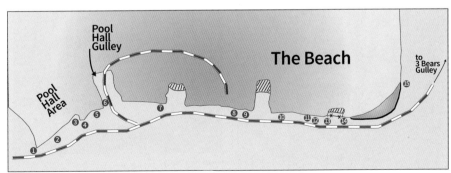

① 10-BALL 5.11b

This is the leftmost route at Pilot. Start 5 feet left of 9 BALL. Power up the big overhang via a seam feature. Pull the overhang and continue up and right, passing a pine tree along the way. A second rope (and belay) should be used to "reel" the climber in to control the enormous swing. You can use the shared 8/9 BALL anchors by running the rope on the other side of the pine tree as a directional, or build natural anchors. The set-up can be a pain, but not as painful as a pendulum into the pine tree. (30 ft.)

② 9-BALL 5.10a ★

Long moves between big jugs on the steep face just left of the 8-BALL corner. Step right at the top to the shared bolted anchors with 8-BALL. (30 ft.)

③ 8-BALL 5.9 ★

The short but sweet overhanging dihedral - a burly, bouldery start in the corner pocket leads to easy face climbing. Bolted anchors. (30 ft.)

④ SCRATCH 5.9

Climb the vertical crack system that runs through the center of the wall, then head up and right over a run out face. (60 ft.)

⑤ SNOOKER 5.8

Snooker isn't as fun as other billiard games, and this route isn't as fun as the others in this area. Start just right of the SCRATCH arête, at the base of the Pool Hall Gully. Climb the short, pocketed face to the top. Natural anchors can be built using rock horns at the top. (30 ft.)

Pull the low bulge on the far right side of the wall beneath two bolts. Climb straight up past the bolts and through a crack in the face, veering right at the top for maximum value. Gear is challenging to find as well as place. (60 ft.)

⑥ 7-BALL 5.7

Starts in the Pool Hall Gully, about 10 feet right of SNOOKER, at some broken flake systems. Climb the short, featured face, navigating under tree branches towards the top. Natural anchors can be built using rock horns at the top. (30 ft.)

Pool Hall Gully

THE BEACH

If approaching from the Pool Hall area, walk past the small Pool Hall Gully that separates the Pool Hall from the rest of the cliff line to find these routes on a discontinuous section of cliff. A good landmark is a large chimney with smooth, Michelin Man features on either side (THE WAVE and HAWAII-FIVE-O, respectively). This area is approximately 10-15 minutes from the bottom of the Three Bears Gully. The routes here consist of technical face climbing on some of the nicest rock at Pilot.

"A few years ago I decided to introduce my friend Chris to climbing. After one gym session together, we headed to Pilot. When we got there, it was raining, and no one else was climbing. But, we had driven two hours, and we were psyched, so I looked around for something easy for Chris. We ended up on SCARFACE. We only did one climb that day, before the rain forced us off the rock, but when Chris got to the top, he let out a loud whoop, and I knew that he was hooked! The proof? We were back at Pilot for the next twelve weekends in a row!" -Aaron Gootman

⑦ SCARFACE 5.6

Like chickenheads? Then say hello to your many little friends! Locate a deep chimney capped by a huge overhang about 60 feet left of the Michelin Man chimney, and 30 feet right of the Pool Hall Gully. A few different options exist on the juggy face – start up higher around the corner and then move left (easier terrain) or start farther left directly off the trail, increasing the difficulty. Bolted anchors. (50 ft.)

⑧ BODY SURFIN' 5.7+ ★★

This a very leadable route on good solid rock. Start at the base of a small, right-facing dihedral left of the Michelin Man Chimney. Layback the start, then navigate through a sea of incut holds and horns to a ledge, finishing

up through the leftmost of 2 prominent roof cracks in a small but pumpy roof. If leading, bring slings for chickenheads on the lower section, and some small stoppers for the crack up high. Bolted anchors. (50 ft.)

9 THE WAVE 5.11a ★★

Mixed. This is the line to the left of the large chimney. Surf along the arête past two bolts, and then continue straight up the steep weakness at the top. A harder start tackles the face left of the arête. If leading, take a light rack. Bolted anchors. (50 ft.)

10 HAWAII-FIVE-O 5.11b ★★

This is the line about 15 feet right of the chimney. Pull a low roof to get established on the face. Step left, and then wander up the thin crack system through crimps and sloping bulges. Next, power out the roof crack to the bolted anchors at the top. Bolted anchors. (60 ft.)

This is a great climb on better-than-average rock for Pilot, making this line worth the stop. Leaders take lots of small gear.

The following two routes share the same low roof start 15 feet right of HAWAII-FIVE-O at a left facing flake. The bolted anchor at the top is set up so that you can drape slings over the top of both routes.

11 LOW TIDE 5.10b

This is the left option. Start at the break and make a move to a stance. Move up and left to the thin face. Eventually the face turns into steep, but juggy terrain. Finish in an easy chimney. (50 ft.)

The sooner you move onto the left face the harder the climbing.

12 THE MAYOR 5.9 ★

(a.k.a. SPINDRIFT)

This is the rightmost, more direct, option. Start same as LOW TIDE, but follow the obvious line straight up to the top. Bolted anchors. (50 ft.)

This route is named and dedicated to Lloyd Ramsey, a.k.a. "The Mayor of Pilot Mountain," who passed away in 2012. (This was Lloyd's favorite route, and he ended most of his climbing days watching the sunset from the top of it.)

13 GOOFY FOOT 5.7

Just right of THE MAYOR locate an alcove capped by an overhang. There are two corners inside the alcove. Climb the left corner to a chimney. Leave the chimney and finish on the face to the anchors. Bolted anchors. (50 ft.)

14 RIGHT BREAK 5.9 ★

This is the corner on the right. Climb the corner to a chimney. Bolted anchors. (50 ft.)

Locate the lone bolt on the slab. Clip into the bolt with slings in order to safely access the bolted ring anchors just below the cliff edge. Bolted anchors. (50 ft.)

15 WALKING ON THE BEACH 5.9

This is the right most line at The Beach, around the corner from the previous two routes. Find a really high foot and crank up and onto the face. Follow the thin crack system along a pocketed face. Bolted anchors. (50 ft.)

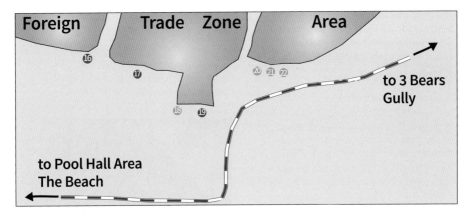

Foreign Trade Zone Area

to 3 Bears Gully

to Pool Hall Area
The Beach

FOREIGN TRADE ZONE AREA

From Three Bears Gully hike left (west) for a few minutes. The area is right where the trail cuts sharply downhill. From The Beach head east along the trail. In about 2 minutes you will walk past low, mostly chossy cliffs. This rock is too small to be worthwhile climbing and too tall to boulder. Pass between two large boulders. As the trail turns left and heads uphill, you will see several small buttresses. The stairs that head straight up the hill take you directly to the base of I GOTTA WEAR SHADES. A good way to get your bearings is by locating the bolts on FOREIGN TRADE ZONE and BAT OUT OF HELL.

16 WIFE'S A BITCH 5.8

She can't be that bad, but this route might be. Begin at a small cliff about 100 feet to the left of COWBOYS AND HEROES. If you can actually find the route and then still want to climb it - follow the short but overhanging face to the top.

17 COWBOYS AND HEROES 5.9

Start about 50-60 feet left of I GOTTA WEAR SHADES. This route is not located right off the main trail. When approaching from Three Bears Gully look for the place where the trail begins to cut down the hill (just below I GOTTA WEAR SHADES). Walk straight along the recessing cliff line. This line climbs the

short, unassuming buttress 20 feet right of a small gully. Climb easily up the corner to a ledge and then climb the face. Scramble up the dihedral to another ledge and then continue up the rippled face to the top. Bolted anchors. (40 ft.)

The next two routes climb the narrow buttress located just before the trail cuts down and around toward The Beach, about 40 feet left of FOREIGN TRADE ZONE.

18 TEFLON TOES 5.11b ★

This route is just left of the very obvious I GOTTA WEAR SHADES. Climb the crack on the left side of the buttress to a large ledge. Continue up the face to an overhang and steep smooth corner. Climb through the steepness to a ledge and easy climbing to the top. 4 bolts, bolted anchors. (60 ft.) Mostly easy with a short, but challenging crux section.

19 I GOTTA WEAR SHADES 5.9 ★★

This route climbs the narrow buttress located just before the trail cuts down and around towards The Beach, about 40 feet left of FOREIGN TRADE ZONE. Climb up the corner crack until it's possible to commit to a step right via some rather awkward moves onto the arête (be mindful of the potential swing). Enjoy the nice (albeit cramped) rest, and then finish on huge holds through overhanging rock to the top. Bolted anchors. (60 ft.)

20 EUROZONE 5.10a ★★

Start just left of BAT OUT OF HELL. It sports a few glue in bolts. Climb past six bolts to bolted anchors (shared with FOREIGN TRADE ZONE). 6 bolts, bolted anchors. (50 ft.)

21 FOREIGN TRADE ZONE 5.10d

This variation to EUROZONE was the original line, but is simply not as much fun as EUROZONE. Climb past the first four bolts of EUROZONE then move right to a corner and another bolt. Continue up past another bolt to the EUROZONE anchors. The sequence at the corner (crux) may prove more difficult to decipher than international politics. 6 bolts, bolted anchors. (50 ft.)

22 BAT OUT OF HELL 5.11a ★★

This route is the bolted line on the right side of the buttress. Climb the thin awkward face past three bolts to a lay down rest. Be careful

with the razor sharp horizontal flake in the steep cruxy section up top. 6 bolts, bolted anchors. (50 ft.)

Topropers watch out for that tree. Some people love it, some hate it. Short people tend to have problems at the second crux.

BAT OUT OF HELL - *The initial FA attempt was thwarted by an unruly winged culprit from deep within the recesses of the large flake below the roof. As John Black was casually cranking his way up the face, he began noticing a rather strange and indistinct noise. At one point the noise got significantly louder, at which point John peeked inside the flake. He came face to face with a large, open-mouthed bat that was not at all thrilled about the ruckus going on outside of his sanctuary. There are a few versions of what happened next, but the most comical one involves John Black uttering a high-pitched noise reminiscent of a 12-year-old girl at a Justin Bieber concert. All versions end with a subsequent FA attempt at a later date.*

Oya Bermek approaching the first crux of BAT OUT OF HELL (5.11a)

LLOYD RAMSEY: The Mayor of Pilot Mountain

When I first informed Lloyd Ramsey that I wanted to do a profile on him for this guidebook he was flabbergasted that anyone would want to read about him in a book, and hardly felt as though he deserved such an "elevated status" (his words). Though some perhaps found his quirks and oddities less endearing than others, Lloyd was a good-hearted man that was a permanent fixture at Pilot for many years. Those facts alone were enough to warrant his mention in this book, but now that he's gone, I think including him is essential to preserve and honor his memory.

Were the park staff ever to give out a perfect attendance award, it's safe to assume that Lloyd would be the leading candidate. Living only a few miles outside of the park, Lloyd spent the majority, if not all, of his free time on the mountain. Though never employed by the state park system, Pilot Mountain was Lloyd's home away from home, and his love for both climbing and this particular crag was evident to all who met him. On weekdays he would show up promptly at 10 am to claim "his" parking place under the apple tree. He would then spend his day in solitude, rope-soloing the popular moderate lines that get overloaded with traffic on the weekends. On Saturdays and Sundays, Lloyd arrived much earlier, and was typically the first to hike in to the crag. Weekends seemed to be more about socializing than actual climbing for Lloyd, as he would make his rounds from group to group, watching others climb and memorizing their exact beta. He would file this information somewhere in his head, and then be ready to recall it again at a moment's notice. Most Pilot regulars were on a first name basis with him, and newbie climbers were usually very appreciative of his extensive and anecdotal knowledge of the cliff.

Lloyd also had the uncanny ability to know exactly when something exciting was going on, and he always wanted to be a part of it. Although you never knew where and when he'd show up, it was a foregone conclusion that he was lurking somewhere on the mountain, just waiting to pop up, often at the most random of times. One of my fondest memories of Lloyd was the very first time I got on Blind Prophet in the Amphitheater. I was at the upper crux and kept taking repeated whippers. All of a sudden I heard a voice coming from up top, on the other side of the Amphitheater. It was Lloyd, "encouraging" me by shouting, "That's why they call it 5.12!" He then proceeded to give me an unrequested run-down of the crux beta of every person he'd ever seen on the route. He asked me how tall I was, did a few calculations in his head, then with a worried look on his face shouted back, "Uh-oh, you're in trouble!" I must admit that at the time his "advice" may not have been that well-received, but what Lloyd may have lacked in tactfulness, he more than made up for in sincerity. No one cheered harder for me than Lloyd when I came back two weeks later and sent the route.

Lloyd passed away at the base of the Three Bears Gully sometime on July 30, 2012. Many of the details of his death remain uncertain, but those who knew him can hopefully find solace in knowing that Lloyd's final moments were spent doing what he loved best in the place he loved most. I think it's safe to say that Pilot Mountain will never be the same without Lloyd Ramsey. No matter how much time goes by, I will always half-expect to see him popping out from behind a rock with his camera, or hear his unmistakable guffaw from farther down the trail. But although in my heart I know that won't happen again, I like to think that he now has a special bird's eye view of everything happening on the mountain.

Clearly I'm not the only one who will think of Lloyd every time I'm at Pilot. This is just a handful of memories shared by others…

"I still laugh when I think about a friend of mine's first encounter with Lloyd. My friend's name is Cassaburo, and when he introduced himself, Lloyd helpfully (although incorrectly) explained that his name meant "donkey house." Needless to say my buddy was not at all amused." - John Liles

"Over the years I have met Lloyd countless times. We have climbed routes, walked the cliff together and had many discussions about climbing. We haven't agreed on everything, but Lloyd's intensity and singular focus on rock climbing at Pilot were constants throughout. He was incredibly outgoing and social at the cliff - always ready to drop what he was doing and help out climbers that were new to the area. He was a constant source of genuine enthusiasm and encouragement for climbers of all ability levels." – Jeff Dillon, Winston-Salem, NC

"I started climbing outside at Pilot, and Lloyd was there watching for my very first lead. When I led "ANY MAJOR DUDE" in 2012, and was finishing on the easy moves past the crux, I could hear Lloyd laughing. He was there standing by the anchors, waiting for me, and as I clipped them he said "I'm gonna have to change the way I look at you!" Climbing is rewarding in itself, but Lloyd sure knew how to make it feel even better." – Adam

"One thing most people probably didn't know about Lloyd is that he had a great voice. I happened onto this when I told him that I was getting ready to sing in a choir piece called "Carmina Burana." Lloyd said he loved the piece and burst into song, singing one of the movements. Who knew?" -Sarah Wolfe, Durham, NC

"Lloyd was helping me with the re-bolting project at Pilot. I was continually amazed at his energy at age 70. He willingly lugged drills, batteries, hammers, etc. up and down the trail, gave great advice, and proved to be quite a good companion. I miss that old buzzard." -Bill Webster, Chapel Hill, NC

"The climbing community is full of colorful characters, and Lloyd was certainly no exception. Amazingly, at 70 years old, he could still out-climb many of us young whippersnappers. He looked at climbing like a game of chess, focusing on each and every move as if he wanted to squeeze every ounce of fun from the experience. It wasn't just a hobby to Lloyd, it was his lifestyle." -Alan Howell, Winston-Salem, NC

23 **PSYCHOTIC REACTION 5.10**

This rarely climbed line follows the overhanging arête that is covered with lichen near the top. (50 ft.)

The area from DURACELL to NUTS AND BOLTS is included in this guide only for historical purposes. Most of the routes are poor quality and very short. The few nice looking routes in the Coppertop area are very hard to set up with topropes. In addition, the park staff would prefer that climbers avoid setting topropes in this area in order to protect the vegetation.

COPPERTOP AREA

This area lies a short walk left of the Three Bears Gully beneath a landmark rust-colored face capped by a large roof. Top rope set-ups have the potential for dangerous swings into trees. All of the routes in this section have natural anchors, so if you insist upon doing these routes, be sure to bring lots of webbing and/or long runners. Also take care on the approach from the cliff top, as it involves a lot of scrambling on steep, pine needle strewn terrain. This fact is exactly why the park staff would prefer that climbers simply not use this area.

24 **DURACELL 5.7**

Start on the left side of the face, and then climb the face to the left of the large roof. (30 ft.).

25 **OSCAR MAYER 5.9**

Climb the laybacks below the obvious roof to a juggy but steep finish through the overhangs on the left side of the roof. Long slings are needed for toprope anchors. (50 ft.)

26 **COPPERTOP 5.10**

An aptly named route – climb straight up the middle of the face, then make sure your battery is fully charged as you blast out the overhangs. (50 ft.)

27 **CLIMAX 5.12**

You've probably had better. This not-as-good-as-the-name-implies route climbs the right side of the face to the roof, and finishes through the large roof crack. (50 ft.)

NUTS AND BOLTS AREA

This little climbed area is just a couple of minutes west (left) of the Three Bears Gully. The main landmark is the large flat roof that hangs about 15 feet over the trail. Bring long runners for natural anchors. The cliff is short, the rock chossy, and the top rope anchors are difficult to reach.

28 **WET SPOT 5.10d**

Climb the broken face and continue out the left side of the roof. (50 ft.)

29 **MR. SOFTEE 5.10**

Follow a crack through a low roof to reach an off-width crack. Follow the offwidth to the top. (50 ft.)

30 **NUTS AND BOLTS 5.11b/c**

Start below the far right side of the low roof. Climb through the white rock to the top. (50 ft.)

THREE BEARS AREA

This popular area is on the left side of the Three Bears Gully, approximately 10 minutes from the parking lot. Most of these routes have bolted anchors, although a few require some easy fifth class down climbing to reach them. Expect lots of company as this area usually sees non-stop action on fair weather weekends.

31 **CREATIVE GERMS 5.7**

This route climbs the face that is 15 feet to the left and around the corner from GOLDILOCKS. Natural anchor. (25 ft.)

32 **GOLDILOCKS 5.5**

This route starts to the left of the right-facing dihedral that is immediately left of PAPA BEAR. Climb the easy, low-angled face to a bolted anchor. A great route for introducing

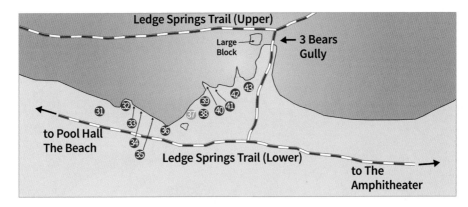

newbies to the sport. This climb has about 15 feet of actual climbing before turning into an easy fifth class scramble. Bolted anchors. (25 ft.)

33 PAPA BEAR 5.10b ★★

Climb the broken crack system (5.7ish) to the five-foot horizontal roof. Find a hand jam in the crack, throw a heel, and crank over the roof and onto the short face above. This route may feel stout to the vertically challenged. To set up a top rope you must down climb easy terrain for about 20 feet to reach a ledge with 3 bolts. Bolted anchors. (25 ft.)

34 MAMA BEAR 5.10c ★★

This route follows the middle set of discontinuous cracks, just right of PAPA BEAR. Pinch your way up the cracks, and then step left towards a dihedral at the roof. A hidden hold unlocks the crux sequence. Anchors are shared with PAPA BEAR. Bolted anchors. (25 ft.)

Variation: Step right, avoiding the roof, and continue straight up to finish on the BABY BEAR anchors.

35 BABY BEAR 5.11a ★★★

If the cracks on PAPA BEAR and MAMA BEAR were too big, this one might be juuuust right! This line is the technical finger crack on the right side of the wall. Don't cheat by traversing in from the right! Once you get off the

ground, tech your way up towards a small triangular pod just before a bulge. Decipher the bulge (crux) and climb past a horizontal crack to the bolted anchors on the right side of the ledge. Take extreme care in setting the toprope on the exposed anchors. Bolted anchors. (25 ft.)

36 GENTLE BEN 5.10b ★★

Start on the arête on the right hand side of the Three Bears face. Climb either side of the arête to the roof. Continue up and right past a thin face to the top. Beware of large chunks of easily avoidable loose rock along the arête. Bolted anchors. (40 ft.)

Variation: Many parties choose to do an easier, less direct finish by traversing left across the arête about midway up and finishing via a hand-sized crack. (5.10a)

37 ANY MAJOR DUDE 5.11d ★★★

The shiny new bolts that recently replaced the archaic pitons elevated this mostly toproped line to sport leadable status for both dudes and dudettes alike.

Start in the corner just left of the large chimney. Balance your way along the interesting orange face past 5 bolts using small but consistent crimps and edges. Traverse right at the horizontal crack below the roof and power up to a reachy, barn-door inducing diagonal rail (crux). 5 bolts, bolted anchors. (50 ft.)

FROM GYM RATS TO ROCK HOUNDS

Though it'd be hard to find the exact statistics, I'd be willing to go out on a limb and say that a very large number of North Carolina climbers were introduced to outdoor rock climbing at Pilot Mountain State Park. For those of us that are "wiser, more experienced" climbers (read: tendencies towards being old and crotchety), it's sometimes hard to remember what those first few forays onto real rock were like back in the day. But whether you started out as a gym rat or a toproper in a meet-up group, we all had very humble beginnings in the sport and moved forward at our own pace. And more than likely, we all could identify with the following rites of passage…

Sexual Innuendos – If taken out of context, just about every other word exchanged between two climbers sounds dirty. When you first start climbing, every statement is surrounded by chuckling and giggling like two 13 year olds with a lingerie catalog. After a while though, you get so used to the lingo that not only can you tell your partner things like "I was relieved to grab that jug because I looked down and saw that my nut had popped out," with a straight face, but you're so accustomed to it that it doesn't even register as funny anymore.

Summit Fever – New climbers are psyched to get to the top, and they could care less how they get there. It doesn't matter in the least how many times they fall, hang on the rope, or whether they are toproping or leading (or aiding…). Vocabulary lessons on sending, redpointing, and the sharp end will all fall on deaf, enthusiastic ears. It's kind of refreshing actually – and can serve as a good reminder that the view at the top is always rewarding.

Information Overload – To a new climber, the climber jargon might as well be a different language. It's just a lot to take in, and it's easy to get overwhelmed. Though it may be tempting to poke fun at a climber using incorrect slang, try your best to put yourself in their shoes and maybe play the role of translator every once in a while.

Butt Shots – For some, rock climbing is a once in a lifetime activity that needs to be documented every step of the way. Unfortunately it takes a while to learn how to position the camera and photographer correctly, so the majority of climbing action photographs are likely to be more bad ASS than BAD ASS!

Sprained Egos - Egos tend to shrink dramatically in the absence of tape, grid-bolting, and flat, cushy landings. Expect to hear the trash talking escalate on the hike in, then fade dramatically with each passing hour of the day.

So for you old geezers out there, don't forget that you too were once a newb. Don't be afraid to lend a helpful hand or offer some sage advice to some enthusiastic beginners. Oh yeah, and for the gym rats who can crush the red taped 5.12 route – be wary of fat guys, old men, or skinny little girls, because odds are good they can out climb you without breaking a sweat. –Erica Lineberry

38 ANY MINOR DUDE 5.11c

A slightly easier (but significantly dirtier) variation of MAJOR DUDE pulls through the obvious crack to the left of the MAJOR DUDE roof. If you choose to toprope the variation, be sure to set up your toprope further left to avoid potential pendulum swings (and bring ski goggles to keep the sand out of your eyes). Natural anchors. (50 ft.)

39 DUDE ON THE CORNER 5.9+

This line climbs the interesting corner feature to the right of those other dudes. Start at the base of HONEY POT. Climb easy rock just right of the smooth face of DUDES. Move up and left (crux) to gain a left-facing dihedral. Climb moderate terrain to the top. Bolted anchors shared with HONEY POT. Bolted anchors. (50 ft.)

40 HONEY POT 5.5

Climb the chimney just right of the DUDES face. Chimney up the back of the corner to the top. Bolted anchors. (40 ft.)

41 EVERY MAJOR DUDETTE 5.6

Climb the face to the right of the HONEY POT chimney. Bolted anchors (40 ft.)

42 HOWDY DUDE 5.7 ★★

Located inside the Three Bears Gully, this is probably one of the most easily accessible routes at Pilot. Climb the face just right of the arête, at a prominent layback flake. Reach around to the left and transition to the left face. Bolted anchors. (40 ft.)

43 BEAR CLAW 5.5
(a.k.a. CRUMBLY HOLE EXPERIENCE)

A popular route despite the poor quality. This is the chimney on the left side of the Three Bears Descent Gully. This chimney is located near the top of the gully. Scrap and claw your way up the chimney. Bolted anchors. (40 ft.) NAME IT, and follow the blunt arête. (50 ft.)

Sarah Hogan trying to be the DUDE ON THE CORNER (5.9+)

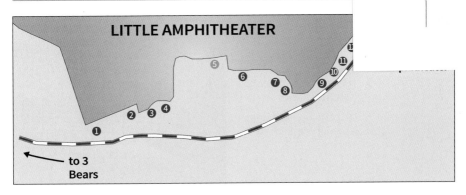

LITTLE AMPHITHEATER

to 3 Bears

LITTLE AMPHITHEATER

The Little Amphitheater is the first area east of the Three Bears Gully. This small area could also be called party central, due to a high concentration of easy top-rope routes less than 15 minutes from the parking lot. This small area is understandably a prime location for scout troops, outdoor clubs, and other large groups. Each route in this section has its own set of bolted anchors, accessed easily from the top.

① KMA 5.8 ★★

This route has variations further left that push 5.10. However the most obvious line ascends the vertical crack on the center of the face on the left wall of the Little Amphitheater. Bolted anchors. (60 ft.)

② DIRTY ROTTEN SCOUNDREL 5.7 ★

Cleaner than it sounds, this line starts on the block below the obvious dihedral. Chimney and stem your way to the top. Bolted anchors. (50 ft.)

③ PLACE YOUR BET 5.6 ★★

If you have time for just one route in the Little Amphitheater, put your money on this one. The arête is a sure bet on this fun and exposed line to the right of the left-facing dihedral. Gym rats may have a hard time with this one, as the line is not as straightforward as others in this area. Bolted anchor. (50 ft.)

④ GRANDPA'S BELAY 5.7 ★

Starts 5 feet right of PLACE YOUR BET. Climb the crack that starts in a shallow left-facing dihedral to a nice stance at an interesting pedestal type feature. Follow the large crack up and left to the top. Bolted anchor. (50 ft.)

Variation: Start at the wide crack right of GRANDPA'S BELAY. Step left at the pedestal to the GRANDPA'S finish.

Climber on the very popular GRANDPA'S BELAY (5.7)

5 EROCKTICA 5.10c ★★

Locate the obvious roof in the center of the Little Amphitheater. Climb through the right side of the roof. Make a series of moves up and left to a hard slab move. Finish on easy rock. 5 bolts, bolted anchor (50 ft.)

A 5.10d/.11a direct start top-rop variation can be done on top rope through the large roof.

OUTHOUSE is a relatively new addition to the list of recorded Little Amphitheater climbs. However, odds are good that this line was first toproped many years ago Recently, Aaron Gootman, Chris Hamilton, and Lloyd Ramsey took an interest in it. After taking note of the unique "outhouse" feature, Aaron and Chris decided to give it a whirl on toprope in February of 2011 while Lloyd photographed. Shortly after that Chris had to take time off indefinitely as he battled four different types of cancers, most recently Acute Myeloid Leukemia. The memories and pictures from that crisp, sunny day, along with the support of his climbing partners, were an inspiration for Chris to keep fighting and not give up.

A toprope ascent of the sport route EROCKTICA (5.10c)

6 OUTHOUSE 5.7 ★

This line begins on the right side of the Little Amphitheater. Clamber up to the namesake feature, two short dihedrals that mirror each other at an overhang. Crank over the "outhouse" on either side, and continue straight up to the top. You can also directly tackle the roof between the corners at about 5.9. Bolted anchors. (50 ft.)

7 PEE BREAK 5.6

Begin on the far right side of the Little Amphitheater. Climb the short, left-facing dihedral to a large ledge eight feet off the ground, then work through the face via a nice flake system to a small roof. Head right at the roof and finish via a crack/chimney feature. This line has been the scene of many first trad leads, and has surprisingly good rock. Bolted anchors. (50 ft.)

8 PEE BREAK RIGHT 5.6 - - CLOSED

This line climbed the face around the corner from Pee Break Left, but is now closed to climbing due to an unfortunate incident involving a climber/hiker collision – the hiker was in the wrong place at the wrong time as the climber took a vicious pendulum swing. May this route serve as a reminder to always consider swing potential when rigging anchors, as well as being mindful of hikers when climbing near the trail. Always keep the trail clear of gear, take extreme care if there is danger of loose rock, and of course, belay so that falls are controlled.

THE AMPHITHEATER

This is where the big boys (and girls) play. Though only a short stretch of rock, there are many high quality routes, most of which are at least partially bolted and can be safely led. This section of the cliff contains many of the highest quality routes that Pilot Mountain has to offer. If you fancy yourself a hardman, you'll probably spend your entire day here. Continue east along the trail from the Little Amphitheater for a minute or so and you won't be able to miss the large horizontal roof that juts out over a slab. You'll be pleasantly surprised at how dry the routes on the left wall will be, even in a heavy rain. Unfortunately the easier slab routes in the middle of the Amphitheater are often nothing more than a nice waterfall backdrop after long periods of rain, especially in the winter.

Safety Note - It is not recommended to set up topropes on the majority of the bolted Amphitheater routes, especially the popular slabs. Any fall will result in a huge swing because of the large roof. If no one in your party can lead climb and you simply must get on these routes, please use extreme caution. Utilize a second belay and clip into some of the bolts for directionals if you can. Otherwise be prepared to get up close and personal with a tree in the event that you fall.

In 1998, a 23-year-old climber got in over his head when he tried to show off how fast he could descend from the top of the Amphitheater via an "Australian Rappel" (face-first). The climber apparently had a military background, and was performing for his friends, who were videotaping the whole debacle. From Accidents in North American Mountaineering 1999 (Issue 52) – "The climber let go of the rope and fell 30 feet to the base of the route. Witnesses on the scene described the climber as out of control as soon as he began his descent. It is not known whether or not the victim was wearing a helmet or gloves. Chances are he was wearing neither." Amazingly enough this guy escaped with nothing but some minor head trauma and a few scratches on his face. This story is included as a reminder to think twice before engaging in ill-advised stunts. Don't forget that there is some truth to the old adage about a redneck's last words: "Hey ya'll, watch this!" Please be safe out there and use good judgment!

The bases of the following four routes are very close to the trail, so please be mindful of hikers and other climbers passing through and don't block the trail.

9 AMPHED UP 5.7 ★

Climb the chimney and face to the left of BUZZARD'S BREATH. Once out of the chimney climb around to the left then back right to the bolted anchors of BUZZARD'S BREATH. Bolted anchors. (60 ft.)

Var. At the top of the chimney section it's possible to climb straight up a bulge and nice face at around 5.10a.

Typical crowd scene at The Amphitheater

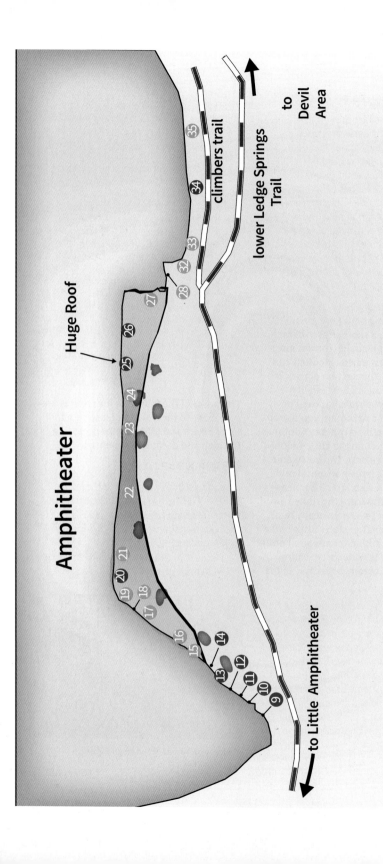

anchors of those routes. From the anchor, rappel straight down to reach the anchor for SURRY or SYZYGY. The OVERHANGING anchor is a little to the right.

13 SURRY COUNTY ETHICS 5.10b

Mixed. Start at a block under a small roof, below two closely spaced bolts. The burly and awkward dihedral is well protected by bolts, but bring a light rack for the thin face climbing that follows. Trend up and left to a vertical crack, finishing at anchors just below the large ledge with a big tree. The crux area is frequently wet. 3 bolts, bolted anchors. (40 ft.)

14 SYZYGY 5.11c ★

Mixed. Climb the bolt line through the overhanging terrain just right of SURRY COUNTY. After maneuvering past the third bolt (crux), join up with SURRY'S last bolt, and finish out on the same crack system and large ledge. 4 bolts, shared bolted anchors with SURRY COUNTY. (40 ft.) Fun Fact: the only word in English with three Ys.

10 BUZZARD'S BREATH 5.8 R/X ★

Almost always toproped. This route is a lot more appetizing than it sounds. Climb the face 15 feet right of the blunt arête, between the two chimneys of AMPHED UP and I'M FLYIN'. There are a few different options to vary the difficulty, particularly towards the top. Bolted anchors. (60 ft.)

11 I'M FLYIN' 5.8 ★

Climb the dihedral/chimney just right of the BUZZARD'S BREATH face. Bolted anchors. (60 ft.)

12 TOO OLD TO ROCK AND ROLL 5.9

Climbers should take care that the loose rocks don't roll on this seldom travelled line that follows the face to the right of the I'M FLYIN' corner. Natural anchors. (60 ft.)

If you insist on top roping SURRY COUNTY, SYZYGY, or OVERHANGING, use the bolted anchor near the cliff rim to access the

Robert Fogle about to launch into the airy crux of MR. HENAR (5.12b)

When I first starting cleaning it, BLACK AND BLUE VELVET was covered in a blanket of velvety soft lichen – that got pretty slick when it got wet! That's partly why I named it what I did…that and I took a good beating on it before I sent it.
–John Black, on BLACK AND BLUE VELVET

15 OVERHANGING 5.11a ★★★
HANGOVER

"O-ho" for short, this route is a classic - great for the leader aspiring to break into the 5.11 range. Start just right of a blocky section of rock. Dance your way up small, incut edges, clipping (but not falling on…) two old pitons. Continue past a bolt to a small ledge, where many choose to place gear in the horizontal. Two options are possible at this spot. The original line traverses right past a bolt, and an easier variation skips that bolt in favor of heading left around the bulge. Both scenarios meet up at the horizontal crack in the roof, where an exciting, but well-protected crux move is waiting for you. For the full value experience, don't stop at the first set of anchors. Instead, traverse right and up onto the steep face above to a second set of anchors. (A medium TCU can protect the traverse on the extension). 2 pitons, 4 bolts (plus 1 more if you do the extension) (60 ft. to first set of anchors, 80 ft. with extension)

16 BLACK AND BLUE 5.13a/b ★★★
VELVET

Climb the swirly but blank-looking face, dancing past four bolts to a bulge. Bruise your way past the bulge (crux) as well as two more bolts to chain anchors. 6 bolts, bolted anchors. (50 ft.)

17 BLIND PROPHET 5.12b ★★★

Start on the right side of the wall 10 feet right of BLACK AND BLUE. Crimp your way past four bolts on technical face climbing to a roof. You may want to bring a 1/2-inch piece for the spicy real estate between the fourth and fifth bolts. Climb out the left side of the roof to a good shakeout stance before follow-

ing the face up to another roof via jugs. Clip the bolt at the lip, then pull onto the upper face (crux). For the 12b finish, climb straight up above the last bolt, then traverse right to the anchors. For the 12c finish, traverse to the right first, then climb straight up to the anchors. 7 bolts, bolted anchors. (75 ft.)

18 BLIND VELVET 5.11a ★★★

This is a popular variation to BLIND PROPH-ET for those not yet into the 5.12 range. Climb BLIND PROPHET proper to the fifth bolt, then traverse left to the BLACK AND BLUE anchors. Again, you may want to plug some gear after the fourth bolt. 5 bolts, bolted anchors. (50 ft.)

19 MR. HENAR 5.12b ★★

This moniker was coined because this line is a combo of both the "heinous" and the "gnarly," Climb the CRACKIN' UP corner to the first bolt. Move past several bolts to a large roof with a permadraw. Pull up and right past the permadraw via some hard finishing moves. 7 bolts, bolted anchors. (80 ft.)

You can also climb about 2/3 of the route to a set of anchors. This 5.10c variation called HENAR LITE contains some of the best 5.10 climbing at Pilot. You get the fun without the hard bit up higher.

20 CRACKIN' UP 5.7+ ★★★

This delightful line is the only true crack climb at Pilot, and is worth the extra work of packing in the rack. It was also one of the first lines to be documented at Pilot. Climb the obvious large layback crack at the left end of the Amphitheater slab. Gear to 3 inches. Bolted anchors. (40 ft.)

Kelly Weinel moving through the lower crux of
BLIND PROPHET (5.12b)

Bennett Harris on ARMS CONTROL (5.11c) one year after his accident. See page 123

Shane Messer pimpin' and crimpin' the lower half of Black and Blue Velvet (5.13b)

Erica Lineberry using "braille" technique on BLIND PROPHET (5.12b)

Erica Lineberry on the often overlooked, but very good, upper section of WHEN SHRIMPS LEARN TO WHISTLE (5.11b)

21 TURKEY SHOOT 5.8 R ★

Named in honor of the repeated gunshots from the good ole local boys down below that were heard all afternoon during the FA. (And can frequently still be heard today!)

Climb the bolted face just right of CRACKIN' UP to a set of anchors just below the huge roof. Take extra care between the widely spaced first and second bolts. 3 bolts, bolted anchors. (40 ft.)

It is possible to toprope CRACKIN' UP from the TURKEY SHOOT anchors. However, it is highly recommended to use gear as a directional at the top of the crack to mitigate the swing factor.

22 MILD MANNERED SECRETARY 5.7 ★

This is the second line of bolts to the right of the CRACKIN' UP corner on the Amphithe-

> *MILD MANNERED SECRETARY is a reference to the first ascensionist, Anne Marie Williams. John Black's girlfriend at the time, her demeanor was apparently anything but the stereotypical climbing chick. Her timid and careful personality would give most the first impression that she would be much more at home behind a desk all day than out on the rocks. I guess the moral is not to judge a book by its cover.*

ater slab. Climb the face past three bolts to a bolted anchor just below the large roof. 3 bolts, bolted anchors. (40 ft.)

Descent: Rap from fixed anchors.

23 ARMS CONTROL 5.11c ★★

Big guns definitely required for this one! Climb the bolt line 10 feet left of the left-facing dihedral on the slab. Four bolts of fairly casual face climbing lead to a small roof and a good stance under and left of an enormous roof. Shake out here before pulling up into the roof and cranking out right on jugs to an exciting mantle finish. 7 bolts, bolted anchors. (80 ft.)

24 PUMP STREET 5.10b ★

A mixed route in a previous life; this route is now a popular sport climb. Climb the face and arête just right of a left-facing dihedral to the COW PATTY anchors. Despite the name this route consists of non-pumpy, technical face climbing on good holds. 6 bolts, bolted anchors. (60 ft.)

25 COW PATTY BINGO 5.9 R ★★

Mixed. This enjoyable line would probably see more action if not for the runout, although there are a few spots for smaller gear. Climb the dark face on the far right side of the main amphitheater wall. Leaders be strong at the grade. 3 bolts, bolted anchors. (60 ft.)

26 OBSEQUIOUS 5.12 X

Not recommended. This toprope line climbs just right of the large vegetated chimney on the right-hand wall of the amphitheater. Climb through the roof to the top. Seldom climbed due to poor rock quality. (80 ft.)

In 2013 volunteers from the climbing community re-routed the hiking trail from SHRIMPS to a point east of BLACK RAIN. It's now cool to use the trail for ropes and gear. As of this writing some work is still needed and hikers still wander onto the old trail. If this happens you might politely point out the new trail.

27 WHEN SHRIMPS LEARN 5.11b ★★★ TO WHISTLE

Climb through easy terrain on the right side of a corner to a high first bolt. Then work up the insecure, but well-protected arête (crux) to a large ledge. Many parties choose to stop at the set of anchors at this ledge, The original line continues up and left along a somewhat chossy-looking (but fun to climb) overhanging face. 10 bolts, bolted anchors. (4 bolts to intermediate anchors.) (80 ft.)

28 SINGLE HANDED SAILOR 5.11c ★

Start in the dihedral on the right most edge of the amphitheater. Climb past three bolts to the roof. Traverse straight left and then continue up and left to the ledge shared with the intermediate anchors of SHRIMP. Continue up the steepening tiers to finish at the arête. The crux is at the very end. Take a selection of longer slings to deal with its wandering nature and a few odd traverses. Like SHRIMPS the upper part looks loose, but is actually pretty solid. 9 bolts, bolted anchors. (80 ft.)

This is a nice 5.10 route if you aid the final few feet or otherwise avoid the crux at the end.

29 WHEN SHRIMPS WHISTLE 5.11c ★★ AT SAILORS

Climb the first half of SHRIMPS to the ledge with intermediate anchors, but instead of moving left, finish on the top half of SINGLE HANDED SAILOR. 8 bolts, bolted anchors. (80 ft.)

30 DIHEDRAL ROUTE

Mixed. Not recommended. Start the same as SINGLE HANDED SAILOR, but move right at the roof and follow the broken crack to the top. Look out for very loose rock in the upper sections. The original finish is not recommended. It's better to climb DIHEDRAL DANCING or POLE DANCING. (80 ft.)

Why I Climb...A Comeback Tale

In the early spring of 2009, I moved to Salt Lake City, searching for a fresh start and a renewed sense of purpose for my life. What I found was a bad job waiting tables and a hard time making ends meet. Along with the current of unfortunate events came a nugget of hope. A friend I met through work opened my eyes to the vertical world and I've been up in the air ever since. When I finally decided it was time to make the sensible move back to North Carolina, graduate school, and normalcy, the passion and the love for pushing my limits through climbing decided to migrate with me. As I began to hone my mental and physical abilities, I started to view climbing through the myopic lens of achievement. Climbing became a source of neurosis instead of a centering force, as weekends without all time hardest sends became self-imposed disappointments. I still enjoyed climbing, but I had lost the joy of communing with nature and friends somewhere along the way. I had lost the vision that had given my life new purpose. On September 25, 2010, my life was set to auto focus. A collision of fate and aluminum resulted in a newfound perspective concerning all things precious, including my motivation to climb. I was at Pilot Mountain working a route called ARMS CONTROL when a bad fall took my finger and nearly my life. As I lie at the base of the crag, shivering from blood loss, the thought of never climbing again rocked me. The only comfort I found came from the warm eyes and caring voices of friends tending to my wounds, not the promise of future redpoints or hard onsights. Somewhere along the way I had forgotten why climbing was so important for me. Some may say that it was unfortunate that it took such a violent and grim accident to serve as a reminder, but let's just say things have turned out just fine. I am grateful and truly blessed to have made a full recovery, and I continue to share my climbing experiences with great friends. Next time you're out at Pilot, or any other crag for that matter, take a minute or so to catch your reflection in the eyes of those around you. That's the real reason I climb. - Bennett Harris, Charlotte, NC

31 DIHEDRAL DANCING 5.7 ★

Mixed. You may need a piece of gear to protect the traverse at the top of the dihedral. Take some longer slings. Climb the dihedral to the roof past three bolts. Traverse right at the top of the dihedral. Follow the top part of POLE DANCING past four bolts. 7 bolts, bolted anchors. (80 ft.)

32 POLE DANCING 5.7 ★★★

Same start as SINGLE HANDED SAILOR. Climb the dihedral to the second bolt. Traverse out right to the arête. Climb the arête until just above the roof. Move left and climb clean rock to the top. Don't panic, the anchor is only a few feet away, out of sight to the right. 7 bolts, bolted anchor (80 ft.)

BLACK RAIN AREA

A short distance to the right of the Amphitheater is the BLACK RAIN WALL, home to just three routes. All are good. The rightmost route, BLACK RAIN, will often have a queue several parties deep.

33 PSYCHO METRIC 5.11a ★

Start under a low roof just behind a large pine tree. Climb straight up past eight bolts to a bolted anchor. (80 ft.)

This was once a choss monster. The loose rock is largely gone, although caution is still a good idea.

34 MY HUSBAND IS GOING 5.7 ★★★ TO KILL ME (AKA START THE CAR)

Scan the top for a tall pine tree at the edge of the cliff line about 60 feet up – the bolted anchors are located just below the top of the cliff beside this tree. Follow the path of least resistance through flakes and a broken crack system to the top. Bolted anchors. (60 ft.)

35 BLACK RAIN 5.9+ ★★★

A great introduction to moderate face climbing. There are several variations within the first 20 feet, ranging from 5.8 (starting significantly farther right than the bolt line) up to 5.12 (most direct, and a bit contrived). The most popular start (5.9+) begins a few feet right of the bolt line and climbs through some polished holds past three bolts to a ledge big enough for a bivy. Follow three more bolts past steepening rock. Use caution while scrambling up the runout section between bolts 3 and 4. 6 bolts, bolted anchors (60 ft.)

BLACK RAIN was originally a John Black solo route – running laps up it sans rope was part of his regular warm-up routine. He later added bolts to make this classic available to the masses. It was so named for the copious amounts of dirt and black moss growing on the lower face – according to Black the ledge above the second bolt was covered with at least 2 feet of fine debris. After their first attempt at cleaning the line, Black and his buddies looked like they'd been working in the coal mines all day.

Just a few minutes beyond BLACK RAIN is another nice collection of mixed routes, a few of which are must-do's. If you desire to top rope ETHICS or HERCULEAN use the bolted anchor near the rim to safely reach the anchors for these routes. It's a short rappel to the anchors, but much safer than the steep scramble.

36 ETHICS IN BONDAGE 5.12c

Stick clip the bolt above a low roof. Make a couple of campus moves over the roof, then head right to a stance (plugging a cam or two if you so choose). Step left to the next bolt, pull onto the thin, upper face and gun for the top. 4 bolts, 1 piton, bolted anchors. (50 ft.)

Variation: For an easier variation skip the powerful start and begin instead on HERCULEAN. Traverse in via the overlap below the first bolt. (5.11d)

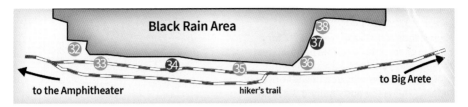

Black Rain Area

to the Amphitheater   hiker's trail   to Big Arete

The always controversial (and bolt-happy) John Black was never afraid to mince words. The term "Ethics in Bondage" was intended to be a somewhat political jab towards the opposing side of the bolt wars camp. John was of the opinion that the traditional purist majority was forcing their rules on everyone else, leaving those with differing views no room to compromise. In John's words, "I'm all for trad routes staying trad. But the rock was questionable – not good enough to take gear. Safety first was my motto when it came to bolting decisions."

37 THE HERCULEAN TEST 5.11a ★★

Mixed. Hercules! Hercules! A bouldery start pulls over a low roof to a technical face. Channel your inner Greek god to blast over the overhangs to the anchors. Bring along some mid-sized cams. 4 bolts to anchors. (50 ft.)

38 DEVIL IN THE WHITE 5.10d ★★★ HOUSE

Regardless of your stance on politics, you're guaranteed to love this one! Make your way up easy, blocky features until you reach a smooth face with grooves. Climb past a couple of bolts to the base of the roof. Make a tricky clip and then jug haul your way out the roof past a couple more bolts to a ledge. An easier variation (5.10b) traverses right after the third bolt, tackling the overhangs from the right side. 5 bolts plus anchors. (50 ft.)

Setting up a toprope requires a significant down climb to reach the anchors. Use caution, or better yet – lead it.

39 STEAMING PILES 5.5

CLOSED TO CLIMBING As enticing as this route sounds, the only loss from its closure is a great vantage point from which to snap pics of climbers on DEVIL. This line followed the low-angled, blocky dihedral right of the orange wall to natural anchors at the top. It was closed due to the potential for rockfall. (50 ft.)

40 DESK JOCKEY 5.7

Though not an area classic, it probably beats sitting behind a desk all day. This line is located 75 feet to the right of DEVIL. Climb the short crack in the middle of the short gray wall, left of the blocky arête and right of a curving vegetated crack. Natural anchors. (50 ft.)

Eleanor Saunders approaching the crux of DEVIL IN THE WHITE HOUSE (5.10d)

BIG ARÊTE AREA
(a.k.a. BUZZARD'S ROOST)

Keep hiking right (east) from DEVIL for a minute or so. After a couple hundred feet look up and you'll see a gorgeous white arête and wonder why you never noticed it before. This is the aptly named Big Arête. As enticing as it may be, do not be tempted to use the Big Gully a couple hundred feet to the right as a short cut to the cliff top for anchor rigging. In the case that you conveniently forget that it is closed, let the permanent wooden fence serve as a reminder.

BUZZARD'S ROOST

The Big Arête area was originally referred to as BUZZARD'S ROOST – so named for the group of 30-40 buzzards that would regularly hang out atop the Big Arête, soaking up the sun with wings wide open. (The sun is Mother Nature's cure-all for parasites and other undesirables nestled inside the bird's wings.) These guys provided a fair amount of shock value to unsuspecting climbers, and were blamed for numerous whippers at the top of MAN OVERBOARD and ANCHORS AWAY, until they eventually got tired of the sun-bathing interruptions and relocated

It's necessary to climb up an easy chimney in order to access the toprope anchors of HUNGER STRIKE and BET YA CAN'T EAT JUST ONE. The chimney starts on a ledge that is also the start of the Big Arête routes.

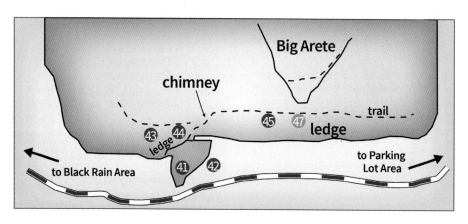

41 HUNGER STRIKE 5.7

This route starts at the left side of a short, detached pillar. Follow the blocky arête to the top of the short, 30-foot buttress. Bolted anchors. (30 ft.)

42 BET YA CAN'T EAT JUST ONE 5.6

This route climbs the white face on the right side of the detached pillar. Bolted anchors. (30 ft.)

43 IBUPROFEN JUNKY 5.8

Nothing Vitamin I can't fix, right? This line starts atop the 30 foot tall detached pillar just left of the Big Arête, and climbs the face at the left end of the pillar. It can be reached via either of the previous two routes, or by scrambling up the chimney on the backside of the buttress. A few variations exist, so choose whatever path looks most appealing to get to the top. Natural anchors. (40 ft.)

Don't Forget to Look Out!

I'm a little better about it now, but when I first started climbing outdoors, I was notorious for climbing to the top of a route where I would immediately lower off, and then proceed to hear every person that climbed after me rave about the spectacular view they got when they turned around. I would tell myself as I was tying in and putting my shoes on, "Make sure you look out this time," and invariably, it would not come to my mind again until I was back on the ground taking my shoes off again. I can't begin to tell you how many times my husband has yelled, "Don't forget to look!" right as I reach the chains!

It's not that I'm afraid to take my eyes off the rock and look out. It's just that I get so caught up with what I'm doing, that I forget to look around and see what else is going on around me. I feel like that's how life is sometimes. We get so inundated at work or so involved in a project of some sort, that we forget to stop and see what else is going on – to "stop and smell the roses," as the old cliché goes.

The times that I forget to look out and just come right back down – does that mean my whole day is ruined, that my climbing experience is somehow tainted? No, of course not. I move on to the next route and continue to have a fun day. But can I ever get back that split second moment of child-like awe that I would have had if I would have remembered to turn around and look at the beautiful rural backdrop of the foothills of the Piedmont?

It's the same with life – we can easily go through it focused on what is right in front of us, never turning around to see what's going on behind us or out of the corner of our eye, but if that's all we ever do, we will be missing out. Maybe not missing out on some gigantic life changing event (although sometimes that may very well be the case), but missing out on the sweet smell of honeysuckle 5 feet off the path, a great conversation with a friend over coffee, or even watching your toddler giggle with delight as he watches the leaves fall to the ground from his perch on my back. As climbers we are blessed with the opportunity to recreate in a beautiful setting week after week. Don't let these sights and sounds ever become commonplace and mundane, and take every chance you can to look out and absorb the wonder!

-Erica Lineberry

Kyle Trettin getting started on BLACK RAIN (5.9)

44 AFTERSHOCK 5.10

This line also starts on top of the short buttress and climbs the steep face on the right end of the pillar. It can be done as one long pitch from the ground, starting on either HUNGER STRIKE or BET YA. Natural anchors. (40 ft.).

The next three routes start at the base of a large ledge about 15 feet above the trail. There is a decent amount of room up there, but groups of more than two or three climbers will want to take extra caution or scramble up in shifts.

This area originally contained several half pitch routes. Recently bolts have been added, chopped, and moved to create three very nice routes; all of which go from bottom to top.

Pilot Mountain's Camp 4?

Back in the early 1990's, John Black and his buddies would often camp for days, and even up to a week at a time on the large ledge that marks the start of MAN OVERBOARD. Tucked safely out of sight from both above and below, their own little hideaway made for a cheap way to extend their climbing time, while avoiding the drive back home (which for many was 2 hours away in Raleigh). It's long gone now, but for quite a while there was a camping stove stashed in a crevice on the ledge

45 MAN OVERBOARD 5.10c ★

Mixed. This is not a sport route! Starts on top of a 20-foot high ledge below the striking Big Arête. Climb past two bolts to a large ledge with a third bolt. Continue up fourth-class terrain to a steep wall. Move up through the overhanging wall and delicately traverse to starboard (right) out onto the point of the arête, and follow the arête to the top of the cliff. Leaders take some small cams and micro-cams. 5 bolts, bolted anchors. (60 ft.)

One of John Black's craziest stories (of the ones he admitted to anyway) happened during the bolting of ANCHORS AWAY. "Well the rock is really good quality there, nice and hard, so my drill battery kept running out of juice. No problem, I'd just put it on a sling around my neck, and change it out. Well apparently all the drilling was attracting quite the crowd at the top. At one point while I had the drill on the sling, one of those young junior rangers popped his head over and said (in the sternest voice he could muster), "You can't do that here! You'd better get up here and talk to the rangers!" Meanwhile my drill bit had been sitting on that sling, and it was so hot that it was melting right through the cord. When I realized what was happening, I pitched right off, and drill parts went flying. I was attached to the bolt below me with a piece of static webbing, which caught me with a gut-wrenching hard stop. In hindsight, I should have just finished drilling the bolt that I was at before looking up, as the excuse that I couldn't hear him over the drill would have been valid."

The crux requires micro-cams. Mess this up and you will be in danger of a big whipper. Unfortunately the landing won't be as soft as diving into the deep blue sea. If setting it up as a toprope, be sure to anchor yourself in or you'll be the one going overboard. It's also not a bad idea for top-ropers to clip a few quickdraws into the bolts as you are rappelling or lowering to keep scary pendulum swings to a minimum.

46 ANCHORS AWAY 5.11d ★

Follow the first part of SMOOTH SAILING to the large ledge. Take the left line up to the shared bolted anchors with MAN OVERBOARD. 6 bolts, bolted anchor (60 ft.)

47 SMOOTH SAILING 5.10a ★★★ (a.k.a LLOYD WOULD HAVE LIKED IT)

The upper part was once called SHORT BUT SWEET. Climb past 4 bolts to a ledge below a beautiful white face. Climb the face past two more bolts to the top. 6 bolts, bolted anchors. (80 ft.)

From SMOOTH SAILING to SKATIN' the cliff is mostly broken, loose, dirty, vegetated, or in some cases all of the above. Over the years dozens of routes have been done in this area. Some routes have probably seen multiple "first ascents". None of them have become popular. Little information is known about these seldom-travelled lines, but if you are feeling adventurous, take your best shot (and if you happen to have information besides what's listed here, please let me know so we can include it in the next edition).

48 HAMBURGER YELPER 5.11b/c

This line is located approximately 60 feet left of the Big Gully, under a large crack in a roof. Pull the roof crack, then continue up the face to the top. Natural anchors. (70 ft.)

49 DEBBIE DUZ DONUTS 5.11

Climb the obvious dihedral 40 feet left of the Big Gully. Natural anchors. (70 ft.)

The next set of climbs is on the right side of the BIG GULLY, just west of the parking lot. The routes also happen to be directly below a popular lookout point near the parking lot, which unfortunately means that unwelcome flying objects are a common occurrence. Be sure to report any reckless behavior to park staff. A helmet might not be a bad idea.

50 SKULL AND BONES 5.8+

This climb starts about 100 feet left of SPANISH BOMBS. Begin below a giant pine tree and follow an obvious corner and crack system straight up to the tree. Rap from the pine tree or scramble up another 10 feet to the top. Natural anchors.

This route was inaccessible before a recent forest fire cleared out the dense Greenbrier thicket. If the route doesn't see traffic in the near future it will be lost to thorns once again.

51 BLOODMOBILE 5.7

This line climbs the prominent arête approximately about 200 feet right of the Big Gully just right of a smaller, narrower gully. Natural anchors. (70 ft.)

52 LOOK BEFORE YOU LEAK 5.7

....or before carelessly hurtling your beer bottle over the edge at unsuspecting climbers. Begins just right of BLOODMOBILE on a ledge 20 feet above the trail. Follow cracks up the left side of the face. Bolted anchor. (If you set as a top rope the anchors are on the face about an arm's reach down from the rim.) (40 ft.)

53 VENUS SCRIBNER 5.10b R ★

Using crimpers climb the short, clean face just right of the cracks of LOOK BEFORE YOU LEAK. This is a fun top rope that is seldom if ever led. Use the bolted anchors of LOOK BEFORE YOU LEAK. (60 ft.)

49) DEBBIE DUZ DONUTS (5.11)

PARKING LOT AREA

This section of rock is home to the eastern most routes in the park that are still open to climbing. Though many more routes exist past this area, park staff has closed it off to climbing in order to reduce the number of people walking to the overlooks near the parking lot. Please respect this closure. Most of these routes require a 60 meter rope!

54 SKATIN' 5.11d ★

Mixed. Start approximately 100 feet right of BLOODMOBILE, just right of an arête, on a slanting block below a low roof. From the block make a hard move up to a horizontal crack, then traverse left to the obvious corner below a bolt. Climb past the old bolt (to a V slot) and then up through a smooth bulge with an incipient crack to a larger crack. Continue up somewhat easier rock to the large, greenbrier-covered ledge 40 feet off the

48) HAMBURGER YELPER (5.11b/c)

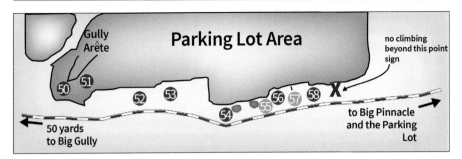

ground. Almost always toproped, either from the cliff top or by gaining the ledge via the lower part of VEGOMATIC. (40 ft.)

Variation: You can keep this line in the 5.11-range by climbing a corner crack to the left of the steep dihedral, and then skatin' left around the crux bulge.

55 THIN TO WIN 5.10a ★★

Start just right of SKATIN' on a large slabby boulder below the low roof. Throw a foot up really high and grab onto the good flakes that enable you to pull the roof. Move right to the corner. Continue past a low set of anchors onto a large ledge. Continue up the left side of the face to bolted anchors. 11 bolts, bolted anchors. (90 ft.)

If 5.10 is your goal, you can also stop at a low set of anchors after five bolts. For those seeking a 5.7/5.8 sport pitch you can rappel in from the top to the large ledge. There are bolted anchors on the large ledge that can be used as a belay anchor. (50 ft.)

Variation. FAT BOY 5.11a ★★

This is an excellent toprope variation. After the burly THIN TO WIN start, move up a smooth, thin face to a tricky bulge. After maneuvering around the bulge, you can step right to the THIN TO WIN anchors.

56 VEGOMATIC 5.8 ★★

A well-protected route with good gear stances makes this route a good option for newer trad leaders. Climb the chimney/crack feature for about 40 feet to a set of anchors below a large

ledge. You can stop here or keep going onto the large ledge. From the ledge you have several options. 1) Keep climbing the crack to the top and bolted anchors. 2) Move a little to the left and finish the 5.7/5.8 bolted upper section of THIN TO WIN (6 bolts to bolted anchors). 3) Stop at bolted anchors on the large ledge then continue up either option 1 or 2. However you do it don't forget to look back and enjoy the views of the rural Piedmont! (90 ft.)

57 CHICKEN BONE 5.7 ★★★

Start 10 feet right of the VEGOMATIC chimney at a slanting block in front of a very low, small roof. Climb the thin face to a ledge. Take a break, then continue up slightly steeper rock to the top. The anchors are located just below the top of the cliff underneath a tree. 10 bolts, bolted anchors. (90 ft.)

This is one of the best routes at Pilot. Expect lines on a nice day.

58 PILOT ERROR 5.7 ★★

Start 20 feet right of the chimney behind a large tree. Fun climbing on a flake system trending up and right, with a few thin for the grade face moves interspersed throughout for good measure. Sustained 5.7 moves all the way make for a long, full-value line. There are two sets of anchors for this climb – one set of hangers at the top of the cliff, and another set of super shuts about 12 feet down from the top, above a small ledge with a tree. (90 ft.)

The following routes, which are located east of the authorized climbing area, are off limits and listed for historical purposes only.

(X) HARD HAT AREA 5.7

(X) BLACK ROUTE 5.11+

(X) SINBAD THE SAILOR 5.12

(X) BACK IN THE SADDLE 5.10

(X) RIDE 'EM COWBOY 5.12

The first FA of CHICKEN BONE had several unlikely witnesses. As John Black was making his way to the top, he first realized something was amiss when he saw something fly past him from above out of the corner of his eye. A few moves later he grabbed a couple of handholds that seemed almost greasy. He glanced up, and promptly got pegged in the forehead with a half-eaten chicken bone. He shouted up to the top, "Hey! Whoever's up there, you'd better save me some chicken!" Upon topping out, he discovered two young boys with a shocked and incredulous look on their faces. It's probably safe to assume that was the last time anything flew out of their hands and over the cliff.

MOORE'S WALL

What do old-school traddies, swarms of pebble wrestlers, and maybe even a few high octane bolt clippers all have in common?

Answer: Moore's Wall

Many aspiring North Carolina hard-persons have used Moore's Wall as a playground to sharpen both their physical and mental skills. Moores is one of the earliest developed climbing areas in the state. For generations the bullet-hard quartzite of Moore's Wall has appealed to a wide variety of climbers.

At first glance Moore's Wall might not be quite as striking as Pilot Mountain, its neighbor a few miles down the road. The two crags are close enough in proximity that one might mistakenly assume that they are similar in characteristics, but we all know what happens when we assume. For every time a North Carolina climber snubs their nose at Pilot, there are at least five others touting the clean, quartzite goodness that can be found in the lines at Moore's Wall.

Moore's in fact couldn't be more different than its semi-chossy cohort. It has twice the number of routes, many of which are more than twice as tall as the longest lines at Pilot. You're likely to see only a fraction of the number of climbers. There are no offical hiking trails; thus no lines of day hikers. There's no threat of getting whipped by a top-rope being thrown over the edge, although you may get dive-bombed by a Peregrine Falcon.

Large groups of climbers are common at Pilot, but almost never seen at Moores for one very good reason. Rigging an easy toprope is next to impossible at Moore's. While Moore's provides great learning ground for newer climbers interested in honing their trad skills under the tutelage of an experienced partner, the majority of routes in each area descend from a single rappel sta-

tion, making large guided groups a headache at best and an epic at worst. Even though there are many wonderful moderate lines, the notoriously creative gear placements and required route-finding skills keeps Moore's Wall from being a true "beginner crag".

That being said, while Pilot might get the prize for the most popular climbing area in the state, Moore's is definitely in the running for "Best Climbing Area" in not only North Carolina, but throughout the Southeast. Here's a sum-up of what makes Moore's Wall so unique.

1. Trad is Rad – More than just a catchy slogan on a t-shirt, this phrase is a way of life at Moore's. The overwhelming majority of the lines here were established from the ground-up, led boldly without the use of fixed protection. If you are going to climb at Moore's make sure you are well-versed in the art of placing your own protection.

2. Extreme Moderates - Steep face climbing and wildly overhanging roof sequences are common on even moderate routes; sometimes a 5.7 can look like a 5.12 from the ground. Impossible looking roofs often reveal giant buckets upon closer inspection. Really good holds can appear at just the right moment, making for exciting climbing regardless of the grade of difficulty.

3. All Around Adventure – Getting to the top of the route is only half the battle. Sometimes finding your way down can be the most adventurous part of the day.

4. Fewer People - Although Moore's Wall is part of the very popular Hanging Rock State Park, the climbing area is far from the main tourist sections of the park. This means that crowds will be at a minimum on most weekends. It is not unusual to have the entire cliff to yourself during the week.

LOCATION
Moore's Wall is located just north of Winston-Salem. From US Highway 52 take exit number 122 (Moore-RJR Drive) and drive east along Moore Road, which will eventually become Mountain View Road. After about 4 miles there will be a Texaco Station on the left, marking the intersection with NC Hwy 66. Turn left (north) onto NC Hwy 66 and continue for 6.7 miles. Next take a right onto Moore's Spring Road (there is also a sign for Hanging Rock State Park). Drive for 0.5 miles and turn right onto Mickey Road. Follow Mickey Road for 0.9 miles before turning right onto Charlie Young Road. When Charlie Young Road ends, make a right onto Hooker Farm Road. Next, take the first right (onto the aptly named Climbing Access Drive) and drive for a short distance to the parking lot and kiosk. The parking area has a pit toilet that is usually pretty clean, as well as a water spigot.

ACCESS
For many years access was a major problem. Local residents hated the weekend traffic on their gravel road. Car vandalism was common and at least one fist fight broke out over climber access to Tim Fisher's property at the end of the old access road. One of the first successes of the Carolina Climbers Coalition (CCC) was an agreement with the park to find an alternative parking location that would not upset the neighbors. Bill Webster, who was the first CCC President, met with the park staff and developed an agreement that a new parking lot was essential. Several options were identified, but lack of funding delayed progress. Several years later and after countless volunteer hours from the climbing community and compromises on all sides, the park staff and climbers finally came to an agreement on a site. Closure on this vital issue was accomplished primarily thanks to Park Ranger Erik Nygard and CCC member Sean Barb. The climbing community is extremely grateful that the NC State Park system chose to spend precious resources to provide this all-important access point. If you ever have the opportunity, take the time to thank the park staff for closing the curtains on the endless feud with local landowners.

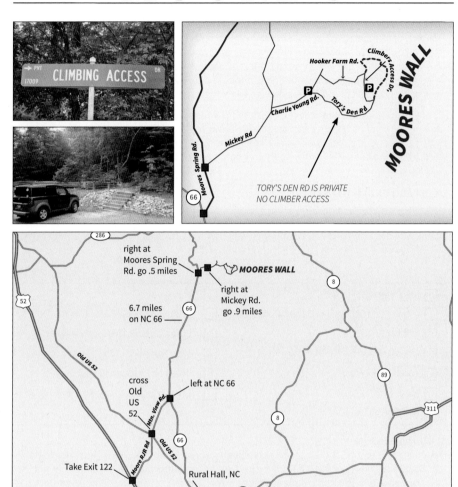

Map labels:

CLIMBING ACCESS — PVT 17009 DR

Hooker Farm Rd.
Climbers Access Dr.
MOORES WALL
Charlie Young Rd.
Tory's Den Rd
Mickey Rd
Moores Spring Rd.
66

TORY'S DEN RD IS PRIVATE
NO CLIMBER ACCESS

286
right at
Moores Spring
Rd. go .5 miles
MOORES WALL
8
right at
Mickey Rd.
go .9 miles
6.7 miles
on NC 66
66
52
Old US 52
cross
Old
US
52
left at NC 66
89
Mtn. View Rd.
8
311
66
Moore BJR Rd
Old US 52
Take Exit 122
Rural Hall, NC
52
65

"To our credit, the arrival of the parking lot we now enjoy at Moore's all started when we (climbers) decided to proactively approach the park administration with a "how can we help you" initiative. In September of 2003 I remember seeing more than 25 climbers show up at the Visitor's Center on a Saturday morning. We trudged up the Moore's Wall Loop Trail from the lake with wheel barrows, buckets, picks, and shovels in hand, and set out to install some water diversion berms on the trail to mitigate erosion. The park was overwhelmed with our volunteer manpower, especially considering that this trail provided no direct benefit to us as climbers. They were also pretty impressed with how strong and fit all of our volunteers were! Almost a year to the day we lended the park a hand again, this time to pick up trash over at the Lower Cascades Waterfall trails – again with 25+ volunteers, and again in an area that doesn't affect climbers. These early volunteer days were a vital precursor to building trust and respect between the park and the climbing community. We not only enabled them to finish their projects faster, but also saved them a ton of money by providing free labor. Without making these efforts, the climber's parking area might never have become a high priority item." - Sean Barb (Winston-Salem, NC)

THE CLIMBING

This cliff band, composed of metamorphic quartzite, offers a wide variety of climbing on mostly vertical to slightly overhanging rock. The steepness of the walls offer excellent exposure and position. Although one will encounter cracks, roofs, and technical face sequences of all types, sometimes even on the same route, quite often the crux is simply managing to keep the ever-increasing pump factor down long enough to get to the top.

There are over 120 established lines at Moore's Wall, enough for climbers of all abilities. In and around the Sentinel Buttress area are several classic routes 5.8 and under, while the Amphitheater is perfect for climbers looking for routes in the 5.8-5.11 range. Harder lines are scattered throughout the entire cliff, with a heavy concentration at both the North End and Hanging Garden.

A 10A AND UNDER TOP TEN...

Looking for a day of classic gear routes that will pack a pump but not leave you crying for your mama? Any of the following 3-star routes would make the perfect choice – all steep for the grade with dizzying exposure, but all laden with bomber gear in all the right places...

☐ Easy Hard (5.5)	☐ Nutsweat (5.9+)
☐ Crow's Nest Access aka Babies Buns (5.5)	☐ Gnatty Pale (5.9+)
☐ Wailing Wall (5.6)	☐ Blue Chock (5.10a)
☐ Almost Seven aka Golden Earring (5.7)	☐ Meat Puppet (5.10a)
☐ Zoo View (5.7+)	☐ Break on Through (5.10a)
☐ Raise Hell (5.8)	☐ U Haul (5.10a)
☐ Air Show (5.8+)	

CLIMBING SEASON

Like most areas in the Southeast, prime climbing season at Moore's is during the spring and the fall. Beware the north-facing aspect of the wall during the winter months. If you're tempted to take advantage of one of those stray 60 degree winter weekends, keep in mind that this rock has been exposed to sub-freezing temperatures for weeks and remains in the shade the majority of the day. The holds will still be hand-numbingly cold, regardless of how warm the air temperature or how many of those hand warmers you stuff into your chalk bag.

It is very possible to have an enjoyable day at Moore's in the summer, but don't forget that despite the respite of shade, you will still have to deal with the same humidity that smothers the rest of the Piedmont during June to August. Afternoon thunderstorms are common, especially during the summer, so keep a vigilant eye on the sky and use good judgment.

GEAR

For the majority of routes at Moore's you will want to have a full rack of traditional climbing gear at your disposal. Unlike the splitter cracks of the Western United States, most routes here follow crack systems that vary in size and shape along the way, so it is difficult to decipher exactly what you will need from the ground. Bring a variety – better to have and not need than to need and not have! Think of what you don't end up using as training weight.

Camming devices are useful for the many horizontal cracks that often double as fantastic incut hand holds from which to place gear. Smaller sizes up through 3 inches is recommended, although a 4 – 5 inch piece may come in handy on certain climbs. For the old school purists, textbook constrictions abound, many of which provide excellent examples of perfect placements for passive gear such as stoppers and hexes. Depending on who you talk to, tri-cams (pink in particular) can be an essential, never-leave-the-ground-without-it piece of gear, or a waste of precious rack space. Micronuts and microcams may prove useful on some of the harder climbs as well.

Though many routes at Moore's offer good gear options, be prepared to have both your mental faculties and physical endurance tested, as the less than obvious placements can often be deceptively difficult to find. That being said, Moore's is a fantastic place to hone your trad climbing skills – if you can place gear at Moore's, you can place gear just about anywhere!

"The rock at Moore's takes gear well, and is of extremely high quality (usually), so it was a natural candidate for ground-up trad climbing. Since people weren't climbing 5.12 and harder too much before the 1980s, many of the routes established had adequate natural gear with the odd pin or bolt. The harder climbs that came later didn't have many good gear placements (if they did, they wouldn't have been hard!), so those are the ones that got bolted. I never had a problem with the supposed "double standard" there, although some do." - John Provetero

"What makes Moore's Wall so special are the little "big" adventures that each climb offers. Don't get me wrong; sometimes the adventure element can be frustrating. It makes every day of climbing a bit more uncertain and projecting an even more fleeting process. But it also packs a lot of mountain into a pretty small space and makes each move of upward progress, each moment of security, that much more of a gift." -

Chris Barlow, a temporary local with a permanent love for Moore's Wall

ACCESS CONSIDERATIONS

In addition to the general rules and regulations about climbing in NC State Parks, please remember the following access issues that are specific to Moore's Wall.

1. LEAVE YOUR DRILL AT HOME – This rule is in effect in all NC State Parks, but rings especially true at Moore's Wall. There are several members of the local climbing community that would gladly serve your head on a platter for the heinous crime of retro-bolting. Don't even think about it.

2. KEEP A LOW PROFILE – Although the parking area itself is not on private property, the back roads that get you there are residential areas. Please be respectful of the neighbors.

3. TOP-ROPERS DEFER TO LEADERS AND RAPPELLERS – Moore's is not a top roping area, however a few routes line up directly over a rap station, making for reasonable top rope rigging after already climbing a route that shares that rap station. (Most notably – QUAKER STATE in the Amphitheater) If your party chooses to run top rope laps on a line, don't cause traffic jams by keeping rappellers or groups that want to lead the route from playing through.

4. NO CAMPING IN PARKING LOT – Local climbers worked hard to secure a parking lot for climbers. Please be out on time and do not don't wear out your welcome with any overnight dirt-bagging. Legal camping is listed on the next page.

PARK FACTS
Hanging Rock State Park

1790 Hanging Rock Park Road, Danbury, NC 27106

Office Phone: 336-593-8480
Email: hanging.rock@ncdenr.gov

Hours
November - February, 8:00 a.m. – 6:00 p.m.
March, April, September, October, 8:00 a.m. – 8:00 p.m.
May - August, 8:00 a.m. – 9:00 p.m.
The park is closed Christmas day.

CAMPING
There are public and private options for camping near Moore's Wall. Hanging Rock State Park has over 70 campsites located in the main area of the park. The fee is a reasonable $9 per site (in 2012) and includes a tent pad, picnic table, and grill. Most sites will hold 2 small tents or 1 large one. There is a maximum of 6 people per site. Water is available on the grounds, along with showers and restrooms, however note that the bathhouse is closed from December 1 – March 15. If you camp here, don't forget about the park hours – make sure that you can get back to the main area BEFORE the gate closes.

Pilot Mountain in the far distance. Sauratown Mountain is the closer peak with towers.

To get to the Hanging Rock State Park campground from the Moore's Wall parking lot, head back the way you came until you reach Moore's Springs Road – then turn right and follow Moore's Spring Road for 5 miles. Turn right onto Hanging Rock Park Road, then follow signs to the camping area.

GEAR SHOPS
Great Outdoor Provision Company – (336) 727-0906
402 Stratford Rd, Winston-Salem, NC 27103

Village Outdoor Shop – (336) 768-2267
3456 Robinhood Rd, Winston-Salem, NC 27106

CLIMBING GYMS
The Ultimate Climbing Gym (at Tumblebees) – 6904 Downwind Rd, Greensboro, NC (336) 665-0662

GROCERIES/RESTAURANTS
Food, Groceries, Gas and ATMs are available at several exits along Highway 52 between Winston Salem and Pilot Mountain State Park. If you are looking for all of the above, a good exit to stop at is 115 (University Parkway).

EMERGENCIES

In the unfortunate event of an accident requiring rescue, call the Stokes County Sheriff (336) 593-8787. The nearest hospital is Stokes Reynolds Memorial Hospital (336) 593-2831 and is located in Danbury, NC, approximately 7 miles east of the intersection of NC Hwy 66 and Moore's Spring Rd. Another option is Northern Hospital, approximately 12 miles north in Mount Airy, NC (336-719-7000). The nearest large medical center is Wake Forest University Baptist Medical Center in Winston Salem, NC (336-716-2255).

Please note that cell reception is spotty at best – in an emergency it may be necessary to drive back towards Highway 52 to get reception.

BOULDERING

If you get tired of lugging your rack around, leave it in the car and join the other pad people. Thanks to a handful of developers in the late 1990's, Moore's is no longer just for traddies. An impressive collection of high-quality boulder problems can be found scattered all along the base of the cliff. The most obvious collection of problems lies just below Sentinel Buttress. Among other good lines this area contains Rodney Biddle's brilliant classic Tsunami (V8). It and others can be reached by hiking as you would for Sentinel Buttress. Hang a right at the aptly named sign that says "Boulders."

If you're willing to do a little bit of exploring off the beaten track, you will be delighted at all the hidden gems clustered in different sections of the park. For directions or beta, try the Carolina Climbers Coalition website, or better yet, make friends with the locals!

"It's sharp. You have to know that going in. But on a positive note, most of the topouts are easy. There are some really great problems here, if you know where to look. Most of them are tall, with just okay landings, so bring a couple of pads and spotters. NEVER forget to fill out a climbing permit, or you will find yourself backtracking the 20 minute hike back to the parking area with a ranger in tow." - Alison Domnas, local pebble wrestler

HISTORY

No one can talk about Moore's Wall without also mentioning the bold, ground-up tradition in which the routes here were established. The men that were involved in the development of this cliff remain proud examples of what one can accomplish with physical strength, a cool head, and nerves of steel.

Though climbing at Moore's may have taken place prior to 1959, the first known ascent was recorded in August of that year (HEADWALL DIRECT), by George DeWolfe and Tom Fawcett. This line was documented as the face just left of EASY HARD in Chris Hall's Southern Rock. This first ascent was a catalyst for the development of many moderates such as SCRAMBLED EGGS and the SENTINEL, as well as a few routes on Hanging Rock itself, which is in the main area of the park, and is now closed to climbing. By May of 1967 there were approximately 30 established lines in the park, according to an unpublished, underground guidebook by DeWolfe.

The mid to late 1970's saw another surge of activity, this time on the steeper faces, thanks to advancements in protection (camming devices, hexentrics, and better nuts). During this period Tom Howard, Tom McMillan, and Bob Rotert established what many consider to be Moore's most classic routes – RAISE HELL, AIR SHOW, ZOO VIEW, and TOO MUCH FUN. Probably the most significant ascents made during this time were AID RAID and WILD KINGDOM, which were sent in 1978 and 1979. These lines helped set a new standard of difficult climbing across North Carolina.

By the time the 1980's rolled around, Tim Fisher, the unofficial "Mayor of Moore's" had entered the scene. Fisher started out climbing the way a lot of us probably did – on a top rope under the watchful eyes of a guide service. However, the rest of us probably didn't go on to nab notable first ascents within 10 months of first setting hands on the rock! Fisher is well-known for his unwavering commitment to bold, ground-up style climbing using little to no fixed protection. In addition to climbing the first ascents of many fantastic lines, Tim has served the climbing community by regularily upgrading old bolts and pins and for purchasing a tract of land that for many years provided the only reasonable access to Moore's Wall.

> *"My personal vote for most important Piedmont-area FA during my era was WILD KINGDOM by Tom McMillan and Rob Robinson. These guys were also the ones who put up DO OR DIVE and QUAKER STATE, which were two of my favorites of all time, anywhere. Back in 1979 and 1980, when I was first ticking the 5.10 routes at Moore's, I used to look at WILD KINGDOM and just shake thinking about what it must be like to be up there and climb well enough to cruise something like that. For the time that was a very futuristic route and it inspired a lot of people to reach inside, train to get better, and learn to control their minds in scary situations". - Mark Pell, on notable Piedmont FA's*

Fisher was joined by a band of colorful characters – among them David Petree, John Provetero, John Regglebregge, Jimmy Overby, and the legendary Eric Zschiesche – in continuing to push the grades in the purist free climbing movement with routes such as POOH CORNER, MIGHTY MOUSE, MIDDLE ROAD, and RECKLESS ABANDON. The staunch ethic at Moore's meant that many early ascents were onsighted. Lee Munson's ascent of SHADOWDANCE marks one of the high points of development at Moore's and remains a sought after tick for the aspiring Moore's hard person.

A young Tim Fisher at the height of 1980's fashion

Among the other VIP's that frequented Moore's during the late 1980's were Doug Reed (who later went on to develop a large part of the New River Gorge) and Porter Jarrard (who can be credited with much of the development at the Red River Gorge). These guys established many hard, classic lines as well, and it is likely that at least one of Jarrard's bold routes on the Fire Wall (P.O.V. 5.12c) remains unrepeated to this day. The 1980's culminated, in terms of difficulty, with Harrison Dekker's ascent of the Zschiesche top-rope project, ZEUS (5.13b).

This left little room for new routes during the 1990's, save a few test pieces such as SUPERCRIMP and HERCULES in the wildly overhanging Hanging Garden. The 1990's also ushered the Meat Puppet crag into the spotlight, an unassuming wall that sits high atop the main cliff. It is likely that most of the routes in this area were climbed long ago, but never recorded.

The invention of crash pads shifted the focus off of the walls to the boulders at the base of the cliff towards the late 1990's. John Provetero, Sean Barb, and Rodney Biddle were just a few of the major players involved in coaxing out the many fine lines found scattered along the base. Thanks to their efforts, Moore's is now considered a destination for bouldering as well as trad climbing.

Harrison Dekker getting addicted to NICOTINE (5.13a)   Eric Zschieche on an early ascent of NICOTINE (5.13a)

The strong traditional ethic that makes Moore's so unique has also been the source of quite a bit of controversy in the local climbing community, causing bolts to be added and chopped over the years. The state park has now put a general ban on any new bolting throughout the park. To comply with their rules as well as show respect for the first ascensionists, do not under any circumstances be tempted to add any fixed hardware to this cliff.

The original "men from Moore's" gang celebrating after a day of climbing

APPROACH (ALL AREAS)

All climbs are approached from the Climbing Access Road parking lot. From the parking lot take the trail that leads past the outhouse and registration kiosk. Follow the wooded trail for approximately 5 minutes until you reach a set of steps leading to an old fire road. Head left onto the road and up the hill. From here, there are two different options for getting to the base, depending on where along the cliff you want to climb. (Navigating the base is pretty easy, so don't worry if you end up at a different section of cliff than anticipated.)

The first option will take you to the right (south) side of the cliff (Sentinel Buttress, Circus Wall, Fire Wall, and Hanging Garden). Look for a narrow trail marked by a sign ("Sentinel Buttress") heading up and right after only a couple minutes along the fire road. This somewhat steep and rooty trail forks after about 3 minutes. Branching to the right will take you to the Practice Rock in the boulderfield. Stay straight on the trail for another 5 minutes to reach the base of Washboard and the Sentinel Buttress area.

The second option is your best bet if you want to climb in the Amphitheater and/or the North End. Continue along the fire road past the Sentinel Buttress turnoff to a second sign ("Amphitheater"), also heading up and right. Follow this trail for approximately 10 minutes until you reach a fork in the trail, also marked by a sign – go left to the North End, and up and right to the Amphitheater.

A third option also exists if you happen to be coming from the main area of Hanging Rock State Park. Though this approach is fairly long and strenuous to reach the majority of routes at Moore's Wall, it might be worth considering if you are camping in the main area. For this option follow the Moore's Wall Loop Trail through the family camping area until you reach the top of Moore's Wall. Look for a large boulder at the top of a gully, then scramble down to the base of the wall. The gully will land you at the Central Wall.

NORTH END

The North End is the perfect playground for those in search of steep, shady walls free of crowds. The climbing is stout and sustained – be strong at the grade and be prepared for tricksy gear and precarious stances at times. A few bolts here and there doesn't mean these are sport routes!

Approach: Take the Amphitheater side trail from the gravel road to an intersection just downhill from the Amphitheater. Bear left at the North End/Amphitheater trail intersection and continue hiking for another 5 minutes, maneuvering over a large tree with a step cut out and past a sign marking "North End" territory. In a couple of minutes, look up and right to see the proud, overhanging face of the Indian Head Buttress, which is home to some of the longest routes at Moore's. For more detailed directions to specific areas at the North End, please see the approach descriptions for each section.

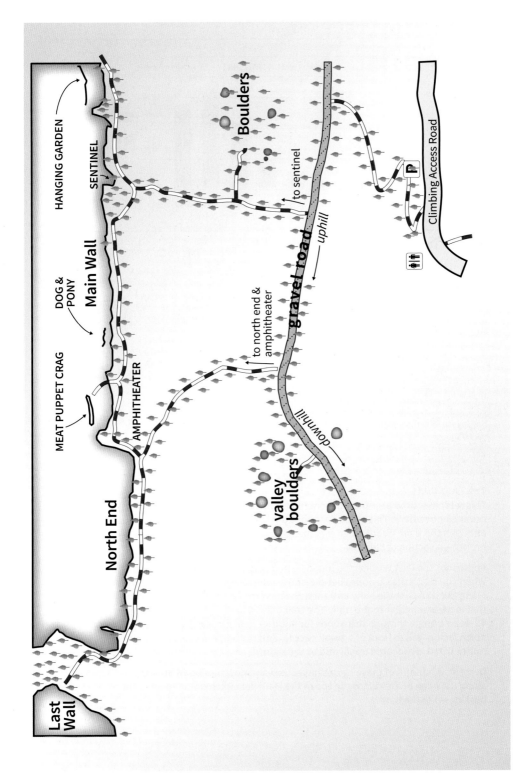

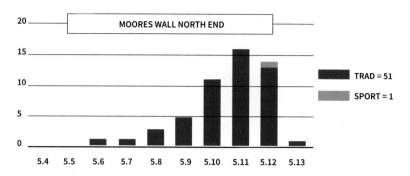

MOORES WALL NORTH END

TRAD = 51
SPORT = 1

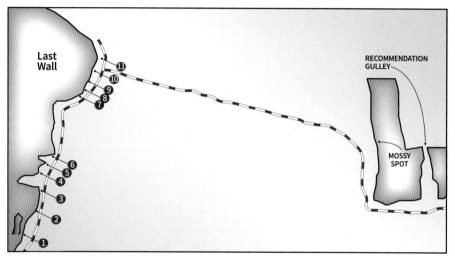

THE LAST WALL

This seldom visited area lies far from the more popular cliffs. Many Moore's regulars have never climbed here. This guide describes ten of the primary routes in the main area, although there are about twice that many developed lines scattered among this shorter, broken-up section of cliffline.

Approach: The Last Wall can be found by hiking past all of the other North End areas. When you reach the obvious Filet-o-Fish Turret and Recommendation Gully, keep walking along the trail past the gully entrance and past the large, east-facing wall on your right that is perpendicular to the trail. The trail takes a hard right as it cuts steeply uphill at a 45-degree angle through the woods for another five minutes. You will arrive at another north facing wall in front of a small cave low on the left hand side of the cliff. All of the routes listed are located uphill and to the right.

Descent: A handful of these routes have fixed anchors, but for all others, walk a faint trail along the edge of the cliff to the top of the Main Vein Buttress, where the trail then circles back down to the base.

1 DIABOLIC 5.12d

This route starts in a steep, low cave. Start in the right side of the cave on very small holds. Pull an extended boulder problem, veering right past small gear at the lip of the roof, and onto easier ground above. Fixed anchors. (35 ft.)

2 TIM'S ROOF 5.11d ★★

Look for a white face capped by a massive roof. Climb easy terrain for 50 feet to a large ledge beneath the roof. Attack the roof on the left side, and hold on until the top. Natural anchors. (80 ft.)

3 NATURAL SELECTION 5.11d ★

This route is located 25 feet right of TIM'S ROOF. Walk past an orange dihedral, then halfway up a staircase of boulders.

P1: Start on a low jug directly in front of an old tree fall. Climb up and slightly left for a few feet, then ease back right through the steepest part of the overhanging prow. Belay from natural anchors on a giant ledge. (5.11d, 35 ft.)

P2: A short pitch of easy, but hairy climbing will take you to the top. (25 ft.)

The next three routes are located at an obvious clearing about 35 feet up the trail. A good landmark is a three-headed tree.

4 ARMS FOR AMERICA 5.10

Climb the vertical crack system that runs through the center of the wall, then head up and right over a run out face. (60 ft.)

5 GIZMOSIS 5.11b ★

Pull the low bulge on the far right side of the wall beneath two bolts. Climb straight up past the bolts and through a crack in the face, veering right at the top for maximum value. Gear is challenging to find as well as place. (60 ft.)

6 FACE THE FACE 5.11c/d ★

On the right side of the wall is a smaller disconnected face with twin vertical cracks. Thin climbing over the twin cracks leads to the top. This scary lead is shorter than its left hand neighbor, but more sustained, and blessed with the same devious gear. (45 ft.)

The Main Vein area is found at another obvious clearing, 60 feet up the trail. This marks the end of the cliffline.

7 TIM'S SPORT ROUTE 5.11c/d ★★

Affectionately named by Tim Fisher's peers because of his strict traditional ethics. Steep climbing leads through bulges past one pin, a bolt with a homemade hanger, another bolt, and then gear to the top. Natural anchors. (50 ft.)

8 STRETCH ARM STRONG 5.12 a/b ★★

Climb past two bolts through a polished dihedral. Next use gear to surmount the overhangs. Natural anchors. (50 ft.)

9 THE HURT LOCKER 5.12c/d ★★★

This is the first route on the left side of the radically steep buttress. Climb past three bolts to pull two roofs through overhangs. Fixed anchors. (65 ft.)

10 THE MAIN VEIN 5.12d/13a ★★★

Climb the left leaning crack past three bolts and through overhangs to the top. Fixed anchors (65 ft.)

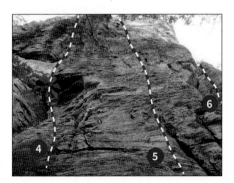

Peregrine Falcons

Peregrine Falcons ((Falco peregrines) are named from the Latin word for "wanderer." This name stems from the long distances the birds migrate during the winter. Owning the title of "fastest bird in the world," these speedsters dive-bomb their prey in mid-air, sometimes reaching speeds of more than 175 mph. Due to the use of DDT in pesticides in the 1960's these birds were pushed to the brink of extinction, as the DDT caused premature breaking of the bird's eggs.

Until recently, climbing at the North End of Moore's was subject to a seasonal closure to protect the birds and their nests. However it has been many years since nesting birds have been seen in the park, so when the closure was lifted in the summer of 2012, it was lifted indefinitely with a new management strategy – to allow climbers to enjoy the cliffs year round, and to close the cliff only in the event that nesting birds are seen. The park rangers have requested that any peregrine sightings be reported to the park (336-593-8480).

"Both THE MAIN VEIN and THE HURT LOCKER used to be R/X routes with cruxes that were unprotected into decking range. I was going for the repeat of THE MAIN VEIN and after pushing through the crux I successfully latched onto the "this route's over" jug. Sheeww. One deep breath..... and the jug blew off in my hand! I don't remember much but the climbers who came running said they heard all sorts of yelling and screaming as well as shrubbery displacement. My partner in crime, Jim Maddox, had taken one for the team and done a running belay down the hill into the briers, Rambo-style. I trimmed the razor boulder on the ground and swung under the low roof at the base and got face planted. I love you Jim! - Seth Tart

"THE HURT LOCKER got its name for a similar incident. An unexpected fall jerked my belayer off the ground as I came screaming in off the 40-degree angle rock. I grabbed the rope, lifted my feet and leaned back like a swing. After the dust settled, my shirtless back looked like a Bengal Tiger had attacked me and the ground looked as if someone had dragged a dead body off. Things were bolder in the past and that was just part of climbing. In that regard things have changed a lot and necessarily so." - Seth Tart, reflecting on memories from The Last Wall

11 YOSEMITE SAM 5.12b ★★

Shares a start with MAIN VEIN. After the first bolt, break out right through the face to follow cracks through overhangs and a roof. Natural anchors (65 ft.)

FILET-O-FISH AREA
The landmark for this area is a distinctive turret-like feature just right of The Recommendation Gully, which lies on the left side of the North End cliffline.

The next four routes start in the gully around the corner and left of the Filet-o-Fish Turret.

① RASTAFARI 5.9

To reach this route, hike up to the top of the Recommendation Gully. Scramble up a short wall, and wrestle through the briars to a separate wall on the left. Follow the flake/crack system up and gradually left.

Descent: Rap from a fixed nut anchor. (70 ft.)

② WAR GAMES 5.12b ★★
This route follows the steep arête that towers over the back of the Recommendation Gully. Scramble up the boulder at the top of the gully, starting just left of the bolt. Climb up the left side of the arête past a horizontal seam. (Make sure to take microcams). Save some juice for the redpoint crux up high. 2 bolts and fixed anchor. (40 ft.)

Variation: A direct start begins beneath the boulder. (5.12c)

"No doubt you're going to war, but it's more pleasure than pain! This route is a load of fun for gear at this grade, but don't mess around as your guns will be ablaze!" -

Seth Tart, on WAR GAMES (5.12b)

"There is a distinct crux on this one. No jug jumping here. The gear is reasonable but may require a forearm sacrifice to place."

Tim Fisher, on ENDURO MAN RIDES AGAIN.

③ THE RECOMMENDATION 5.12b ★

A short but powerful crux leads to an easier, but pumpy finish. Climb the bolted line that begins partway up the gully. (60 ft.)

Descent: The original finish was to a fixed gear anchor just above the fourth bolt. The route was retro-equipped with a controversial bolted anchor that at the time of this writing, is still there. In the event of their disappearance, keep climbing for another 20 feet and rap from a higher set of anchors.

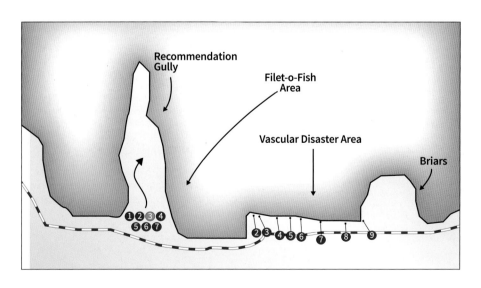

Recommendation Gully

Filet-o-Fish Area

Vascular Disaster Area

Briars

3) THE RECOMMENDATION (5.12b)

5) FILET-O-FISH (5.12a)

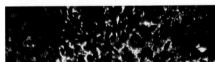

7) ROOF AWAKENING (5.11b)

An early FILET-O-FISH (5.12a) ascent for Porter Jarrard

Seth Tart heeding THE RECOMMENDATION (5.12b)

4 ENDURO MAN RIDES AGAIN 5.11d ★

Better be confident on slopers or you'll take the ride (again and again). Start at the base of a large slanted tree a little way up the gully at a shallow, overhanging dihedral littered with slopers. Follow this weakness through a series of steep Michelin-Man bulges. Fixed anchor. (70 ft.)

Descent: Rap station at the top.

5 FILET-O-FISH 5.12a ★★★

Named in honor of Tim Fisher, this line is almost as good as it gets – superb rock, stellar position, devilishly sustained, and bomber (though not obvious) protection. Starts just right of ENDURO MAN, along the right edge of the turret.

P1: Climb 5.7 terrain to access the base of the turret. (35 ft.)

P2: Angle up and left to a shallow dihedral. Move up the dihedral and then climb up and right through roofs and bulges, toward a fixed pin. At the pin head up and right to surmount the final roof. There are plenty of jugs at the top if you've got the juice to get there. Double ropes recommended. (60 ft.)

Descent: Rap off of ENDURO MAN anchor

> *"Even though Doug Reed suggested FISH FOR BREAKFAST to Tim Fisher back in the late 1980's, it wasn't climbed until more than a decade later (2000), and at the time of this writing, it still remains unrepeated. One fall was taken on an old-school free climbing ascent, and no fixed gear was added to the route. According to Fisher, this line is a "burly 90 foot pitch that will get your attention."*

6 FISH FOR BREAKFAST 5.12a/b ★★★

Need another excuse to eat your Wheaties at breakfast? How about this link-up of FILET and ROOF AWAKENING. Climb FILET but instead of finishing on the ledge, traverse right

underneath it and finish on ROOF AWAKENING. (80 ft.)

Descent: Same as ROOF AWAKENING

7 ROOF AWAKENING 5.11b ★★

This route was originally rated 5.10+ by the first ascencionists who claimed "we didn't know any better. "

P1: Start same as FILET and work your way up to the ledge 20 feet off the ground. Alternately, clamber up the first 15 feet of FILET-O-FISH to the same ledge. If necessary, gather some mental mojo by clipping the fixed aluminum bong to decipher the crux through the enormous roof. Belay just after the roof. (60 ft.)

P2. Scramble to the top.

Descent: Traverse left above the RECOMMENDATION to the large pine tree, then rappel from the tree down through the big cave. Alternatively, you can rappel from trees down and to the right.

VASCULAR DISASTER AREA

The following seven routes are located on the steep wall in between the Filet-O-Fish Turret and the Indian Head Buttress. For many of these routes, the second can be belayed from the ground, making for a convenient training opportunity for parties that are looking to run repeated laps up steep, pumpy terrain.

1 MINI-MOUSE 5.10 b/c

Start on the left (and often wet) side of the MIGHTY MOUSE chimney. Climb up easy rock and then traverse left beneath the roof to gain the crack on the face. Follow the crack, then trend right to finish at the MIGHTY MOUSE anchors. (80 ft.)

2 MIGHTY MOUSE 5.11d ★★★

This classic was once upon a time rated 5.11b, but over the years a few key holds have broken off in the crux area, slowly but surely pushing the grade up into the .11+ range. The gear, however, remains bomber, rendering this line one of the most well-protected of the

Seth Tart almost through the business of
ENDUROMAN RIDES AGAIN (5.11d)

grade at Moore's. Start left of the bolts on NICOTINE. Climb up the funky chimney to an interesting "seat" perched in an alcove. Step out right and blast through a steep face to a horizontal crack and a band of rust-colored rock. Traverse right along the rusty band to a blocky vertical crack. Manage your pump through more moderate terrain to a fixed anchor with a great view. (80 ft.)

Descent: Rappel from fixed anchors

③ SUPERMAN'S DEAD 5.12b/c R ★★

Better grab your super hero lycra for this one – this variation to MIGHTY MOUSE is mighty tough. Climb through the crux of MIGHTY MOUSE, but instead of traversing right, trend up and slightly left following the steep line to an overhang. At the overhang move up and right to the MIGHTY MOUSE anchor.

④ NICOTINE 5.13a ★

Mixed. The first 5.13 at Moore's, and one of the first in North Carolina. Begin at the stacked boulders towards the left end of the obvious undercut roof. Smoke your way past five bolts and 2 fixed pins. (75 ft.)

Descent: Rap from fixed anchors.

⑤ MIDDLE ROAD 5.12d ★★★

This route was originally rated 12c. However, several holds have broken and significantly increased the grade. This aptly named line lies in the middle of the wall, between NICOTINE and BOOGIE. Crank past the low first bolt to reach a sloping ledge. Move right and travel past two more bolts, a fixed pin, and a fixed stopper. Finish on the BOOGIE ledge and anchors. Bring a #3 camalot for the top. (60 ft.)

Descent: Rap from anchors.

> **BOOGIE TIL YA PUKE** *has a choose-your-own adventure start. The original line traversed in from VD (there once was a fixed stopper that protected this option, but it's long gone). Nowadays the most popular way is to boulder through the MIDDLE ROAD start, then traverse right. Porter Jarrard also did a direct start right below the crux, which is likely unrepeated due to the R/X rating. Pick your poison!*

⑥ BOOGIE TIL YA PUKE 5.12b ★★

Mixed. Great movement on even better rock. Burly and sustained, with one hard move after another. This pump-fest culminates with a few long pulls off of a redpoint crushing sloper before finishing on steep but juggy terrain. 3 bolts, fixed anchor. (50 ft.)

Descent: Rap from anchors.

⑦ VASCULAR DISASTER 5.11b/c ★★★ (a.k.a. VD)

A classic North Carolina sandbag that should not be missed. Start 20 feet right of BOOGIE on two obviously chalked holds beneath the low roof. Pull the V3 boulder problem start from a dead hang (shorties will need a cheater block to reach the start holds), and head straight up through a pumpy series of juggy bulges and horizontals to a fixed anchor. Gear is solid but tricky to place, and the bouldery start is unprotected. (75 ft.)

Descent: Rap from fixed anchor.

8 INDECENT EXPOSURE 5.11d ★★

This route climbs the exposed arête to the right of VD. Start same as VD and climb up to a few feet below the black roof. From here, fire up and right, following the hairline crack through a polished face to the base of a rectangular roof. Turn the right side of the roof and follow the arête to the top. Natural anchors or traverse 10' left to VD anchors. (75 ft)

9 NEVERMORE 5.11b ★★

This route is found right around the corner from VD. Start under the left side of a roof 20 feet off the deck. Climb to the roof. Next, step left to follow the short dihedral. Climb the corner to the hand slot at the base of a very large roof. Pull the roof directly rather than bailing out left.

Descent: Rap from fixed anchors (55 ft.)

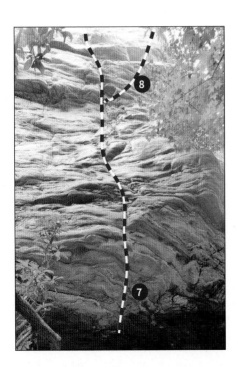

10 JOY LOADER 5.10b/c ★★

This route lies 20 feet right of NEVERMORE, beneath a low roof system. Be strong at the grade because you won't get gear until after pulling the roof sequence. Make for the sinker seam under the roof, then crank up and over the surprisingly juggy roof. Follow sculpted holds through a bulge to a stance, then step right to a large crack system. Follow the crack until it ends. Traverse right to another crack before eventually moving back left again through deceptively steep terrain. Finish on easier ground to fixed anchors.

Descent: Rap from fixed anchors. (100 ft.)

11 VISUAL SPLENDOR 5.10d

Tricky gear and committing moves make this route not for the faint of heart. Located 15 feet right of JOY LOADER, at a left leaning crack on the right side of the JOY LOADER roof system.

P1: Follow the crack and then trend right, aiming for a large crack/flared hole. Climb the steep headwall through the main business to a huge quartzite jug. From here bust out right with a few more moves to easier terrain to a belay ledge with natural anchors. (5.10d, 120 ft.)

P2: From the right side of the ledge, follow the crack system in the middle of the wall. Enjoy great rock quality and stellar exposure as you climb straight up the gently overhanging headwall to a roof near the top. Exit the roof up and right through a large V-slot. Natural anchors. (5.10d, 40 ft.)

Descent: Walk off to the left and scramble down a ways to the edge of the cliff (level with the end of P1) and rap from fixed slings. Note: It is also possible to reach this rap station from the end of P1 by traversing left from the belay ledge.

Erica Lineberry fiddling with crux gear on MIGHTY MOUSE (5.11d)

"*I went ground up for the FA of SUPERMAN'S DEAD after seeing all of the unclimbed rock left of MIGHTY MOUSE. I survived the business down low to find the headwall dicey with no gear. Almost through it, I slipped off a piece of lichen and looked down at the long swinging fall into the side buttress and screamed like a girl. My belayer, Tim Fisher, tried to sooth me yelling,"You're ok, you're ok, piece a cake up there." I regrouped and pushed on through it (not that I had a choice at that point…). Then he got up there and yelled,"It's steeper than it looks up here. Glad you didn't fly off that one. And the name stuck.*"

– Seth Tart

Seth Tart powering through the crux of SUPERMAN'S DEAD (5.12b/c R)

Rob Fogle feeling a VASCULAR DISASTER (5.11b/c)

The Taste of Humble Pie

"Having grown up in Eastern Tennessee, I cut my climbing teeth on sandstone, and thought I understood the "Deep South Climbing Experience." I grew up hearing the stories of harrowing run outs, bold first ascents, and seemingly mythological figures who spent countless days trudging through rhodos and steep gullies in search of the next spectacular line. As a teenager in the late 1990's, I remember hearing about Moore's, and its reputation as a place to get really scared. It wasn't that I didn't believe those stories. It wasn't that I doubted the boldness of the local activists. It was that I just figured "How bad could it really be?" After all, I'd climbed in some pretty wild places – from R/X routes in Eldo, to ground-up FAs in the Winds of Wyoming and the Cordillera Blanca of Peru, not to mention the mother of all scare-fest climbing areas – the Black Canyon of the Gunnison!

I adopted Moore's Wall as my home crag when I moved to North Carolina from Colorado in the summer of 2008. Staring up at the 200 foot panel of white rock of the Fire Wall, doubt started leaking into my cool attitude. Still, I kept telling myself – "How bad can it really be?" Things all went fine for my first few pitches at Moore's, temporarily plugging up those leaks of doubt. But then my wife and I hiked over to the North End, and I racked up below the mega classic Vascular Disaster. Were there bolts every eight feet up the iron-gray wave of overhanging rock, VD would be your standard 5.11 jug haul with just enough sequential beta to keep your brain working. But there aren't any bolts on it...

I bouldered over the initial bulge, firmly establishing myself irreversibly on the wall. The first few moves felt good on positive holds and decent stemming; the gear was solid but required a good bit of finagling to make it so. In my experience, things don't fall apart all at once in these situations; it's more of a subtle, cumulative effect. You have to climb a bit higher than you wanted, so you overgrip and get a tad pumped. Then, you realize that you have to punch it again, so you reverse a move and put in another piece, further swelling your forearms. Then you make five unnecessary moves blindly reaching over a roof for what just might be a hold. Once you find the one that is, you pull up and the search for protection starts all over again.

This is what happened to me; only, by the time I found the gear, I was irrecoverably pumped, gasping in the humid air, and staring down the arc of rope to my last piece. I blindly stuffed a cam above my head, and then the doubt returned in a torrential flood as I questioned how good the cam really was, then rapidly began downclimbing, my feet skittering beyond any sense of composure. My onsight attempt ended in a final gutteral utterance that was a combination of both demand and sheer desperation – I screamed "TAKE!" and slumped down several feet on the rope. I had nothing to be proud of – I didn't even take the whip.

I did manage to finish the route and even redpoint it soon thereafter (having comfortably identified all the key holds and gears placements while lowering down), but the level of commitment and boldness that sixty-foot pitch of climbing required still haunts me just a bit."

- Chris Barlow (temporary local with a permanent love for Moore's)

NUTSWEAT AREA

The following routes are located on the largest and rightmost of the three North End formations. This is the first major area you will encounter when approaching the North End from the Amphitheater.

Approach: You will reach NUTSWEAT about 5 minutes from the left edge of the Amphitheater. On the way you'll pass the very distinctive and impressive Indian Head Buttress, which juts out over the trail.

Descent: Unless otherwise stated, routes in this area can be descended from a single 70m or double ropes by way of the communal NUTSWEAT anchors. Another option is to top out and then make several shorter rappels into the gully right of Indian Head Buttress.

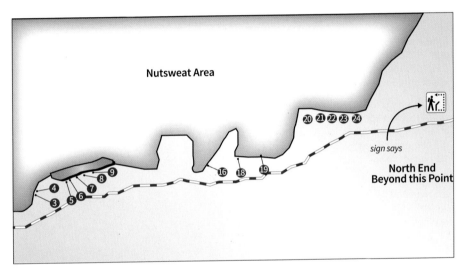

1 SNAP CRACKLE POP 5.10c

Start about 50 feet left of SHADOWDANCE, just left of the dirty start of FIDDLERS. This route follows the prominent steep crack system. Belay at an obvious ledge. (50 feet.)

Descent: Decide between the lesser of three evils – leave your own gear and rap down, continue climbing another 15 feet up and rap off of the nest of ancient, rotten fixed gear (not recommended), or keep climbing through moderate, but dubious rock to the top, then hike/rap down the gully to the right.

2 FIDDLERS ON THE ROOF 5.9+

Start about 40 feet left of SHADOWDANCE, at an overhanging dirty corner.

P1: Climb through the corner, then head right to an arête. Belay at the base of a corner. (5.9, 60 ft.)

P2: Follow the corner up to another roof. Pull through the center of the roof (crux) and keep climbing to the top. (5.9+, 70 ft.)

3 SPICE 5.11b/c R ★★★

Despite the spice, this route is nice. It shares a start as well as the first 30 feet with SHADOW-DANCE. Start on SHADOWDANCE then move left to a left-facing corner. Follow the corner toward an exposed arête. Gear is small and tenuous to place, but take every opportunity to protect when you can, as the spicy runout comes right after the main business. Climb the arête until it meets the small roof (some parties choose to belay here). Next traverse right beneath the roof to a steep corner crack, which eventually gives way to a juggy finish on the ledge above NUTSWEAT. With a 70m rope and mindful rope management, this line can be done in one long pitch. (110 ft.)

Descent: A new fixed gear anchor was recently added at the top of this route.

④ SHADOWDANCE 5.11d R (★★★ 5.10d first pitch only)

Start at an obvious corner system leading to some aesthetic finger cracks, about 200 feet right of VD. It is commonly done as a classic 5.10d pitch to the first set of anchors. The upper portion is rarely done.

P1: Follow the corner to a ledge. Commence with a technical dance up aesthetic finger cracks to a committing move to a jug at the top of the corner. Step right to an intermediate bolted anchor. (5.10d, 65 ft.)

P2: The second half of this route is serious business and therefore not as popular as the well trafficked first pitch. However, it is a worthwhile endeavor for those confident at the grade. There is a lot of runout on steep, 5.10 terrain with small and deceptive gear. For the full value experience, climb past the intermediate anchors and around to a right-facing corner. Skirt left around the large roof to easier ground. Belay on the ledge above NUTSWEAT. For those going all the way, this route can (and should) be done as one pitch. (115 ft.)

The next four routes all start on the right-trending, blocky ramp in the center of the cliff, about 25 feet right of SHADOW-DANCE. With good rope management, they can all easily be done in a single pitch.

⑤ NUTSWEAT 5.9+ ★★★

Stellar position and awesome exposure make this route a must-do for the grade. Unless your party wants to practice their jugging

skills up high, make sure both the leader and the second are solid at 5.9. It can be a bit runout on the easier terrain, but there's good pro when the climbing gets harder. Casually work up and right along the blocky ramp to a small open book, then head up and left to a stance at the base of a green corner. (stop here if you are going to break this route into two pitches). Follow the green corner until it is possible to step left into another corner. Crank through this corner (crux) then make an exciting, airy traverse out left to an amazing jug haul finish. Belay at a fixed station in a small cleft. Bigger gear may prove helpful up top. (100 ft.)

6 DEATHWISH 5.10c ★★

Don't be scared away by the name. This over-hanging pump fest is actually well-protected. Climb NUTSWEAT through the green corner to the roof, but then continue up and right through some steep, thin, vertical cracks. Work your way back left across a ramp and into a burly chimney. Belay above the chimney in the trees or downclimb to the NUTSWEAT anchors. Note: As with NUTSWEAT, some break this into two pitches. (100 ft.)

7 BAT ATTACK 5.12a ★★

Start the same as NUTSWEAT, but early on start to trend right into the obvious right-facing corner, passing a couple of bolts. Climb the corner and flake to a steep section high on the wall. Lieback and crimp up the steep wall to a nest of pins. Rappel here, or continue up past a bolt to a large horizontal crack. Follow the crack out right to the top of RECKLESS ABANDON. (95 ft.)

> "I remember one time when I belayed Eric Zchiesche on NUTSWEAT. When he got to the final juggy roof, he cut both feet loose and pedaled them wildly in the air – all while hollering like a cowboy!" - John Provetero

> "Eric Zchiesche is the one who figured out the no hands rest at the crux. The next time I led it I decided to give his beta a try. I stuck my leg in the hole and prepared to shake out…but then promptly got stung by some angry bees! Needless to say there was no rest for me!" - John Provetero, Moore's pioneer, on RECKLESS ABANDON

8 NEW WORLD MAN 5.12c

This variation is the direct finish to BAT AT-TACK. Climb straight up after the second bolt of BAT ATTACK, continuing past a third bolt to the top.

9 RECKLESS ABANDON 5.11a ★★★

Scramble up and right along the ramp. Keep trending right past a bolt to a cramped ledge. Step right, then blast up to a deep hole in a vertical crack system. Keep an eye out for the unique, no hands rest mid-crux! Finish on a steep crack that eases up towards the top. 90 feet.

Descent: Rappel from slings at the top of the cliff.

Variation: A very serious direct start on the arête was done by Doug Reed and Tim Fisher. It goes at 5.11c R/X, and the little gear you do get is difficult to place.

The next few climbs are located on a small, recessed cliff about 50 feet uphill of the trail.

10 SNAKE DEN 5.8

Pick the path of least resistance up the face left of the NORTH END CORNER. (100 ft.)

SNAKE DEN and NORTH END CORNER are two climbs whose origins are unknown. It is unclear whether these routes were climbed during the early years of development, or whether the lines sat untouched until the 1980's, when the rest of the North End was developed. The names were made up for easy reference in this guidebook, as are a few other names in this book.

11 NORTH END CORNER 5.6

Start at a right-facing corner system on the left face of the recessed alcove, left of the chimney. Climb this corner system and then continue to the top. There are a few loose sections. (100 ft.)

12 UNBROKEN CHAIN 5.10b/c ★

The more familiar route name JUGGERNAUT was used for many years because the second ascent party thought they were the first.

This is a high-quality hand crack that would perhaps get more love if the rock quality was better towards the top. Look for the steep

crack about 20 feet off the deck. Climb the strenuous, overhanging crack and face, veering to the right of a small Hemlock tree near the top. Follow the face to a tree ledge and belay. (100 ft.)

Descent: Traverse right to a fixed lowering station around a large tree.

13 JUGGERHEAD 5.8

This route begins 15 feet right of UNBROKEN CHAIN at a fist crack. Follow the crack until it ends, then trend right to the featured arête. Finish at the UNBROKEN CHAIN rap station. (100 ft.)

14 THE WINDIGO 5.11c

This route was done in the late 1980s, but was not previously documented. It is a challenging line with an outrageous position on the big Indian Head feature. The protection is adequate but not easy to place – be strong at the grade. Start 30 feet right of UNBROKEN CHAIN at the base of a left-facing corner.

P1. Climb the corner until it turns into a traverse right under an overhang. At the right end of the overhang, climb up the corner to the big ledge underneath the Indian Head. Continue up the corner to a smaller ledge that is directly under the imposing east face of the Indian Head. On your left is the steep wide crack that is the second pitch of NEVERMORE CHIMNEY. (5.11c, ft.)

P2. Climb the line through the very steep face about 15 feet right of the wide crack. After the business, climb from the ledge up and right to a belay just below the top of the Indian Head. (5.11c, ft.)

Descent: Same as INDIAN HEAD.

15 THE LARK'S TONGUE 5.8 R

This newer line is located on the left side of the NEVERMORE CHIMNEY. Start in the corner and transition left to cracks and a featured face to a large ledge. Look for small gear up and left to protect the impending bulge. Crank past the bulge, then climb to another ledge up and left. Sling the name-sake feature and scurry up and right to the top. Though the climbing is not difficult, the gear is less than desirable. Bring some brass, small TCU's, and a #5 friend.

Descent: Same as NEVERMORE CHIMNEY

> *"According to Tommy Howard, Rich Gottlieb climbed this line sometime back in the 1970's, and the name was his. This was back in the pre-Peregrine era, and the ravens used to hang out in full force over on the North End of the cliff, hence the Edgar Allen Poe names."* - Tim Fisher, *on NEVERMORE*

16 NEVERMORE CHIMNEY 5.9

This route starts left of INDIAN HEAD in an obvious chimney. Jam and stem your way through the chimney to a crack up and over a bulge. Finish at a tree with slings. (100 ft.)

Descent: Rap from the tree.

Note: Not much is known about a most-likely unrepeated second pitch which may be in the 5.10 range

17 INDIAN TOE 5.12a

This route is located 20 feet right of NEVER-MORE CHIMNEY, in a corner with a very steep seam splitting off to the right. Boulder up the seam-like feature past a fixed stopper and onto the short but sweet face just left of the V-slot. This is a great option for accessing INDIAN HEAD. (65 ft.)

Descent: Rap from NEVERMORE trees, or continue to INDIAN HEAD.

18 INDIAN HEAD DIRECT 5.10d ★★

This line is seldom done despite being the longest and one of the most spectacular routes at Moore's. Double ropes are recom-mended. Start beneath the massive prow of the Indian Head Buttress. Use a V-slot with an overhang down low for reference.

P1: Climb the rightmost of the two chimneys and continue through the overhang to a large ledge. (5.7, 40 ft.)

P2: Maneuver past the short but awkward crack through a bulge, then face climb on easier terrain to a smaller ledge at the base of a steep, dark-colored corner. (5.10d, 70 ft.)

P3: Head up the exposed, overhanging corner, aiming out toward the prow, utilizing rests when you can. Head up and left through over-hanging chimneys, then savor the exposure through the open book crux before relaxing on easier terrain to the summit. (5.10d, 80 ft.)

Descent: Either scramble right and down to the trees and rap with 2 60m ropes, or scramble up and left to rap down the Indian Head Gully with one rope.

Variation: The original start for the first pitch started in the loose corner to the right of the chimney.

19 THE CORNER 5.9+

Start below an obvious left-facing corner about 25 Feet right of INDIAN HEAD. Follow the corner to the left side of the roof. (50 ft.)

Descent: Rap from trees.

20 WALKING THE GERBIL 5.10d

Up, right, and around THE CORNER is an al-cove with a chimney in the corner. This route starts just right of the chimney and follows the face through a bulge to a short right-facing dihedral. Continue up the dihedral, and at the top, step right to crank through the overhang. Finish on a tree ledge further up the face. (50 ft.)

Descent: Rap from trees.

21 BODACIOUS 5.10d

Looking for an adventurous combo? Climb GERBIL, and finish on P2 of BODACIOUS. Start at a thin flake 10 feet right of GERBIL.

P1: Use the flake as well as the face to its right to make your way to a ledge. Pull the overhang directly above you and climb to the tree ledge. (5.10a, 50 ft.)

P2: Move to the right along the ledge to the base of a very nice looking steep, thin crack

(there is also a much easier crack to the right). Climb the thin crack and face to the top. (5.10d, 50 ft.)

Descent: Scramble to the west back down to the tree ledge, then rap from the trees.

22 BURLY BOY 5.10c

Climb the obvious wide crack just right of BODACIOUS. Continue through the wide-crack roof and continue to the ledge. Take large cams. (50 ft.)

23 NAME IT, CLAIM IT 5.8 ★

This line has been claimed numerous times as an FA, although it was likely climbed very early on in Moore's climbing history. Start right of BODACIOUS, on a face just right of a wide crack. Follow the line of least resistance up the face to the BODACIOUS ledge. (50 ft.)

Descent: Rap from trees.

24 CORRIGATION CRACK 5.6 ★

About 30 feet right of BURLY BOY is a well featured wide crack. Climb the featured wall and crack to the ledge. (50 ft.)

25 INCONSPICUOUS 5.10a

Another short and steep route ending on the BODACIOUS tree ledge. Start just right of NAME IT, and follow the blunt arête. (50 ft.)

Descent: Rap from trees.

26 A PRIORI 5.11a

This is the striking finger crack that is along the corridor on the trail to the North End. It can also be done as a highball boulder problem. The name was coined by local climber Sean Barb for being an obvious line that remained shrouded in mystery and had maintained a sense of first-ascent-style adventure over the years.

Close Encounters of the Serpentine Kind:

Triangle climbers Matt Westlake and Chris Sproul were enjoying an afternoon out at the North End one day in the fall of 2011 when they found a small but fiesty copperhead inside a helmet that had been left unattended on the ground below UNBROKEN CHAIN. Chris thankfully noticed the hitchhiker before donning his hard hat, although he was so startled that he dropped the helmet, sending the terrified serpent flying. A bit unnerved about leaving their packs on the ground without knowing the snake's whereabouts, they searched and searched, only to eventually find the snake putting on a clinic in camouflage a mere 5 feet away from where they'd been standing.

Copperheads are more common, but Rattlesnakes can also be found at Moore's. This Rattlesnake was seen in the Amphitheater.

I have fond (for lack of a better word) memories of an epic afternoon on seldom travelled territory in the North End back in 2008. What started out mildly enough as an alternate start into FIDDLERS ON THE ROOF quickly turned into an adventure up SNAP, CRACKLE, POP and beyond – ending with loose rock, greenbriar, and quickly fading light. After fumbling around in the dark and a few pitch-black rappels down the gully, my partner and I finally reached our packs and started hiking out a little before midnight. Thankfully my partner had cell reception so that we could contact our significant others just moments before they sent a search party out after us."

- Erica Lineberry, Charlotte, NC

AMPHITHEATER

Climbers of varying skill levels will find a high concentration of excellent routes in this area. The left (western) side of the wall is sometimes called the Sun Wall. If you can't figure out why, climb there on a summer afternoon (and don't forget the sunblock). The flip side is that on chilly spring mornings, these routes are the first to warm up. Routes along the right side of the Amphitheater can be nice warm-weather options, but will be frigid as cooler weather approaches.

Approach: Hike in along the Amphitheater Trail, bearing up and right when the trail to the North End forks off to the left. The first routes you reach are EXCELLENT ADVENTURE and WAILING WALL.

Descent: The standard descent for all routes on the left side of the Amphitheater (EXCELLENT ADVENTURE to STEP AND FETCH) is via anchors located above QUAKER STATE. Bring a 70m rope if you have one, but if not, a 60m rope will be exactly (read: barely) enough to get you down with rope stretch. This rappel station can be the scene of traffic jams, so if there are other parties climbing in the area, please be considerate and don't belay or toprope from these anchors. Be extremely careful when making your way out to this anchor, as it requires an exposed traverse. It is recommended that you stay on belay until you are safely secured at the station.

There is an alternate descent option located at the top of DROMEDARY, that makes for a convenient getaway on higher-volume days, especially for routes ending on the left side of the Sun Wall. From the WAILING WALL tree, hike towards the top of the cliff. You will encounter a short (8 feet) fifth class section. Instead of climbing up, head down into the cleft-like feature to find a wiggly but bomber fixed-gear anchor. For routes that finish on DROM-EDARY, this anchor is pretty easy to find, nestled in a cleft at the top of the chimney.

Rappel anchor for WAILING WALL

For routes on the right (eastern) side of the Amphitheater (BREAKING ROCKS IS HARD TO DO to SHIT HOOK), you have a few options. 1 – Rappel from the anchors on the BREAKING ROCKS ledge. 2 – Follow the trail along the top (climber's right) towards the Main Descent Gully. 3 – Follow the trail along the top (climber's left) to the QUAKER STATE anchors.

Rappel anchor above QUAKER STATE

① EXCELLENT ADVENTURE 5.6

Adventure? Perhaps. Excellent? Hardly. If you are short on time, pass this one up in favor of its 3-star neighbor to the right. Start about 10 feet left of the WAILING WALL corner, and scramble left along a ledge to a crack.

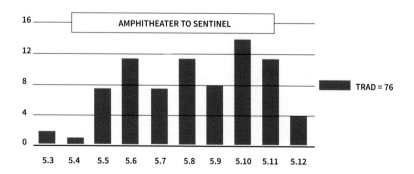

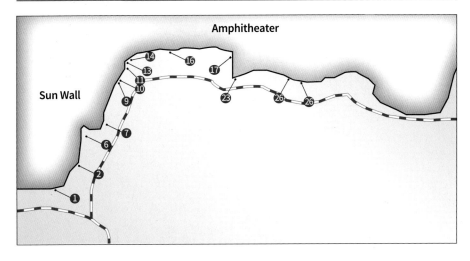

Follow the crack and then angle up and left, skirting left past two roofs. Double ropes might be nice. (110 ft.)

② WAILING WALL 5.6 ★★★

Probably the best of its grade at Moore's, this is a must-do for both new trad leaders as well as experienced climbers. Start on the left side of the Ampitheater, just right of an obvious arête at a short chimney. Take one of many variations to gain a ledge just left of a roof. You could belay here, but most parties do this route in one pitch. Step left past the broken crack system and out onto a steep face, navigating through a sea of awesome horizontal cracks with amazing exposure and all the gear you could dream of. Make sure to have mid- to large-sized cams on hand towards the top. Exit the wall through an obvious notch and belay from above. (120 ft.)

③ U-HAUL 5.10a ★★

This is a combination of three different variations to WAILING WALL that add up to a very nice and distinctive route. Mostly 5.6 climbing with a brief and well-protected crux up high, this route is a good one for the aspiring 5.10 leader. It can be done as a single pitch if long slings and good rope management is employed.

P1: Climb the first few feet of WAILING WALL until your feet are just above the roofline on the left. Traverse left to the arête and climb up to the ledge just left of a roof. (5.6, 50 ft.)
P2: Instead of trending left into the horizontals on the face, stay right of the regular WAILING WALL line by climbing straight up the broken crack system. Aim for the U-shaped break in the roof about 15 feet right of the WAILING WALL exit notch. (5.10a, 70 ft.)
Descent: Look for the fixed gear anchor atop DROMEDARY in a small cleft behind the finish.

SNAKES: The next time you're tempted to toss your leftover crackers in the bushes, think again. While it's true that all those little crumbs will be gone the next day (unlike that candy bar wrapper), the problem comes with the pesky rodents that end up taking residence at the base of the cliff in hopes of finding more of those little crumbs. And actually the real problem is the long, slithery friends that show up in response to the arrival of all the furry ones. In addition to several species of non-venomous snakes such as rat snakes and black racers, poisonous snakes such as copperheads and even timber rattlers are becoming more and more of a common occurrence at Central Piedmont crags.

Climber following the first part of the classic
WAILING WALL (5.6)

> *"I remember one summer when I, along with 2 other ladies (one of whom was experiencing trad climbing for the first time), decided to climb WAILING WALL. My partner had decided to break the route into two pitches so our inexperienced friend could see a trad anchor. Upon reaching the first belay however, we noticed that black clouds were moving in at an alarming rate. I took off for the top, and as the last member of our party was cleaning gear, the sky opened up. At the top I made a split second decision that it was too dangerous to cross over the slick rock in the wind and the rain to reach the exposed QUAKER STATE rap station. Instead we opted for the seldom-used walk off (to the right across the cliff top and down to the Meat Puppet Gully), which still involved some serious bushwhacking through trees and briars. We finally found the trail and made our way down. We were soaking wet but happy to be safe. Lesson learned: Always have a back-up plan!" - Stephanie Gilliam Raleigh, NC*

④ DROMEDARY 5.8 ★

A decent route that doesn't see a lot of traffic. A few large pieces will help keep the top from being runout.

P1: This route shares a start with WAILING WALL, but moves up and right. Climb cracks to a ledge beneath a roof. Surmount the roof with as much grace as you can muster, then head right to another larger ledge underneath the AID RAID roof. (5.8, 40 ft.)

P2: Follow the easy chimney to the top. (5.7, 60 ft.)

⑤ AID RAID 5.11c/d ★★

This route features stellar position and a nearly-horizontal roof. Bring aiders if you're worried about your second's ability to pull the roof. The first ascent was originally done on aid, then Bob Rotert onsighted the FFA a few months later.

P1. Climb DROMEDARY or GUTTERBALL to the large ledge. (40 ft.)

P2: Siege the obvious roof crack. Nearly-horizontal finger locks eventually yield to jugs. Scramble to the summit via 5.5 terrain, or stop to belay in the alcove above the lip of the roof. (5.11c/d, 100 ft.)

⑥ GUTTERBALL 5.7 ★

This route climbs the obvious ramp and chimney system located between WAILING WALL and FIVE EASY PIECES. Start at the ramp that slopes up and right. It can be done as a long single pitch or comfortably broken into two shorter pitches.

P1. Climb the right-leaning ramp to the AID RAID ledge. (5.7, 40 ft.)

P2. Continue up the DROMEDARY chimney to the top and the fixed wire anchors that serve the lower Amphitheater. (5.7, 60 ft.)

⑦ FIVE EASY PIECES 5.11a R ★

You might want more than five pieces for this direct series of five roofs.

Start below and left of the large RAISE HELL block. Climb out of the cave on extremely bad rock. The rock quality dramatically improves at the first roof – follow the crack to four additional roofs. (100 ft.)

Note: Its possible to avoid the death choss at the start by doing an easy solo of the first 15-20 feet of GUTTERBALL. At the top of the GUTTERBALL ramp toss your lead rope down to your belayer and start climbing at the crux roof, above most of the cream-cheese rock. (120 ft.)

⑧ THREE EASY PIECES 5.10b/c ★

This variation to FIVE EASY PIECES starts on RAISE HELL and traverses in left to the vertical crack. This avoids the rotten rock and two of the five roofs (including the crux). You will want long slings to avoid rope drag. Climb through an easy bulge (5.7) to a harder bulge (5.10b/c) and then to the top. (100 ft.)

⑨ RAISE HELL 5.8 ★★★

This route is deservedly popular – sustained, solid, and well-protected. Bring lots of medium to large cams. Start on top of a large, obvious block at the base of the Sun Wall.

QUAKER STATE: A Carolina Classic By Brian Payst

"Ever since I started climbing at Moore's I had been drawn to QUAKER STATE. It just sits there and says, "climb me." Over the years, I've been in and out of North Carolina and on and off of QUAKER STATE, but never led it. It was in my head and just didn't seem like it was going to happen. I mean, it was QUAKER STATE. I'd seen Porter Jarrard dance up it, hanging his rack from a gear placement and running it out to the top. Tim Fisher does it as a warm up, carrying just the pieces he needs. No way was I going to keep up with that.

Then one day in 2009, I just made up my mind that QUAKER STATE had to get done. I'd climbed harder sport routes, and I was feeling pretty good about my fitness.

Thus QUAKER STATE became a minor obsession. I spent time at work thinking about it and compulsively checking the weather forecast for the right conditions. Finally I saw my chance. It was one of those first cold fronts of the year days – when the summer

QUAKER STATE (5.11a) on the left and NUCLEAR CRAYON (5.10c) on the right

humidity is cut away and the air feels like it could suck the moisture from your skin. Hiking up the trail I just kept getting more and more psyched. I had a big goofy grin on my face; finally getting my chance to move past the psychological barrier QUAKER STATE had been for years.

After a warm up, I took a lap on it just to make sure it still felt doable. It did, so I pulled the rope.

QUAKER STATE starts with a somewhat sketchy move over a small lip onto a slab. The gear is a good nut placement, but you don't want to blow the moves getting established on the slab. After the second piece I felt settled and was looking at the first crux. Pulling through the steep crack / overhang of the crux, I skipped the mid-height placement in favor of the rest I knew was above. A good no-hands-ish (it's not totally no hands, but you can shake at the expense of your calves) rest and moved the gear around for the next section. Thin moves on solid crimps and edges and I had arrived at the gear below the crux. This was a surprise as I had no idea it was so bomber. . A mid-size stopper slots in a horizontal crack - it's just one of those placements you dream about.

QUAKER STATE has beautiful flow and the moves just link up one into the next. The crux is thin and slightly barn door inducing, but I knew there was a hold out right I wanted to get. Problem was, I seemed to have forgotten where it was. Settling for decent, if not what I wanted, crimps I just kept moving until I latched the good hold at the end of crux and then grabbed the undercling that denotes the end of the physical business. Now I had a decision to make. My last gear was 10-15 feet below me and the next placement was over to my left. Unfortunately I had racked the cams on my right and needed one for that placement. Knowing that it was almost done and there was another killer rest just ahead I opted for running it out to the rest. A few feet further and almost home free.

Eventually I found a good cam placement and headed for the anchors. I think I let out a whoop as I called to be lowered.

I took one last lap on TR before leaving that day. That time I found the key foothold that puts me on track for the crux. Between the two TRs and the lead, I climbed QUAKER STATE three times that day and I loved every single one of them. It felt good to have a project and to have it go. To this day, I still smile when I think about it. If that doesn't make something a classic, I don't know what does."

Follow the vertical crack system, then head left to a wider crack that splits a small roof. Climb the wide crack through the roof (crux), then step left onto the face to finish up the steep, knobby wall (recommended), or move right and follow the shallow chimney to the top (easier). (100 ft.)

10 DO OR DIVE 5.10a ★★★

This is a North Carolina classic with good, albeit sparse, gear through the crux. Botch the sequence and you'll join ranks with the many who have taken the "dive" rather than the "do." Start on the same large block as RAISE HELL. Climb straight up the vertical cracks to the small roof. You can get good gear under the roof, but with the somewhat runout crux looming ahead, you will also want to fish around for two key small stopper placements just above. If you can't find them, look again. Next, power through the overhang to a crack. Continue past a second crux to the chimney. You can either follow the chimney to the top, or, for a full-value finish, step left and climb up the face. (100 ft.)

11 QUAKER STATE 5.11a ★★★

A very aesthetic line that features two well-protected cruxes and ends with a somewhat runout section (5.8) towards the top. Though seconds and topropers may tout the grade as soft, the tenuous gear stances bring most leaders to a consensus 5.11a. Start just right of the RAISE HELL block below a small bulge. Pull the initial bulge and follow the cracks past a triangular pod. Savor the rest. Next tackle the thinning crack on the steep face. Trend right as the crack ends, and get gear as high as you can. Once past the thin face crux follow big holds to the top. (100 ft.)

Note: Because this route is directly below the standard Amphitheater rappel anchors, it is common for parties to rig a toprope on QUAKER STATE after climbing one of the easier lines in the vicinity. To avoid a traffic jam of climbers waiting to rap down, please refrain from toproping here unless you are the only party in the area.

12 COMMAND PERFORMANCE 5.11d ★

A wildly exposed, intimidating line – an alternate finish to QUAKER STATE that packs quite a punch! Climb QUAKER STATE through the crux, and then trend up and right to ascend the dramatic, overhanging prow to the right. Fixed stoppers were placed on the first ascent, but disappeared shortly after. Bring small wires in addition to a standard rack. (30 ft.)

Descent: Scramble down the back side of the prow back to the QUAKER STATE anchors.

13 NUCLEAR CRAYON 5.10c ★★

Although maybe a two move wonder, those moves are definitely full value. To find this line, locate the lone bolt on the right side of the Sun Wall. Follow the left facing flake up to the bolt, then blast your way through a sequency steep section (crux). The terrain above the crux is much easier (5.8ish). Make your way up the face to the roof, then traverse left and up to the QUAKER STATE anchors. (100 ft.)

14 ALMOST SEVEN 5.7 ★★★
(a.k.a. GOLDEN EARRING)

Another popular moderate, and rightly so! Start in the vegetated corner on the right end of the Amphitheater beneath an unmistakable hand crack. (Some parties prefer to start in a curving crack 10 feet right of the vegetated corner and traverse left to the hand crack.) Follow the hand crack to the roof. When the crack ends, traverse left to the QUAKER STATE anchors. Staying low on the traverse makes for easy climbing, but the gear is up higher, so depending on whether you want to be on speaking terms with your second, you may have to shuffle up and down a bit. (100 ft.)

15 STEP AND FETCH 5.8 ★★

This is a great alternative for finishing ALMOST SEVEN that avoids all of the traversing shenanigans. With proper rope management and/or double ropes this can easily be done as a single pitch. For two separate pitches, belay under the large roof. From the sloping ledge at the top of the ALMOST SEVEN crack, skirt underneath the roof, moving up and right to the steep face above. Follow jugs to the top. (120 ft.)

Descent: Scramble to the top of the cliff, then back to the left and down around to the QUAKER STATE rap station.

> *"Several years ago I was climbing NUCLEAR CRAYON. Directly, to my right was a guy leading ALMOST SEVEN. I happened to look over just as he started to tackle the crux just below the roof. He started to do a really high step when suddenly there was a scream of despair and seconds later a wave of odor that hit me like an outhouse in a heat wave. The poor guy had shit himself while making the crux move. The strain and high step had apparently loosened the ole sphincter to the detriment of all. The defeated leader lowered off to a water bottle cleaning. The route wasn't climbable until the next rain."*
>
> *- Bill Webster, Chapel Hill*

16 HIGH WIRE 5.8 ★

This long route requires a bit of route-finding skill, and culminates with an exposed aerial act high up on the face. Start at the wide "refrigerator crack" left of BREAKING ROCKS. Climb the left of two cracks in the main inside corner. The first 50 feet of the crack are wide with sparse gear, but very easy (5.4 or easier). Where the crack steepens, climb up and left around a steep prow, eventually heading back right to finish on an aesthetic right-facing dihedral. Be careful of the loose rock as you approach the top. Belay from trees. (160 ft.)

Descent: Scramble off the top and back left to the QUAKER STATE anchors. Scope out your route carefully to avoid greenbriar thickets.

17 BREAKING ROCKS 5.9 ★ IS HARD TO DO

Although generally a true statement at Moore's, not so with this route – in fact a very large rock broke off some time in the mid 1980's, rendering an interesting start that you will either love or hate.

Start in the deep alcove with a flaring corner on the leftmost side of the right wall of the Amphitheater. Negotiate the alcove to gain the crack system above – continue up the line of cracks trending up and right to a ledge. (80 ft.)

18 YOUR CHEATIN' START 5.8

Not a fan of the start, but love the rest of BREAKING ROCKS? Try this variation to avoid the initial awkwardness. Start at the base of HIGH WIRE. Climb up an easy crack just right of HIGH WIRE until it is possible to step right. Continue past two rubble-covered ledges then traverse right to join the regular BREAKING ROCKS route at the top of the initial dihedral. This alternate line would clean up nicely with a little more traffic. (80 ft.)

Scott Gilliam finishing the crux of NUCLEAR CRAYON (5.10c)

19 DOAN'S PILLS 5.9

Why name a route after a medication for headaches and backpain? You'll have to wait until the end of the route to find out. This very un-Moore's like route is an odd but fun line that starts from the BREAKING ROCKS ledge. From atop the ledge, scramble up and left to an obvious dihedral. Stem your way up the corner until you can traverse right under the huge roof using a horizontal crack. Don't forget about your second as you maneuver around the bulge along the traverse. Continue past a rap anchor to a nice gear belay ledge. (50 ft.)

20 ZOMBIE WOOF 5.10c ★

Not recommended for larger or claustrophobic climbers (unless you are willing to climb a slightly harder and significantly more exposed variation on the outside of the crack). This route is a unique experience for sure. Start atop the BREAKING ROCKS ledge. Climb up the DOAN'S PILL'S corner (5.8). Some parties choose to belay here, but most do the line in one continuous pitch from the top of BREAKING ROCKS. When you reach the big roof, head left and allow yourself to be swallowed by the overhanging chimney. Squeeze, slither, and tunnel your way up through the slot to the summit. Some leaders choose to abandon their rack and helmet. Take a 4" camalot. (60 ft.)

Descent: Find the cliff top trail and head right to the descent gully or left to the QUAKER STATE anchors.

21 FINGER LOVE 5.10a ★

A beautiful specimen of thin vertical crack high off the deck. Yet another route that starts from the BREAKING ROCKS ledge. Scramble up and left a short way to the obvious finger crack. Lovers of the finger lock will find this fantastic, well-protected crack a dream come true until rudely awakened by the burly and ungraceful exit to stage right at the top of the crack. Same awkward finish as DOAN'S PILLS. (50 ft.)

22 INDIAN SUMMER 5.11d / 5.12 TR

Looking for a hard line to toprope? Set up an anchor on the BREAKING ROCKS ledge. Climb the start of BREAKING ROCKS, then start trending up and right along the face.

Variation: A slightly harder toprope variation climbs directly up the face between BREAKING ROCKS and STAB. (90 ft.)

Bill Webster at the crux of STAB IN THE DARK (5.11a)

Climber approaching the crux of ALOOF ROOF (5.8)

23 STAB IN THE DARK 5.11a (5.8 R) ★★

A must-do for the grade – well-protected crux followed by two slightly runout sections over moderate (5.8) terrain.

Locate the short, but prominent hand crack perched atop the low roof on the right side of the Amphitheater, and start around the corner to the right. A bouldery start leads to good gear below the roof, then traverses left around the corner to take your best stab at the steep face and crack. Finish up on the sometimes poorly protected arête. The combination of swing and rope stretch could make for an unpleasant fall for your second, so belay attentively. (100 ft.)

24 WALK IN THE LIGHT 5.10b/c (5.8 R) ★

A more direct alternative to STAB. Start in the same place, but instead of heading left at the roof, continue straight up a crack to the 5.8 R face/blunt arête, finishing at the same ledge as STAB. (100 ft.)

25 ALOOF ROOF 5.8

Those not strong at the grade may want a lesson in pump management before tackling this route on the sharp end. This line starts just right of STAB. Climb the right side of the roof. Follow the crack system then head left to the BREAKING ROCKS ledge across a slabby runout. (100 ft.)

26 SHIT HOOK 5.8+ ★

A lot more pleasant than it sounds, but do take care because a few holds have broken off over the years. This is a full value 5.8! Climb the amazingly thin flake right of ALOOF ROOF. From the small tree continue up the steep face to a crack. Follow that crack, then head left to the BREAKING ROCKS Ledge. (100 ft.)

Variation: Continue up the face rather than left to BREAKING ROCKS. End at a tree with slings, then rap down and left to BREAKING ROCKS ledge.

Matt Westlake carefully negotiating the thin flake of SHIT HOOK (5.8+)

"The one time I climbed ZOMBIE WOOF, I got stuck. I was following Tim Fisher, and the gear I was cleaning somehow caused me to body wedge in the giant crack. It took me quite a while to be able to clear the gear around my body and squirm through!" - John Provetero, Moore's pioneer

"I probably have 50% more biomass than John Provetero, but somehow managed to fight through the slot on my one and only time on this squeezefest. In the tightest part of the slot I had to blindly re-tie my knot so it didn't get in the way and hang the rack off the side of my harness. I still ended up with abrasions across my chest and a shredded t-shirt after about an hour of forced exhalations and tiny forward movements."

– Bill Webster

LITTLE AMPHITHEATER
The next six routes are located in an area known as the "Little Amphitheater," which lies between the Amphitheater and the Meat Puppet and Main Descent gullies.

Descent: The descent for all lines except MY WIFE'S PAJAMAS (which has its own anchor) walks off the top and heads right and down the Meat Puppet Gully.

① BLUEBERRIES 5.7

Hike west (right) from the Amphitheater to a large, but low overhanging cave feature that is next to the trail. This route starts at the end of a small roof about 20 feet left of the cave. Climb straight up from the left edge of the roof. (80 ft.)

② SUPERSATURATION 5.9

Start the same as BLUEBERRIES, but head right and up to a left-facing corner higher on the face. From there continue straight up to the top. (80 ft.)

③ POPEYE EFFECT 5.8

Steeper than it looks from the ground – so keep your spinach handy! To start, locate the blunt corner formed by the cliff as it turns sharply uphill and away from the trail. A good landmark is a V-shaped notch about 25 feet up. Follow the crack system that heads towards the notch, then climb straight up through the notch and wander up the arête. Scramble and scurry your way over mostly third class terrain to the top. (80 ft.)

④ MY WIFE'S PAJAMAS 5.6 ★

This nice route has varied climbing that starts on a slab and ends with a steep finish. Start 25 feet right of the corner formed by the cliffline where it merges back along the trail, at a vague, left-facing seam by a small tree. Wander up the slab past a few bulges, aiming for a slanting, right-facing dihedral towards the top of the cliff.

At the dihedral pull up and left onto the short headwall and enjoy the exposure as you pump your way to a tree with slings near the edge of the cliff. Note - Some parties aiming for the Meat Puppet Area find this route to be a better approach option than using the gully. (80 ft.)

Descent: Rap from the belay tree or top out and head up and left, back around to the gully.

⑤ BUBBALICIOUS 5.12a ★

Often ogled, but rarely climbed. This route climbs the intimidating, overhanging prow about 30 feet right of MY WIFE'S PAJAMAS, at a high point in the trail. (60 ft.)

⑥ SUSPICIOUSLY DELICIOUS 5.11c ★

The big, gymnastic moves on this one give this route a sporty feel. Just right of BUBBALICIOUS, climb the quartzy face to a jug rail beneath a roof. Traverse left and gorilla your way out the notch in the roof and continue up. (60 ft.)

"POPEYE EFFECT definitely lives up to its name in the early portion of the climb, so by the time you get through the first section into third class terrain, you are ready to heave a sigh of relief. Well...not so fast. Instead of relief, I was greeted by a couple of sassy slitherers - one on either side of me. Corn snake on my left, approaching. Black snake slithering upon me from the right - molting, cloudy eyes, pissed off. No, neither snake is venomous, but that was not registering in my mind.

After a moment of La Freak-Out, I considered my options and decided on a downclimb and traverse before heading back up to the top, leaving the snakes to their own devices. Snakes alive!"

- Sarah Wolfe

MEAT PUPPET CRAG

This small crag is located above the main cliff band, just below the stone tower and Moore's Knob. Not much is known about the history of this small crag. It is likely that the actual first ascents of these routes were done well before 1994. Though they don't receive much traffic, many of these lines feature tough, bouldery starts that lead to moderate terrain and very rewarding views of the top of Moore's Wall and surrounding Piedmont region.

Approach

There are several options to access these routes:

1. MEAT PUPPET GULLY - Scramble up the narrow, steep gully 30 feet right of BUBBALICIOUS. At the top of the gully a trail heads up and left, passing some old timber along the way, where the cliff will appear on your right.
2. MY WIFE'S PAJAMAS: Climb this route or any of the other routes west of the main Amphitheater and bushwhack your way up to the Meat Puppet Area.
3. MAIN DESCENT GULLY – Scurry up a wider, more obvious gully about 80 feet right of BUBBALICIOUS, and 50 feet left of

RELAPSE. Keep your eyes peeled for a narrow, indistinct trail branching up and left. This trail will merge shortly with the same trail as the Meat Puppet Gully.
4. Hike the Moore's Wall Loop Trail from the main area of the park to the stone tower, then descend the gully.

Descent: All routes descend by topping out and scrambling off left to bushwhack down and back around to the base.

1 HOWLIN' YOWLIN' 5.5

This route on the far left end of the wall climbs a short crack to a wide, right-facing dihedral to the top. (50 ft.)

2 UNDERCOVER LOVER 5.9+

This route lies just a few feet right of HOWLIN' YOWLIN', across from a small tree. Start at a notch in some interesting horizontal fins reminscent of the Grandmother Mountain boulders. A big move to gain the upper fin leads to casual and adequately-protected 5.6 face climbing to the top. (60 ft.)

3 HEAD LIKE A HOLE 5.8 ★★

NIN fans will appreciate this nice line that makes a good warm-up option for its beefier

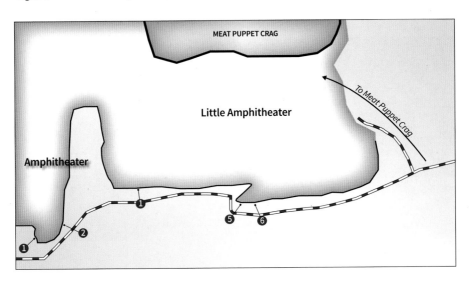

neighbor to the right. Begin on the left side of a large, pointed flake-type feature 15 feet right of UNDERCOVER. Follow the horizontal up the left side of the point, then continue up and left along juggy, diagonal flakes. Continue up the vertical face to the top. (80 ft.)

4 MEAT PUPPET 5.10a ★★

This just might be the softest 5.10 at Moore's. The well-protected crux makes this line a great option for newer 5.10 leaders. Start on the right side of the pointed flake and work up to an interesting and awkward crux at a roof. Beach yourself atop the overhang, then continue to the top, where a steep, juggy bulge makes for a photo finish at the top. (80 ft.)

5 BEELZEBUBBA 5.6 ★★★

This humble line boasts some of the best views at Moore's. Due to its out-of-the-way location it might also be one of the cliff's best kept secrets! Located on the left corner of the wall just before a small depression in the cliffline, this route starts on an easy ramp, then traverses left (be mindful of the two trees growing uncomfortably close to the cliffline) and follows the stunning white arête to the top of the cliff. The finish is steep for the grade, but jugs and gear placements abound. (100 ft.)

The Meat Puppet approach gully

6 MOONWALK 5.11a

Locate a block on the left side of a large overhang, about 50 feet right of BEELZE-BUBBA. From the block, take the path of least resistance through three progressively smaller overhangs to reach the top. (80 ft.)

7 NEW MOON 5.10

It may not be the best of the grade at Moore's, but it is guaranteed to be better than the movie. Climb up the face, passing the first overhang on its left side, and the second on its right until you reach a tree. (80 ft.)

Main Descent and Meat Puppet gully split off

Jorge Castro heads for a rest. HEAD LIKE A HOLE (5.8)

THE CENTRAL WALL

This sprawling area lies between the Amphitheater and the Sentinel Buttress Area, and can be reached conveniently from either trail that branches off from the fire road. The Central Wall has areas of clean, solid rock with great climbs as well as sections that are broken, loose and low-angled. The highest concentration of quality routes is towards the right side of the Central Wall, although there are hidden gems scattered throughout the area.

Descent: There are a few options. Regardless of the option you choose, be safe and use good judgment.

1. Most routes, especially those on the left side of the wall, can be taken to the summit, at times with an additional short pitch over scrambly (and often loose – be careful!) terrain. Upon topping out, access the summit trail, and follow it back left to a junction near a large boulder, where you can then follow the RELAPSE descent gully down and back around to the base.

2. Some routes on the right side of the wall have a rappel station located near the finish. (See descriptions for BLUE BALLS and CENTRAL CLEFT)

3. A quicker, but more exciting option scrambles down the fourth class rock to the (climber's) right of WASHBOARD. (see pg 189 for more detailed info). Though the climbing is easy, it consists of very exposed sections of rock sandwiched between ledges, and a fall would more than likely end in death or at best a pile of broken bones. Please take extreme caution and do not try this option if you are unfamiliar with the descent route. (If both climbers are confident in leading/placing gear, down-leading this terrain can make the consequences less severe).

① RAZOR'S EDGE 5.12a

This route will definitely have appeal for boulderers, featuring never-ending edges with no rests on steep rock. Climb to the bolt on RELAPSE, then allow yourself to get sucked out left onto the super steep razor blade arête. Cut through the first 25 feet, then step inside the right face of the arête to the top. (50 ft.)

Descent: Walk off and head left down the Main Descent Gully.

② RELAPSE 5.11d R ★

This route was done as a highball boulder problem in the pre-pad era. The short pitch climbs the overhanging arête along the inside of a very wide chimney/cleft about 50 feet right of the descent gully. An obvious landmark is a lone bolt on the face. Climb up past the bolt then up the crack to the top. Take small to medium gear. The runout is on much easier rock. (50 ft.)

Descent: Walk off and head left down the Main Descent Gully.

DOG AND PONY AREA

The next three routes are located 40 feet right of RELAPSE, on a small buttress that sits up above the trail. These routes are somewhat short but they are extremely steep and burly. You will get pumped!! Scramble up third class terrain directly to the buttress, or if its wet, go up the Main Descent Gully and turn right above RELAPSE. From here scramble down and across exposed rock to reach the base. Descend from slings on a tree to the main trail.

③ MARTIAL LAW 5.12a R/X ★

This route features steep climbing and good gear, but also multiple cruxes with decking potential on the jagged terrain behind you. Climb smart. Start on a small platform on the left side of the wall. Grab the low jug and crank thru overhangs into a seam under a roof. Don't fall on the roof and hold it together thru the overhanging headwall. Finish under a big boulder at the top. (40 ft.)

④ NATURAL BORN KILLER 5.12b ★★

Locate a bolt in the middle of the face, just above a low roof. Move left at the first bolt, passing a second bolt to a stance under a square roof. Pull underneath and out the left side of the roof onto extremely steep terrain. Move slightly right and climb up the overhanging arête to the top. 2 bolts. (50 ft.)

⑤ DOG AND PONY SHOW 5.11b ★★

Start as for NATURAL BORN KILLERS. Pull through the low roof and climb to the bolt. Move right above the bolt onto the face. Then up and slightly left to a stance under an overhang. From here the choice is yours - finish up and right or up and left - whichever looks more enticing. 1 bolt. (45 ft.)

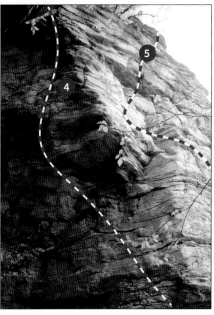

⑥ WALK DON'T RUN 5.7

This line starts in a short, left angling shallow crack just right of a high, imposing roof. Climb directly up through a small roof past a small tree. Head for the overhanging corner that leads to a large roof. Work around the roof to the right and continue up and left on a vertical face, ending at a tree. Be mindful of a few sections of less-than-stellar rock quality. (100 ft.)

Variation: An easier (5.5) variation climbs a more wandering line that avoids the overhanging corner, as well as some of the sketchier sections of rock.

WALK DON'T RUN – *Though the original name was unknown, Durham climber Matt Westlake coined this moniker in 2010 after he and partner Tom Drewes rediscovered this line. The name references an old Ventures tune by the same name. Though completists may find it worth exploring, this "forgotten oldie" of a line is not exactly a classic – no need to get there fast.*

7 TURDSLINGER 5.6

About 50 feet right of WALK DON'T RUN, this aptly named route climbs the easy crack that angles up and to the right. Bypass the nasty slings in a flake in favor of a tree on a ledge. (100 ft.)Descent: Walk off left to the main descent gully trail.

8 BLUEBALLS 5.6 ★

A rather uncomfortable name for such great position on reliable jugs. Start in the right-most corner above a distinctive, skewer-like tree about 100 feet left of DOLPHIN HEAD. Do an easy scramble to a fun and near-vertical headwall (or take a less steep variation off to the left). Stem your way up the amazingly exposed overhanging chimney (a very unique endeavor!) and exit out of a V-notch, scurrying up and right to a large belay ledge. More traffic would probably clean up some of the questionable rock. (100 ft.)

Descent: On top of the buttress, find a free-hanging, one-rope rappel from slings and cord on the right-most side of the ledge. This drops down the steep back side of the buttress into the Kennel Fodder Gully. Give up?

Walk off to the left and take the Main Descent Gully to the base.

9 HORN DOG 5.5

This line starts on the left side of the Kennel Fodder Gully, near the bottom. Traverse around the arête on a ledge, and then negotiate through a hodgepodge of roofs, face climbing, and some questionable rock until you reach the arête at a wide ledge. Stay left of the arête as you continue up to the top of the buttress, then step right to the BLUE BALLS rappel. (100 ft.)

10 KENNEL FODDER 5.11c ★

In spite of less-than-perfect rock in some sections, the sustained nature of this line and the fantastic finger crack finish make this one well worth a look. This line starts a little ways up the gully left (east) of SOUTHERN EXPOSURE. Climb up the center of the steep, left wall, taking the path of least resistance to a ledge. Start from the left side of the ledge and follow the weakness above, eventually angling up and right. The powerful bulging finger crack is found at the last 20 feet. (80 ft.)

Descent: Rappel from the sling anchor at the top.

The next three routes descend by topping out and hiking left along the summit to the Relapse Gully, or by rapping from a rap station creatively rigged from a tree and a chockstone. The Tree/Chockstone station is directly above the aptly named CHOCKSTONE RAP LANE. For what its worth, the farther right you get, the more bushwhacking this option will require, especially if you don't know the top of the cliff like the back of your hand.

11 TRI-SOCKETS 5.7

Bring the tri-cams for this one! This line starts in the gully, opposite of KENNEL FODDER. Work your way up the less-than-vertical face, gradually heading up and right. Mantel onto a ledge just right of two small pockets. Climb to an overlap and somewhat dubious rock.

The Kennel Fodder Gully

Continue up and right (crux) to a couple of shelves. Finish by following cracks and flakes to the horizontal just before the belay at the Tree/chockstone rap station. (80 ft.)

12 CHOCKSTONE RAP LANE 5.6

Start right on the edge of the Kennel Fodder gully, just right of a wide crack. Climb the face, stepping right around a roof (crux) and then back left. Follow the slightly overhanging face up to and through a short, deep cleft, finishing at the Tree/chockstone rap station. (80 ft.)

13 CENTRAL CLEFT 5.6

Start left of SOUTHERN EXPOSURE and DOLPHIN HEAD in a deep, left-angling cleft. Stem your way up the cleft. Pull the roof on the right side before stepping back left and climbing up a slightly overhanging shallow corner. Finish by moving through another deep cleft to Tree/chockstone rap station. (90 ft.)

183

HORN DOG, TRI-SOCKETS, CHOCKSTONE RAP LANE, CENTRAL CLEFT: Back in 2008, Scott Gilliam decided to explore new (forgotten?) territory, by resurrecting several lines on the Central Wall. As with a few lines in the North End it is unclear exactly when these lines were first climbed. Regardless of the official FA, Scott has brought some attention to these lines, providing them with some much needed TLC. If you're looking for a little adventure on moderate terrain, give these routes a try!

14 SOUTHERN EXPOSURE 5.7 ★

Follow the shallow corner just left of DOL-PHIN HEAD up to a slabby face. From there, traverse left and slightly up, through lichen, until underneath a short chimney. Climb up the broken face and exit through the chimney (a 5" piece is helpful but not essential in the chimney) to the top.

Descent: Tree/chockstone rap station. (100 ft.)

Variation: There are several different link-ups and variations combining different sections of SOUTHERN EXPOSURE and DOLPHIN-HEAD, all at about the same difficulty and all with good gear.

15 DOLPHIN HEAD 5.6

Trend right up the corner passing a small tree on the left. Follow the corner/crack up and left over an increasingly slabby face to a notch in the overhang. Aim for the nose of the Dolphin Head feature. Climb over the nose and then straight up to the top. Belaying just under the dolphin's nose can elimi-

Climber moving up and left toward the namesake feature of DOLPHIN HEAD (5.6)

nate unwanted rope drag, but is unnecessary with proper rope management.

Descent: The downside to this route is that there isn't a convenient way to get down. There are rap stations on either side of the finish, but it takes some bushwhacking to find either. If you are not familiar with the area, your best bet is to cut your losses and walk off to the right to reach the Sentinel Buttress rappel. (120 ft.)

> "Seems like every time I ever led WELCOME TO MOORE'S, the key pro at the base of the corner would pull out as I went above it…always scary!" - John Provetero, Moore's pioneer

16 WELCOME TO MOORE'S 5.10d R ★★

An intimidating but satisfying line. Double ropes are recommended.

P1: Climb the easy but dirty corner left of EASY HARD to a ledge below a short left-facing dihedral. (5.5, 70 ft.)

P2: Pull through the overhang and aim towards a diagonal crack a little bit right of the main corner. Get gear as high as you can, then step back down and traverse left to the corner/crack system. Climb up the steep dihedral and jug-laden face (crux) to a ledge and natural belay. (5.10d, 50 ft.)

Descent: There is a descent gully on either side, as well as a rappel tree hiding in a fourth class chimney 50 feet right, and 10 feet down.

Variation: A more direct variation that climbs directly to the center of the traverse can eliminate the need for double ropes.

17 EASY HARD 5.5 ★★

The name says it all - easy climbing at the beginning with a small, sloping crux at the top. About 40 feet left of HEAD JAM, climb the flake system in the center of the small buttress to a fixed anchor at a tree in an alcove. (110 ft.)

Descent: A full 60m rappel from the fixed anchor will get you down with stretch.

18 HEAD JAM 5.5 ★★

Sound awkward? It is. Although the commitment factor might make it feel a bit sandbagged, the uniqueness factor makes it worth doing at least once. Bring a 4-5" piece.

The start of WELCOME TO MOORES (5.10d)

Climber approaching the massive chimney/roof of HEAD JAM (5.5)

Start in the wide chimney to the left of BLUE CHOCK. Pull left and around the big chockstone, collecting style points by performing the head jam move, then follow the corner system to a ledge with a large tree. (110 ft.)

Descent: Same as EASY HARD.

The following four routes share a common start at a large lieback flake above a dead tree next to the base of the cliff, about 30 feet right of HEAD JAM.

There are three options to descend routes from PLASTIC CAT to HOPSCOTCH. These routes effectively end on a long ledge that slopes down and right.

1. Climb an easy bit to fixed slings that are about 30 feet up from the large sloping ledge that can be used as a downclimb. The slings are directly above HOPSCOTCH. The slings are impossible to see from the ledge, but they can be found just to the right of a solitary tree that grows from the rock.

2. Scramble down and right over the broad ledge. In several lcoations the terrain steepens. Its easy but an unroped fall would likley be fatal. See photo on page 189.

3. Climb a long easy pitch to the summitt. Find the cliff top trail and follow it to the right. Look for the side trail that leads to the Sentinel Buttress anchors.

19 PLASTIC CAT 5.12b R ★★

A test-piece Moore's route featuring difficult, sequential climbing and poorly protected sections. A very serious undertaking that likely has not seen more than two ascents. Climb the easy layback flake to a seam below a bulge. Power out past a fixed pin and bolt (crux), then find gear wherever you can through several overhangs up to a ledge. (140 ft.)

Variation: A much harder start (5.10 X) climbs the unprotected face to the left of the flake.

20 BLUE CHOCK 5.10a ★★★

A stellar route with great moves and a unique finish. Gear is good but small and sometimes a tad tricky to place (take some brass nuts and smaller cams). With good rope management you can climb it in one pitch with only minor drag. Double ropes are recommended.

P1: Follow the obvious left-facing flake up to a stance below a corner. (5.6, 50 ft.)

P2: Climb straight up, then left past a black overhang to a pumpy stance below a right-facing feature and seam (crux). Tackle the crux and move straight up to a good stance. From here, there are two choices - the original line traverses right about 15 feet, intersecting with TOO MUCH FUN. A more common way is to traverse right about 5 feet and pull directly through the bulge. Continue up and right into the left-facing corner and climb the corner to a sometimes, ungraceful beached-whale finish. (5.10a, 90 ft.)

21 TOO MUCH CHALK 5.8

A little known variation that links up the easier terrain on BLUE CHOCK and TOO MUCH FUN.

P1. Same as BLUE CHOCK (5.6, 50 ft.)

P2. Instead of heading up and left (as for BLUE CHOCK), continue 10 more feet straight up to the next ledge. Then climb up and right around a steep bulge, continuing to the WASHBOARD finish variation of TOO MUCH FUN (5.8, 80 ft.)

22 TOO MUCH FUN 5.9+ ★

But certainly not "too much gear". Protection is adequate , but not plentiful. Aside from that, this is a nice line with several finishing variations that add to the fun.

P1. Climb the first 45 feet of BLUE CHOCK to a good stance. You can belay here to avoid rope drag. Traverse right around the bulge until you reach a shallow corner with a bolt overhead. Climb past the bolt (crux) to another stance and belay. (5.9,100 ft.)

P2. Choose your own adventure:

1. Trend up and right on easier terrain (longest option, and same finish as WASHBOARD (5.6)

2. Climb up and left until you are level with the base of the BLUE CHOCK dihedral, then traverse right along the overhang (5.8)

3. Finish up and left on BLUE CHOCK (hardest option) (5.9).

23 MUCH TOO BOARD 5.6 R ★

Though a bit runout, this link-up of the previous route with the following one eliminates rope drag, allowing for a pleasant single pitch experience. Find the pointy block to the right of the original layback flake start. Pull the bulge and ease onto the slabby face, aiming for the bolt. A blue tricam is great to have down low. Skirt around the TOO MUCH FUN corner crux by stepping right along a thin horizontal. Finish on the arête marking the left side of the WASHBOARD headwall. (120 ft.)

24 WASHBOARD 5.6 ★★

An enjoyable and well-protected outing that some say gives WAILING WALL a run for its money. Start at the base of the large dead tree lying across the approach trail. Climb the shallow corner past a couple of small trees to a left- facing flake/bulge feature. Pull around the bulge on the left side and navigate up through steep horizontals to a large ledge with a small pine tree. Don't cheat yourself by bailing right, and don't kill your partner by belaying from the tree. (120 ft.)

25 HOPSCOTCH 5.3

Very popular with beginners due to the featured face and low angle. However, novice leaders should exercise caution as a fall on some sections would result in hitting ledges or the heavily-featured low-angled face. This route has been the scene of many injuries and at least one fatality. Don't assume that easy means safe.

Many variations exist. The most popular is to start from the top of a large block just off the side of the trail and then move right of the overhang and up through easy rock. Descent: Rap from slings by a tree. See page 189.

The low-angled, broken area that lies sandwiched between HOPSCOTCH and SENTINEL CHIMNEY is known as the Egg Wall. There are several lackluster and undocumented lines that meander up this face. Descent: Rap from a slung chockstone by a tree.

26 SENTINEL CHIMNEY 5.4

Climb the obvious (often wet and grimy) chimney in three or so pitches. (300 ft.)

Descent: Top out and hike around right to the Sentinel Buttress rap station.

The start to routes 19-22.

RAPPEL ANCHOR

4TH CLASS DOWN-CLIMB

STAY ROPED OR DON'T FALL!

SENTINEL BUTTRESS AREA

The Sentinel Buttress juts out proudly along the right side of Moore's Wall, and is the home of numerous classic lines. These are without a doubt the most famous collection of routes at Moore's. The left side of the buttress is known as the Circus Wall. According to Bruce Meneghin, one of the early pioneers at Moore's, this section of cliff was named in honor of the large number of novices who could be seen thrashing about on the ultra-classic (but ultra-steep) moderates weekend after weekend. Apparently it could be likened to a three-ring circus at times! The right side of the buttress is the Fire Wall, whose fiery orange "Billboard" section can be clearly identified from Hooker Farm Road on the way to the parking lot.

Approach: This area is best accessed via the first trail that forks right from the fire road.

CIRCUS WALL

This wall boasts one of the highest concentrations of high quality routes in not only the State, but much of the Southeast. Most crags would be considered lucky to contain even one of these amazing lines, as each one is deserving of classic status. The routes are characterized by steep-for-the-grade moderate terrain with insanely big jugs and the potential to place as much gear as your forearms can handle!

Approach: AIR SHOW and BREAK ON TROUGH are approached via easy climbing up the Egg Wall. ZOO VIEW to CHEAP SEATS are approached by one of the many easy routes up the Crows Nest ledge.

Descent: All CIRCUS WALL routes descend via a rappel from a fixed anchor at the top of Sentinel Buttress. A single 60m rope rappel will barely reach the Crow's Nest ledge with some stretch. From there, another shorter rappel will reach the ground from fixed anchors around a large block.

THE FIRST ASCENT OF BLUE CHOCK

One of the Kinnaird brothers related to me that they were so excited about the prospect of doing the FA on this classic line that they couldn't wait until the weekend. They were in high school at the time and skipped out. What chance does American Lit and Algebra have when stacked up against the FA of one of the best routes at Moores? However, with the Ying, comes the Yang. They were grounded for a month by their mother. Hope it wasn't prime climbing season.

Bill Webster, Chapel Hill

❶ AIR SHOW 5.8+ ★★★

Everything about this route screams classic – steep face, bomber gear, and multiple crux sections. 5.8 doesn't get much better than this jug-fest! Falls up high will certainly please the crowds, but will more than likely be all air. Start back in the chimney that separates the Egg Wall from the Circus Wall.

P1: Work your way up the Sentinel Chimney and Egg Wall face past a dead tree until you reach a good ledge. (5.4, 100 ft.)

P2: Continue up another 20 feet or so until you can step right to a corner system. Fire up the corner and past a small roof. Catch your breath as you make your way to a shallow right-facing dihedral capped by a small roof. Stand tall in the dihedral and exit the corner on the left side to easier rock and the top. (5.8+, 140 ft.)

❷ BREAK ON THROUGH 5.10a ★★★

It may be a one-move wonder, but the rest of the climbing is pretty wonderful too. A great option for the Moore's climber to "break on through" to 5.10's.

P1: Start same as for AIR SHOW (5.4, 70 ft.)

P2: Traverse right to a quartzy crack system. Work your way up the steep corner and face, then head up and left to a bulge. Surmount the bulge (crux), latch onto the jug and follow the steep, jug-laced face to the top. (5.10a, 150 ft.)

Dick Hain powering through the lower crux of AIR SHOW (5.8+)

Sarah Wolfe approaching the crux of BREAK ON THROUGH (5.10a)

Sarah Wolfe launching off onto BREAK ON THROUGH (5.10a)

The next four routes start from the Crow's Nest, the large ledge at the top of the first pitch of Sentinel Buttress.

③ ZOO VIEW 5.7+ ★★★

Climbing Magazine once featured this mega-classic. It is known by almost every North Carolina trad climber and shows up on many a climber's Top Ten tick list. This is full-value 5.7 at its finest, so it may not be the best choice for those just breaking into the grade. Think carefully about rope management and the use of longer slings to avoid rope drag higher up.

P1: Gain the Crow's Nest via any of the lower SENTINEL BUTTRESS routes (5.3 – 5.9, 80 ft.)

P2: From the Crow's Nest, gather your gumption, then traverse along thin horizontals past a bolt to a crack (stay low for better hands and feet), savoring the instant exposure. Follow the crack up to an alcove underneath the biggest 5.7 roof you'll ever see. Crank up and over using the gigantic handlebar holds, and continue to the top, where the terrain gradually eases off. (If you are not confident about your second's ability to pull the roof, its not a bad idea to belay in the alcove, breaking the route into two pitches). (5.7+, 140 ft.)

Note: The original line climbed up and left of the bolt instead of the lower traverse commonly done these days.

④ CONNECT-A-CRUX 5.10a ★★★

Unless you want to get booed off the CIRCUS WALL, do NOT attempt this link-up if there are other parties in the vicinity. On low traffic days, however, this variation takes a scenic tour across the CIRCUS WALL, hitting the cruxes on three of the most classic lines at Moore's.

P1: Make your way to the CROW'S NEST. (80 ft.)

P2: Traverse past the bolt to the crack system (crux for ZOO VIEW) and continue up for about 15 feet. Trend left onto BREAK ON THROUGH, and crest over the bulge (crux of BREAK ON THROUGH). Once above this roof, traverse left on easy ledges until you can see the open book crux of AIR SHOW above you. Negotiate the dihedral and continue to the top. Take at least a 60m rope and a whole lotta slings!

⑤ BIMBO'S BULGE 5.10c ★★★

A must-do for those solid at 5.10. Thin, thought-provoking face climbing leads to a roof.

P1: Make your way to the CROW'S NEST. (80 ft.)

P2: Walk left on ZOO VIEW for a few feet then climb straight up the steep face on thin horizontals. After about 25 feet, start veering left and then up towards a triangular corner/roof. Pull the left side of the overhanging corner and move up the face and crack to the base of a second overhang. Move left and then up through the namesake bulge to easier face climbing and the top. (5.10c, 120 ft.)

Warning: As this guide was going to print a key hold and gear placement broke off. The rating may be harder than 5.10c.

5 BIMBOS BULGE (5.10C)

Katie Hughes approaching the big roof of ZOO VIEW (5.7+) (below) and above the roof (top)

CIRCUS WALL 1-5

(SENTINEL)

1

5

3

2

1

6 CHEAP SEATS 5.9

The one disappointing route in this area, and it starts so well. Climb a short, steep, clean face directly above the Crows Nest. After a really nice start the route rapidly goes downhill. Continue to the top by wandering up a slabby face and taking in some steeper features. (5.9, 110 ft.)

> "One of the very first times I climbed outdoors I saw a guy drop 30 feet from the intermediate belay on ZOO VIEW. My climbing partner was a nurse and we helped with the rescue. He got helicoptered out but ended up only sustaining a broken ankle, along with a few bumps and bruises. The next year when I got on ZOO VIEW those memories got in my head a little bit. Once I pushed past it however, I loved it – and still do!"
>
> - Diane Joseph, (Chapel Hill)

SENTINEL BUTTRESS

The next six routes climb the distinct prow of the Sentinel Buttress, which is located between the Circus and Fire Walls. Several of the routes lead to the Crows Nest, a spacious ledge at the right end of the Circus Wall. A few have second pitches that take you to the top. There are many different ways to climb this feature, all of them fairly easy. Following are the standard named routes, but you can climb just about anywhere you want.

For many years a unique rap station could be found at the top of Sentinel Buttress. It was built in a machine shop by Ira Warrenfelt. It included several bolts, a pulley, a hanger to allow the rappeller to clip in, and a stainless steel plate that held the whole thing together. It was so funky-looking that many instinctively felt it was somehow unsafe. When it was recently replaced, it turned out to be in GREAT shape and could have stayed for many more years.

In 2012 this new rappel station was the scene of a fatal accident (not the fault of the new gear). A skilled climber made a rapelling error and fell over 200 feet to the ground. This tragic accident should remind us all that the seemingly-simple act of rappelling can be fatal if not done correctly. Please take the time to double and triple check your set up before committing to the rappel.

1 SENTINEL 5.3

Start about halfway between SENTINEL CHIMNEY and the well-travelled CROW'S NEST ACCESS line, at the extreme left end of Sentinel Buttress's north face.

P1: Climb the steep juggy face straight up to the Crow's Nest. (5.3, 80 ft.)

P2: Walk to the right end of the Crow's Nest. Continue trending up and right, traversing under blocky roofs. Once past the roofs, head straight up to the top of the cliff.

2 CROW'S NEST ACCESS 5.5 ★★★

a.k.a. BABIES BUNS. This line probably sees more traffic than any other at Moore's, as the first pitch is the most common approach pitch to the Circus Wall routes, and the second pitch is the rap lane for the entire right side of Moore's Wall. Use good judgment as other climbers will often be both above and below you.

P1: Climb any one of the many variations up the blunt arête that juts out below and right of SENTINEL CHIMNEY to the Crow's Nest. The climbing on the left side of the face is a bit easier, but the right side offers better gear options. (5.5, 80 ft.)

P2.: Follow the obvious crack system at the right side of the CROW'S NEST ledge, topping out to the right of the Sentinel Buttress rappel anchor. (5.5, 110 ft.)

3 SENTINEL DIRECT 5.5

Locate the short, left-facing corner about 30 feet left of SENTINEL SUPER DIRECT.

P1: Climb the corner to a ledge, then step right and climb up another corner, eventually wandering up and right across the face to a ledge at the base of a chimney (Little Crow's Nest). (5.5, 50 ft.)

P2: Follow an easy chimney up to the Crow's Nest. (5.5, 50 ft.)

P3: Finish on SENTINEL. (110 ft.)

4 BIG JUGS 5.5 ★

Surprisingly, this pitch is seldom done even though it climbs clean, steep rock at a reasonable grade. The start is located near the junction of the north and east faces of the Sentinel Buttress, a few feet to the right of and down from the start to SENTINEL DIRECT. Climb a short slab section up and right to gain the steep face and a crack on the north-facing part of the wall.

Climb the steep face and crack to the Crow's Nest. (85 ft.)

5 GREAT ESCAPE 5.9

Start just left of Sentinel Super Direct. Locate the crack underneath the initial SUPER DIRECT roof (on its left side). Climb the crack, skirting to the left of the first roof. Traverse left under the second, larger roof, until you can head up to the Crow's Nest. (80 ft.)

6 SENTINEL SUPER DIRECT 5.9+ ★

The burly business down low is worth the fantastic position on the more moderate terrain above the roof.

Start at the thin crack under a roof (on its right side), just left of a large cave at the low point on the buttress.

P1: Head up the crack and grunt your way past the roof (crux). Next follow the cracks until you reach the second roof. Pass the roof on its right side and then traverse back left above the roof. Belay at the base of a chimney (a.k.a. Little Crow's Nest). (5.9, 80 ft.)

P2: Chimney up to the Crow's Nest (5.4, 50 ft.)

P3: Finish on Sentinel

Variation: An alternate option pulls an overhang midway through the traverse (5.7) and

belays on the face above.

FIRE WALL

The Fire Wall is the more serious side to the Sentinel area. Wild, overhanging faces and thin, technical cracks make a great playground for climbers interested in bold and committing sends. Be aware that despite the large number of bolts and fixed pins scattered about the wall, the Fire Wall is anything but a sport wall. Many of the routes feature exciting runouts and creative gear-finding expeditions. RP's (small, brass micro-nuts, named for their maker, Roland Pauligk) and other small nuts are useful on many Fire Wall routes. Unless otherwise mentioned, descend all lines by topping out and heading left to the Sentinel Rappel.

"My one and only lead of EDGE OF FIRE almost ended up with a huge whipper. After clippng the bolt I looked up at what seemed like a sea of holds. After thinking "whats the big deal" I started up, only to be stopped. I downclimbed to the bolt. Up again and down again. Just couldn't figure out the sequence. Up, down, up down. By the time I managed to get the crux I was utterly, totally pumped.

However, instead of doing the sensible thing which would be to just drop off onto the bolt, I kept going. The easy but steep rock above the crux tortured my forearms. Stopping to place pro was not an option. Up, up, up, with almost no ability left to close my fingers on the holds. The ledge came at the last possible moment before lactic acid totally overcame my muscles.

With my chest flopped over onto the ledge and ass and legs hanging over the brink I rested in this foolish looking position until enough stength came back to complete the ledge flop. Enormous fall averted, but no style points awarded!

- Bill Webster, Chapel Hill, NC

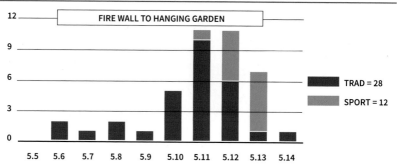

❶ EDGE OF FIRE 5.11b/c ★★

An impressive route to be sure! This pumpy route is a fine example of the "pro or go" dilemma. The lone bolt has been the recipient of many long, clean whippers over the years. The original route (as described below) climbs the flaring chimney just right of SENTINEL SUPER DIRECT.

P1: Climb the chimney and follow a series of blocky ledges. At the left end of the prominent ledge beneath GO DOG GO, move up past a large, detached block to a stance below the prow that forms the left edge of the Fire Wall. Follow the prow to a tricky ramp. Put your gear placing skills to the test as you work up the ramp to a bolt. Unlock the sequence to crank past the bolt. Move up and left through the crux to easier ground. Race straight up to the large ledge. (5.11b/c, 100 ft.)

P2: Scamper left and up easy terrain to the Crow's Nest (5.0, 40 ft.)

Variation: The now standard start is to climb SENTINEL SUPER DIRECT to the base of the ramp.

❷ GO DOG GO 5.12a ★

This route scraps its way up the Fire Wall arête.

P1: From a slanting ledge below and left of WILD KINGDOM, climb a small corner crack to a bolt just left of a small roof. Move left above the bolt to a thin ledge and a dowel that takes a wire. Head right to the jug at the base of the arête. Next climb up past two more bolts, some RP placements and a fixed pin (back it up) to reach a steep, white wall. Traverse 20 feet left to the EDGE OF FIRE ledge. (5.12a, 85ft.)

P2: Finish same as EDGE OF FIRE. (5.0, 40 feet)

❸ UNDERDOG 5.12b/c R ★★★

This direct finish to GO DOG GO packs both bark and bite. The runout occurs on 5.11+ terrain along the overhanging white face. Climb GO DOG GO to the base of the white wall, but instead of traversing left, continue straight up the face. Be sure to get a crucial #2 RP placement before committing to the runout. Continue climbing past a bolt, two fixed pins, and one more bolt to the anchors. (100 ft.)

❹ WILD KINGDOM 5.11d R ★★★

It doesn't get any more classic than this. There are several fixed pins found along the first pitch – the pin stack at the start is in good shape, but the rest should be backed up. Double ropes are recommended, particularly on the first pitch. Start on the obvious large block at the base of the Fire Wall. Most parties choose to scramble on top of the block to belay. By doing this the belayer can spot the climber until the first pin is clipped. Many parties also choose to clip the bolt on POV right after the crux to protect the second.

P1: Clip the fixed pin stack then follow the left crack, moving left on slopers to the large dihedral/roof system. Move up the dihedral

FIRE WALL

Seth Tart looking more like the top dog on UNDERDOG (5.12b/c)

past one pin and two bolts, then pull the roof (crux) and step right. Pass one more bolt, then trend right to a left-facing ramp and bolted belay at the base of a large orange section of rock known as the Billboard. (5.11d, 130 ft.)

Note: An additional set of anchors exists just after the crux for parties wishing to toprope the majority of the first pitch. Though not original these intermediate anchors (referred to by locals as "The Party Anchor") have been in place for many years.

P2. Use the thin crack, a few face holds and slopers to move past two bolts and a pin along the aesthetic orange "Billboard" face. Aim up and left to a ledge with a natural gear belay. (5.11d, 70 ft.)

Finish Variation 1: A direct, alternate finish climbs directly through the summit roof past another 3 bolts, 1 pin. Very sustained. (5.12a)

Finish Variation 2: An easier, but more runout variation follows easier ground up and left. (5.10 R)

5 WILDLIFE 5.12b R/X

This additional variation to WILD KINGDOM is very serious and committing, and has probably only been done once. Don't get in over your head, and be extremely careful with loose rock. Climb the WILD KINGDOM dihedral to the end of the crack under the double roof. Instead of following WILD KINGDOM to the right, traverse left (unprotected) along the lip of the roof to the edge of the face. It may also be possible to pull the roof past two pins, finishing on UNDERDOG, where a crux bolt takes away some of the sting. (110 ft.)

6 P.O.V. 5.12c

Yet another variation to WILD KINGDOM that incorporates the business of the first pitch crux, but then continues directly up on desperate crimpers. This has probably seen only one ascent and the rating is uncertain. Climb the WILD KINGDOM dihedral, but instead of heading right continue straight up past two

bolts to a small arête. Fight your way past two final bolts before heading to an easy crack on the left shoulder of the wall. Fixed anchor. (140 ft.)

7 RIDERS ON THE STORM 5.11a ★

The first line established on the Fire Wall, this route opened the doors to the imposing Billboard section. Start from atop the WILD KINGDOM block.

P1. Start as for WILD KINGDOM, but move into the right-hand crack system. Traverse right along the overhang at the large roof to a bolt. Move up and right, avoiding the roof, then up the face to the base of the crack. (5.11a, 130 ft.)

P2: Follow the crack to a sketchy pin, then make an easy traverse right to the ledge at the far left side of the Hanging Garden. (5.10b, 100 ft.)

"WILD KINGDOM was really a visionary route on the part of Tom McMillan. It was truly groundbreaking, as Tom employed tactics that, to my knowledge, no one else in the state had used to establish a free route – utilizing a combination of aid and fixed protection in preparation to establish a genius free climb! I am not sure how much time Tom spent equipping the route before we did our bottom to top ascent. However, before we did it, he had equipped it with strategic placements that would enable the route to be free climbed with a reasonable amount of protection. Although these tactics were something new for all of us, the beauty, audacity, and difficulty of the route seemed to justify the means of establishment. Tom and I managed to do the first bottom to top ascent in 1978, resting on one piece of gear exiting out of the overhanging dihedral on the first pitch. Neither of us had the endurance and strength needed to make the final moves. At the time this was probably the most sustained and difficult route in North Carolina. A year later Rob Robinson, known for his incredible hang strength, came to Moore's Wall for a visit. Together he and Tom were able to complete the first free ascent." -

Bob Rotert, on the importance of WILD KINGDOM

Variation: Instead of bailing onto the Hanging Garden ledge, keep trending up and right to link-up with WILD-EYED SOUTHERN BOYS for a sporty ending to a very long second pitch. (5.12a, 150 ft.)

The next five routes are located on a slabby area below the intimidating Hanging Garden.

8 STAIRCASE 5.6 R

This moderate line just right of the FIRE WALL once saw a lot of traffic; however numerous accidents over the years (some of which were serious) led to an understandable decrease in popularity. Be very careful should you decide to attempt this route, as a fall from an un-protected 5.5 crux means a guarenteed crash onto a large ledge.

P1. Climb the shallow groove just right of the Fire Wall to a face leading to an obvious belay ledge. (5.6, 80 ft.)

P2. Climb the unprotected (5.5 R) face above to another ledge at the base of a crack. (80 ft.)

P3. Follow the groove to the top. (5.5, 50 ft.)

Descent: Walk off via the Hanging Garden Gully.

MIDLIFE CRISIS - *This line was bolted and established by a group effort in 1995. Many of the other developers in the area disagreed with their tactics – it added a bolt to a route that previously had a bold start (SAND TRAP), and added a pin to a variation of that same route that had also been done sans fixed protection. Unfortunately, the addition of fixed gear to portions of the older routes renders them somewhat obsolete, with most climbers choosing to follow the bolts rather than the natural line. Almost two decades later, however, many climbers have found more than a few redeeming qualities in this line, especially as an approach pitch to the Hanging Garden.*

9 MIDLIFE CRISIS 5.10d

This mixed line is found on the face right of STAIRCASE, directly below the HANGING GAR-DEN ledge. Despite the slabby appearance, this route can pack an unexpected pump. Climb past bolts and pins to a tree with slings at the base of the Hanging Garden. Supple-ment with a light rack. (100 ft.)

BROWN DOG – *Although the original FA party is unknown, this line was given some attention by local climber Sean Barb some-time around the early 2000's. It was a line he liked to rope solo often, and he nicknamed it BROWN DOG in honor of his faithful four-legged companion, who would curl up beside his rope and wait patiently for his return. It offers a good warm-up option for the Hanging Garden, which can be accessed by topping out on this route and tunneling through some briars to arrive in the vicinity of POOH'S CORNER.*

---

10 BROWN DOG 5.10a

This line features two roofs – one down low, and the other at about 30 feet. Start on the buttress below the Hanging Garden, about 150 feet right of the Fire Wall, underneath two roofs. Pull through them both, then wander up and left, aiming for a leaning finger crack just below ZEUS. (100 ft.)

Descent: Rap from a ratty nest of slings or continue into the trees.

There are numerous undocumented lines nestled amid the lichen on the wall leading up to the Hanging Garden Gully. Some are worth doing, others aren't. In the spring of 2012, Triangle climbers Matt Westlake, Sarah Wolfe, and Juneko Grilley-Olson took an interest in this section of cliff after noticing a few obvious cracks on the hike over to DOUBLE OUGHT. The following two routes are the fruits of their labor, which yielded routes that, though not classic by any means, will probably clean up rather nicely with traffic, and offer a few moder-ate options on the right side of the cliff.

Both routes descend by rapping (with a 60m rope) from a large tree with fixed slings atop a ledge on the right side of the wall.

⓫ FLAKY 5.7

Locate a large dirty gully, before the Hanging Garden Approach Gully. Ascend a large flake on the right side until it ends. Veer up and right over moderate terrain to reach an easy, lichen-covered slab. Escape left through a gap in the foliage and belay from a large tree. Beware the slick mossy start and a few patches of bad rock. A 3" or 4" piece is handy. (120 ft.)

Descent: Scramble down and to the (climber's) right to access the rap station on the lower ledge.

⓬ GOOD, BAD, AND NOT TOO UGLY 5.7

The last half is the ugly. The first half is the good. Continue hiking past FLAKY up a steep dirty slope to a small opening in the rhododendron on your left. Look for a short, right-

angling just-bigger-than-fingers size crack and follow it to a greenbriar-infested ledge. Continue up the low-angle lichenous face to a tree with fixed slings. (100 ft.)

Juneko Grilley-Olsen exploring on FLAKY (5.7)

HANGING GARDEN

This area contains a collection of not only the hardest routes at Moore's, but also some of the few outright sport routes found at the cliff.

Approach: From Sentinel Buttress, continue right along the cliff base, passing the Fire Wall and getting a sneak preview of the entire Hanging Garden up above. To access this area, scramble up to a ledge, then look left for a steep, narrow gully heading up and left. The gully is located below an orange wall capped by a huge rectangular roof, only a couple of minutes from Sentinel Buttress. (If you reach the large orange and white block, you've gone too far.) The gully is mostly fourth class scrambling, with a few easy fifth class moves thrown in. If you can climb in the Garden, you certainly won't have any trouble making it up the gully, but be aware that it can be especially dicey in wet weather, especially when toting a heavy pack. (There are a handful of climbs that start in the gully). The gully ends at a trail that will take you directly to the base of POOH'S CORNER, a striking feature that can be seen from the road. Walk left along exposed terrain for the rest of the Garden routes.

It is also possible to reach the Hanging Garden from above by topping out on the Circus or Fire Wall, hiking along the top, and rapping in.

Descent: At the end of the day, a 70m rope will just barely see you to the ground from any one of a number of slung trees at the base of the Hanging Garden, should your party be less than enthused about shimmying back down the gully.

Note: Up until recently, the majority of the hardware in this area consisted of original, hardware store style bolts. In the summer of 2013, a team of local climbers (Tim Fisher, Todd and Cassin Mullenix, and Greg Loomis) took it upon themselves to replace

many of these anchors, along with several bolts and fixed quickdraws. A fixed sling on ZEUS was so tattered that it was easily pulled apart by hand. The new stainless steel anchors, protection, and fixed cables will hopefully last for many years to come. However as always, inspect all fixed gear thoroughly before entrusting your life to it.

THE ROBBINS EDICT

"Royal Robbins wrote a book for early climbers like my brother Steve and I. Were it not for this guide, we would have had no one else to teach us! The hallmark foundation of that book was "the leader must not fall." We used that edict throughout our climbing careers. I can count on one hand the number of times I have fallen on lead. That meant that we took climbs by siege – climbing from one rest stance to the next, placing gear along the way. (If a rest was not to be found, we would down climb (without weighting the rope) to a previous rest."

- Frank Orthel

---

1 WILD-EYED SOUTHERN BOYS 5.12a (5.10 R)

This line is actually on the far right side of the Fire Wall, but is included in this section since it is accessed from the Hanging Garden. Locate a very high bolt on the right side of the Fire Wall. Scramble up to that bolt, clipping a hard-to-see pin along the way, then traverse right for 10 feet before beginning the business. Let the pump factor build before surmounting a final crux bulge and pulling onto lower angle terrain. 1 pin, 4 bolts, no anchor. (50 ft.)

Descent: Top out and walk left to the Sentinel Rappel.

Note: For efficiency's sake, some parties choose to finish at a beefy bail biner on the fourth bolt, and lower back into the Garden. This avoids the upper crux and keeps the route around 5.11c.

2 **RED TIDE 5.11d X**

This toprope problem on the left side of the CATNIP wall can be rigged from the CATNIP ANCHOR. (60 ft.)

3 **CATNIP 5.11b**

Climb the path of least resistance past seven bolts on a slightly overhanging orange face approximately 100 feet left of ZEUS. Bolted anchors. (60 ft.)

Variation: Stay left at the third bolt for a harder variation. (5.11d)

ZEUS WALL

4 **PRIMAL RAGE 5.13a** ★★

At the far left of the Zeus Wall, just before turning the corner to CATNIP, you'll see an obvious roof/arête feature 20 feet up with 2 bolts on it. Climb moderate, blocky terrain (bring a few small cams "just in case") to a small perch beneath the roof. Stick-clip the first 2 bolts from the perch, then fire a giant move to the lip of the roof (first crux). Get re-established, then power your way out left through the second crux. From here, technical face climbing leads to a balancy finish at the anchors. (6 bolts, 60 ft.)

5 **ZEUS 5.13b** ★★★

One of the few true sport climbs at Moore's – savor the steepness and exposure! Start 5 feet left of HERCULES, down and right from a large hanging block. Thunder up the insanely steep wall using crimpers and some devious moves past six bolts and one pin. Bolted anchors. (60 ft.)

6 **SEASON IN HELL 5.13c** ★★★

This variation to Zeus adds another bouldery sequence up high. Climb ZEUS up and through the roof crux to the fourth bolt, then trend up and right. Throw big past the next roof, then follow jugs past one more bolt. Traverse right onto easier ground to bolted anchors. Bring a couple of smaller pieces (orange TCU/pink tricam) to use after the second roof. (5 bolts, 60 ft.)

7 **ARMAGEDDON 5.13d** ★★★

Another ZEUS variation, climb SEASON IN HELL to the last bolt, then head straight up and left via side pulls. (5 bolts, 80 ft.)

8 **HERCULES 5.14b** ★★★

The hardest route at Moore's and one of the hardest in the state, this route requires even more strength and better footwork than its mythological neighbor to the left. Start 10 feet left of PYGMALION. Follow seven bolts to bolted anchors. (60 ft.)

The two bolts to the right are for a not yet completed direct start.

9 **DOUBLE DARE 5.13a** ★★

This PYGMALION variation dares to tread left into the steep, intimidating bulge at the fourth bolt. A thin face leads to a roof sequence and a final push to a set of bolted anchors. (8 bolts, 80 ft.)

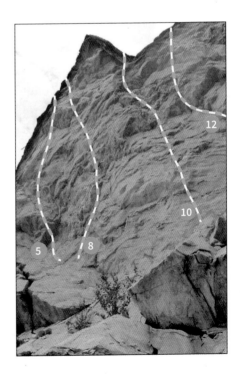

10 PYGMALION 5.12d ★★

Ready to step up your game? Be prepared to get technical – and be on the lookout for the hidden clipping hold. This is the third bolted line left of POOH'S CORNER, just left of STARS AND BARS. Begin in a left-facing dihedral, and follow five bolts to anchors. (60 ft.)

Descend the next six routes by rapping from the STARS AND BARS anchors on the left side of a large ledge.

> *"This route will steal your thunder if your jock strap is loose!"*
>
> *- Seth Tart on LIGHTNING THIEF (5.12c R)*

11 LIGHTNING THIEF 5.12c R

From the start of STARS AND BARS reach out left into an undercling (good gear). Pass through a quartzite band with very little gear, if any, and head for an obvious left leaning 2.5" slot that silhouettes against the sky. Once past the slot, climb the much easier headwall to the STARS AND BARS anchors. Note: This route is easily toproped from STARS AND BARS, which is advisable before a redpoint attempt, due to the seriousness of the fall potential in the quartzite band section.

12 STARS AND BARS 5.12b ★★

One of the more popular lines in the Hanging Garden area, starting just left of POOH'S CORNER. Take a light rack to supplement the three bolts and fixed pin. With a rebel yell, blast through the initial boulder problem, past a low bolt and a pin. From here the holds get better but the pump stays on you as you pass two more bolts and pull over a moderate roof on the way to the top. Bolted anchors. (60 ft.)

13 ARIES 5.12d

Considered a squeeze job by some, this tough line has a powerful boulder problem start that shares start holds with STARS AND BARS. Angle up and right towards PORTER'S POOH. After the last bolt you can join PORTER'S POOH or head straight up. After mantling

Harrison Dekker (aka Conan the Librarian) working ZEUS (5.13b)

the lip traverse left to the STARS AND BARS anchor. (60 ft.)

14 PORTER'S POOH 5.11d ★★★

Once you've ticked POOH'S CORNER, you might want to consider this equally classic, but much more strenuous line. Your forearms might never forgive you, but it will be worth it! Stem and jam up the first 20 feet of POOH'S CORNER, then follow a horizontal crack trending up and left. Head up a ridiculously steep wall where the top is guarded by one send-thwarting crux move. (60 ft.)

15 POOH'S CORNER 5.11b ★★★

One of the best routes at Moore's – a must-do for 5.11 leaders. This wildly overhanging corner is a guaranteed pump-inducer! Start behind two hemlock trees at the right end of the Hanging Garden, beneath an obvious crack/corner system. Slab your way to a shallow right-facing corner, then work your way up to the steep, prominent corner. Grunt

HERCULES is a line that truly lives up to its name. Bolted by Porter Jarrard in 1988, this route didn't meet its match until nearly a decade later when Seth Tart and Howie Feinsilber both climbed the line within one week of each other in September of 1997. Howie found a 5.13d variation (HOWIE'S HERCULES) that goes up and around the crux between bolts 1 and 3, while the original line still remains unrepeated and is now thought to be closer to 5.14b. One of the hardest and most impressive climbs on the East Coast; HERCULES is more than just an everyday sport climb. Perched 150 off the deck in the Hanging Garden, HERCULES offers 80 feet of adventure on an imposing, 120-degree overhanging face. According to writer Chris Huffine in a 1997 issue of Boulder Dash, "HERCULES includes a V10 crux section on open-handed slopers and no feet, topped off by two full lunges to marginal holds, followed by a crimp ladder that puts you two-thirds of the way up before getting a quick rest…but it's not over yet; it's still a sustained crimp ladder to the top that can ruin your day if you lose focus."

past the powerful crux to a well-deserved no-hands rest at a ledge. Climb up and left out the roof via jugs. (60 ft.)

16 COME OUT SWINGING 5.11d R

Start 15 feet right of POOH CORNER, just left of the low roof at the edge of the wall. Pull around the roof into the distinct right-angling crack/seam that leads to a large ledge. Climb off the right side of the ledge onto the imposing headwall above – sparse gear and bouldery moves for about 15 feet will lead to a series of fun roofs. (60 ft.).

The next three routes are located inside the deep, narrow cleft to the right of the Zeus Wall. All are located on the left side of the cleft and can be reached by rappeling from the tree or downclimbing the right-hand wall.

17 SUNSPOT 5.8

Climb the flake and face to the left of BLACK'S ROUTE. (50 ft.)

18 BLACK'S ROUTE 5.11d

The original line climbed the flake, then stepped right to a line of bolts to the top, however the bolts have been chopped. (50 ft.)

19 SOLAR FLARE 5.10a

Follow the flake to a ledge and then climb up and right of BLACK'S ROUTE to the tree. (50 ft.)

20 VOODOO CHILE 5.10d R

This route is located just right of the narrow cleft. Climb the face, angling up and right to a ledge with a tree. (40 ft.)

FIRST IN FLIGHT AREA

This small area is the large, imposing roof on your right as you ascend the gully.

Approach: To reach these climbs, keep heading straight up the gully (don't head left towards POOH's CORNER and the rest of the Garden routes). A fourth/fifth class scramble heads up and right to an exposed ledge beneath the roof. It is also possible to reach these routes by climbing any of the Hanging Garden Gully routes, then traversing left along the ledge.

Descent: These routes all descend via a large tree with fixed slings atop SUPERCRIMP.

21 SUPERCRIMP 5.13c/d

This rarely repeated sport route ascends the monstrous roof system on the right side of the Hanging Garden. Start in a short, left-facing dihedral. Using less-than-super crimps, boulder your way past six bolts to the summit. (40 ft.)

22 FIRST IN FLIGHT 5.12a

Although this line has bolts, bring some extra gear unless you want to take a (long) flight. Start right of SUPERCRIMP. Clip a rusty bolt and take off out the roof past another bolt and fixed pin to the top. Gear belay. 2 bolts, 1 pin. (40 ft.)

23 FIGHT OR FLIGHT 5.11

Just right of FIRST IN FLIGHT, this line cranks out the roof from the obvious left-facing dihedral. Don't fight the exposure unless you want some flight time! 1 pin. Gear belay. (40 ft.)

HANGING GARDEN GULLY

The following four routes are located partway up the Hanging Garden access gully.

Descent: The best descent for the routes in this area is to rappel from the large block atop GNATTY PALE. One 60m rope will get you back into the gully, or double ropes will see you all the way to the ground.

24 DOUBLE OUGHT 5.8 ★

An interesting route that requires concentration and some route-finding skills. Start about 60 feet up the gully, only a short distance before it tops out into the Hanging Garden area. Climb past discontinuous cracks, funky face holds, quartzy crystals and some overhanging rock. Finish on a large ledge underneath an enormous roof. (100 ft.)

25 GNATTY PALE 5.9+ ★★

A relatively new addition to the cliff, this balancy line offers interesting and varied climbing up the face in between HODADICAL MASTER and DOUBLE OUGHT. Start just right of DOUBLE OUGHT. Climb easily to a single bolt. Climb past the bolt (crux) and continue to the roof (the bolted anchor at the top of P1 of HODADICAL will be on your right). Step left and maneuver over the roof, following the clean, pale streak up and through the obvious crack. Pull over a small overhang to a large ledge underneath a giant roof. Take small to medium gear. (110 ft.)

26 HODADICAL MASTER 5.11c

This route (as well as WHIPPING POST) was rap-bolted, which at the time went against the cultural grain - much like the counterculture character this line was named after. Nowadays almost all parties stop after the first pitch (an enjoyable, very un-Moore's like slab.)

P1: Find the bolted line towards the bottom of the Hanging Garden gully. Climb past three bolts to a two-bolt anchor (5.10a, 40 ft.)

P2: Blast out of the overhang past another bolt onto a broken face. (5.11c, 90 feet)

27 WHIPPING POST 5.10a ★

One of the longest routes at Moore's, this one-move wonder starts on a ledge just before the start of the Hanging Garden Gully. Climb past two bolts, the second of which protects the bulge crux. Then enjoy fun, 5.8 face climbing, with a bit of crack thrown in, to a platform with an anchor. (130 ft.)

Seth Tart living up to the name HERCULES (5.14b)

Rob Fogle high atop the Piedmont via PORTER'S POOH (5.11d)

Scott Gilliam repeats his challenging GNATTY PALE (5.9+)

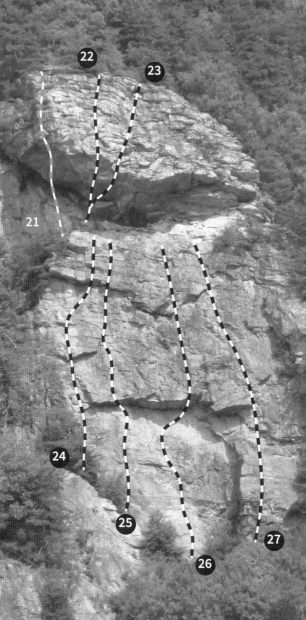

FIRST IN FLIGHT AREA 21-27

Aimee Ahrons tip-toeing up the 5.10a first pitch of
HODADICAL MASTER (5.11c)

INTRODUCTION

And now for something completely different… Stone Mountain is on the opposite end of the spectrum from the vertical to steep quartzite climbing found throughout the rest of the region. This amazing cliff offers sanctuary for those wishing to give their biceps a break in exchange for putting their mental muscles (and calves) to the test. With superb friction climbing that appears to have been hand-delivered from the west coast, Stone offers almost 600 feet of full-value slab paddling through a sea of impeccable granite. But while the highly acclaimed rock quality and unique climbing style might be what puts Stone on the map, it's the jaw-dropping runouts that make it infamous! In fact, the notoriety of the runouts at Stone even gave birth to a unique belay technique – the Stone Mountain Running Belay. Almost everyone who has climbed at Stone has a definite opinion about it – and it's never lukewarm.

LOCATION

Stone Mountain is located 15 miles northwest of Elkin. From I-77, take the exit for US Highway 21 North. Drive for approximately 8 miles, and then turn left onto Traphill Road (there will be a sign for the park). Follow Traphill Road for 4 miles and turn right at the park entrance (John P. Frank Parkway). Continue for another 4 miles, passing the park office along the way, until reaching the parking area by the first restroom on the left.

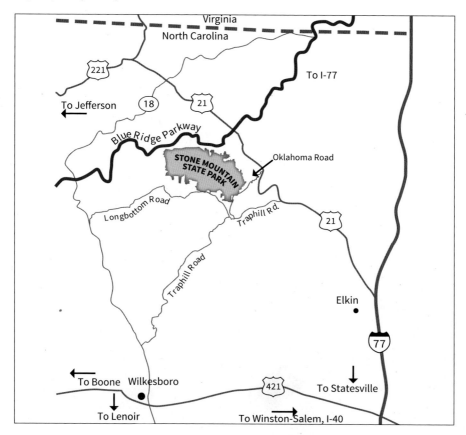

Statements like "Once you go slab, you never go back," and "Friends don't let friends climb slab," are just a few of the many definitive statements you might hear with regard to this area. But whether you're allergic to slab or are a slab fanatic, none can argue the uniqueness of Stone Mountain climbing, as well as its value as a resource to the Piedmont climbing community. Here are just a few of the things that make Stone stand out…

A FRICTION FIX
Stone offers some of the best friction climbing in the country.

A DUAL NATURE
You don't have to head all the way to the west coast if you're down to get your friction on. Because of the style of the climbing it's common for beginners to successfully follow 5.10, but because of bolting ethics, even the easy routes can prove mentally challenging for the leader. This means that climbers of all experience levels are in for an exciting day!

FAMILY FRIENDLY APPROACH
A 5-minute stroll up a gravel road is all it takes to get started on a slab-a-delic journey. The park has many wonderful hiking trails, including a 5-mile loop that goes past a lovely stream, a waterfall, and several spectacular views from the summit of the mountain. As an added bonus, the large field and historical homestead at the base of the cliff can provide a scenic and educational backdrop for any non-climbing family members and/or friends that might be tagging along.

WINTER WONDERLAND
The South Face wallows in the sun making it a wonderful climbing venue when temperatures are too cold for most other locations. Unfortunately, the place can become a furnace even on a mild day when temperatures are in the 60's. While climbers at neighboring crags are blowing on their hands and stuffing hand-warmers in their chalkbags, Stone-masters will be quite comfortable even with temps hovering around freezing, provided the sun is out.

EASY ACCESS
There is plenty of parking, convenient camping, and climbers are on good terms with park staff (Don't give the author cause to retract this statement for the next edition.)

ADVENTURE
I f you want an entire cliff to yourself with steep, stellar routes there are three words for you: The North Face!

Historic Homestead

Kid Friendly

THE CLIMBING SEASON

The premise behind the climbing at Stone Mountain is based almost entirely upon the concept of friction – therefore attempts to climb here during seasons that offer any conditions other than cold and sunny may prove to be futile. In other words, Stone can be a glorious place to be in the winter and at the same time a miserable hellhole in the summer. The one exception is found along the North Face – the all-day shade can make for pleasant climbing during the fall and spring. However, as with all other Piedmont areas, beware of the tangible humidity of the summer, where the granite is guaranteed to be drenched in sweat regardless of the shade factor.

GEAR

Repeat to yourself: "Stone is not a sport crag." Despite the amount of bolts you may see on a topo, this is perhaps the biggest lesson to be learned at Stone with regard to gear. (And keep in mind that while three bolts may not sound entirely unreasonable for one pitch, upon doing the math you'll realize that spaced out across 150 feet means a lot of "no fall territory," which might be a good deal more than your typical sport cragger is bargaining for.) A light rack, a handful of quickdraws (6-8), and a sharp mind-over-matter attitude should be sufficient for most of the routes at Stone. Again, 20-30 foot runouts between bolts are the norm rather than the exception here, but are not given an R or X rating because of the low-angle of the cliff. (That means that when you do see an R or X rating, you'd better take notice, because these lines are very serious.) Climbing above your limit at Stone may mean you wind up losing a lot more than a bail biner, so use good judgment and know your limits.

> "One descent method we would employ on the first or second pitches (not recommended) was to simply hand over hand down the doubled rappel rope, batman style, but not hooked into the harness or anything! Due to the slab angle, it really didn't feel hard or insecure." – pioneer John Provetero (Raleigh, NC)

ACCESS

In addition to the general rules and regulations about climbing in NC State Parks, please remember the following access issues that are specific to Stone Mountain.

DON'T GET WET AND WILD

The mountain is considered closed to climbing whenever the rock is wet. This should not come as a surprise, as wet slab can be likened to a rough neighborhood slip and slide, with far worse consequences than grass stains on your clothes.

NO NEW ROUTES ARE PERMITTED AT THIS TIME.

Stone is basically climbed out – any new routes would be squeeze jobs or very contrived. If you are looking to get your FA on, head elsewhere.

Don't forget to fill out a permit!

YOU DON'T OWN THE CLIFF

Stone can get pretty packed on fair weather weekends, which can cause some traffic problems on some of the classic routes. Be respectful and considerate of other parties above and below you. Remember how blessed you are to be able to climb in such a spectacular setting – enjoy the view while you wait in line with a smile on your face, or else find another route!

PARK FACTS

Stone Mountain State Park is open year-round, weather permitting. The park may be closed during periods of snow or ice and is closed on Christmas Day. If in doubt, call the park for a list of helpful resources that stay up to date. Be sure to be out of the parking lot by closing time. The park opens at 8:00 A.M. throughout the year, closing times are:

- November-February: 6:00 P.M.
- March, October: 7:00 P.M.
- April, May, September: 8:00 P.M.
- June-August: 9:00 P.M.

EMERGENCY SERVICES

For rescues, call the main park number (336) 957-8185 or the county sheriff (336) 838-9111, or 911. The closest hospital is in Elkin – Hugh Chatham Memorial Hospital (336) 835-3722. The hospital address is 180 Parkwood Drive.

GEAR SHOPS

It's best to stock up elsewhere before coming to Stone Mountain, as gear shops are nonexistent. Your best selection is probably going to be in either Winston-Salem or Boone, both about an hour and a half away.

CAMPING

Camping is available year round in the park. There are 88 sites, all of which are equipped with a tent pad, picnic table, and fire ring, and 41 of which also have electrical and water hook-ups for trailers. Drinking water, bathhouses with hot showers, and RV dump stations are also available. There is a limit of 6 people per site, and sites are $20 per day (or $15 for ancient hard persons over the age of 62.) Reservations are highly recommended, but only required for group sites.

Shadows on the South Face

GROCERIES/RESTAURANTS

There are numerous options for food, gas, and ATMs along I-77 in either direction. The country store just outside the park offers miscellaneous camping-related sundries, a small fast food menu, and a surprisingly good selection of ice cream.

A PH.D in FRICTION

Think your slab skills are on par with the Stonemasters of old? Take this "tour de test piece," and work your way up through the ranks. This tick list will walk you through the historically significant lines (most of which are classics) in the order they were established – get through this dirty dozen all on the sharp end and you will be a friction force to be reckoned with…Oh, and for a real comparison with the first ascensionists, all but the last one should be done sans sticky rubber.

- [ ] The Great Arch (5.5)
- [ ] No Alternative (5.5)
- [ ] Grand Funk Railroad (5.9)
- [ ] Indian Lookout (5.8)
- [ ] Rainy Day Women (5.10a)
- [ ] Mercury's Lead (5.9)
- [ ] Pandora's Way (5.9)
- [ ] Electric Boobs (5.10a)
- [ ] The Great Brown Way (5.10c)
- [ ] Bombay Groove (aka Yankee Go Home) (5.10a)
- [ ] Last Dance (5.11c X)
- [ ] The Discipline (5.12a)

THE RUNNING BELAY

As previously mentioned, Stone is the birthplace of the "running belay." Though rarely used, it actually works and is worthwhile to learn. Here's how it works.

Do not anchor the belayer! The belayer must be able to run! If the leader falls, the belayer takes off running through the woods as fast as he/she can. Since falling speed on a slab is significantly slower than through mid-air, the running belayer is able to take up the slack in the system at the same speed as the falling leader, hopefully ending with a catch at the highest piece of protection.

Please note that the running belay doesn't work in every circumstance at Stone - it only works on friction and pitches starting from the ground. Oh yeah, and it won't be too helpful until the leader has clipped into at least one piece of gear.

Drawing reprinted with permission from Dixie Crystals guidebook

BOULDERING

Though for decades climbers walked right past the boulderfield without so much as a passing glance, sometime during the 1990's a handful of committed pebble wrestlers took some initiative and began developing the area – namely Steve Pope, Kenny Hibbits, Eric Zschiesche, Bill Hoadley, Bill Mulvey, Richard Williams, John Provetero, and Jim Horton.

Standout lines can be found on the aptly named Trailside Arête (located just beyond the climber's kiosk), and on and around The Patio Boulder and the Whale Boulder (located down and to the right of the climber's kiosk). Just as with roped climbing, Stone is a great winter destination for bouldering as well. The sloping, slabby features feel fantastic in cool, crisp conditions, and since most of the boulders are free standing, they dry out very quickly after a rain. So if you are looking for a break from the everyday Stone friction fest, bring a pad down to the base and get exploring – there's no guarantee you'll be any less gripped than you would be on the dome, but at least the falls aren't as far!

I think Jim Horton said it best in his Boulderdash article (#29) on Stone Mountain bouldering, circa 2001…

"Hey, ya want to go to Stone Mountain? If you say that to most boulder toads they'll probably look at you like you just asked them to go play 18 holes of golf…Stone Mountain…yes, that's right, the place with all the scary runout slabs. Well, as with any large piece of rock, there are several smaller pieces below it, ripe for the intrepid boulderer…if you're looking for a big jug haul you're going to be sorely disappointed. But if you like slapping your way up sloping arêtes and doing the seemingly impossible you'll find yourself smiling at the top of most of these lines."

Stone Mountain pebble 'wrasslin'

"As the winter season drew to a close I started working a line dubbed Rage. It's one of the hardest lines I've had the pleasure of getting to know…this thing seems to keep building in difficulty until you're standing on top of it. As a matter of fact you might fall off after you're standing on top. One night I was thinking about this problem and actually fell out of the bed. Another time I was telling a friend about it and he fell down. I just hope you're sitting down while you're reading this so you won't take a nasty little tumble yourself. This thing's rough!"

- Jim Horton, on Rage (Boulderdash #29).

HISTORY

The story of Stone Mountain climbing begins long before the advent of modern day sticky rubber. Each first ascensionist had courage, foresight, a mind of steel, and definitely a pair…of semi-sticky Italian high-tops. George DeWolfe and John Thorne got the party started in May of 1965 when they climbed ENTRANCE CRACK to the Tree Ledge. At that time "The Dihedral Crack" (what is now known as THE GREAT ARCH) seemed way out of their league. However, DeWolfe came back towards the end of that summer with Randy Constantine, ready to tackle the line. Their attempt was unfortunately thwarted by heat, humidity, and a bit of dehydration, a heartbreaking 150 feet from the summit. By the time they had a chance to return in the fall, Fess Green and Bill Chatfield had already claimed the FA for their own. Not to be outdone, DeWolfe returned the very next weekend with John Palmer and Robin Wright to establish "Punt Flake" (the line now known as NO ALTERNATIVE), much to the chagrin of their contemporaries. The rest of the 1960's passed quietly by as climbers shuffled in and out of the area, establishing a few new lines, but for the most part repeating what had already been done.

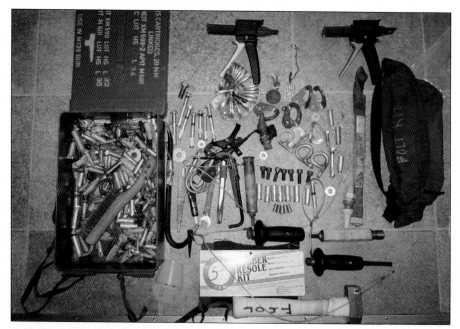

Bolting kit, old school style! (courtesy of Paul "Thor" Pelot)

However, by the time the 1970's rolled around, several FA-hungry hardmen had appeared on the scene – some just passing through, but many were young locals anxious to make their mark. Bob Mitchell and Will Fulton put up the line GRAND FUNK RAILROAD, which held the title of hardest route at Stone for three years. Then, high school student Tom McMillan and Jim McEver's upped the grade with RAINY DAY WOMEN. As the area's first 5.10, RAINY DAY WOMEN was a snapshot of what was to come over the next few years.

NC Hardman Bob Rotert

Other important developments during this time period came from McMillan and his classmate Bob Rotert on their spring break in 1973 (MERCURY'S LEAD, PANDORA'S WAY, and ELECTRIC BOOBS), as well as lines put up by Washington DC climbers Chris Rowins and Chris Kulczycki. None of the locals could deny their strength and skill as they sent longtime projects like THE GREAT BROWN WAY and classic 5.10's such as BOMBAY GROOVE, TEFLON TRIP, and BANANA BREATH, but many looked on their arrival with resentment for "encroaching" on their territory (hence the reasoning behind "YANKEE GO HOME," the alias for BOMBAY GROOVE).

The 1970's also shed some light on the imposing North Face of Stone Mountain, with many bold ascents made by climbers looking for new rock and a place to escape the heat and the crowds of the South Face. The classic INDIAN LOOKOUT was the first line established on the North Face.

A young Paul "Thor" Pelot on the North Face

Climbers then methodically worked their way to the right, ticking off the obvious lines first (STAINLESS STEEL and ZIN SLIDE were among other early ascents), then filling in the gaps over the next decade or so.

Stone received a makeover in the early to mid-1980's with the arrival of Spanish Fire rock shoes as well as a guidebook. Old classics were being downgraded left and right, and new, harder and bolder lines, were spreading like wildfire. After the footwear related frenzy subsided, would-be first ascensionists started running out of room on the mountain, and therefore moved on to other areas. Stone remained in somewhat of a slump, if you will, until the Carolina Climber's Coalition arrived in 1997. Partnering with the state park, a very extensive rebolting project began, which ended up replacing almost

400 bolts and rappel anchors on the South Face of the mountain. In 2009 another rebolting initiative replaced many (but not all) of the bolts on the North Face routes. In addition to improving traffic flow on busy days; this rebolting project also negated the once common practice of sliding stopper cables over hangerless bolts. Nothing was done to remedy the runouts (after all, that's part of the charm!), but there is now an added security in knowing that that bolt catching your 50-footer is gonna hold!

Nowadays Stone is a very popular place midwinter, as young and old climbers alike are rediscovering the wonders (and sometimes terrors) of Southeastern slab climbing at its finest!

THE CLIMBING

Stone offers a host of easy to moderate terrain as well as bold, stout test pieces. Wandering up a giant slab while enjoying fantastic views of the surrounding Piedmont can be a wonderful way to spend a sunny winter day. Ironically, a typical day at Stone carries the potential for providing both a relaxing day of slabbing for the newbie follower, while at the same time a hair-raising, mind-blowing head game for the leader. Almost all of the lines here were established from the ground-up, with the majority of bolts being placed by hand by the first ascent party. On the South Face, only SCIMITAR and BETWEEN THE WAYS were rap bolted. That being said, 20-30 foot runouts are considered well-protected by Stone Mountain standards, and 1-3 bolts spread out over 150 feet of easy terrain is rather commonplace.

"It was an awesome little guide at the time... Dixie Crystals came out about the same time as the first sticky rubber shoes. So with the new info, and much better shoes, we were able to get around pretty good. Stone Mountain was early "sport" climbing for us and it was one of the few places that you could go with just a rack of draws and do a bunch of pitches in one day."

- Mike Grimm (Boone, NC), on the release of Dixie Crystals: A Climber's Guide to Stone Mountain in the early 1980's.

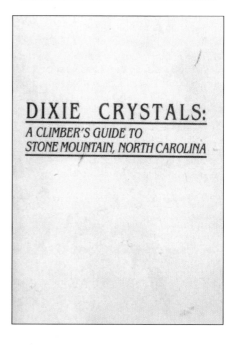

DIXIE CRYSTALS:
A CLIMBER'S GUIDE TO
STONE MOUNTAIN, NORTH CAROLINA

The most notable aspect of this smooth, granite dome is that the rock is almost entirely devoid of features, save a few cracks, the occasional overlap, and a water groove here and there. Smearing on the granite can be likened to climbing on sandpaper – so long as your foot is weighted correctly, there will be plenty of grit to keep you from slipping. Stone is the perfect teacher for climbers interested in learning how to trust their feet. High-stepping, balancy footwork is rewarded here, whereas dynamic displays and lunges to non-existent jugs won't get you very far.

With that in mind, leave your high-performance, down-turned shoes at home. Stone is the place to break out the flat, comfy shoes. And for the full-value effect? In every crux sequence picture yourself without the benefit of sticky rubber on your feet – and marvel at how many classics

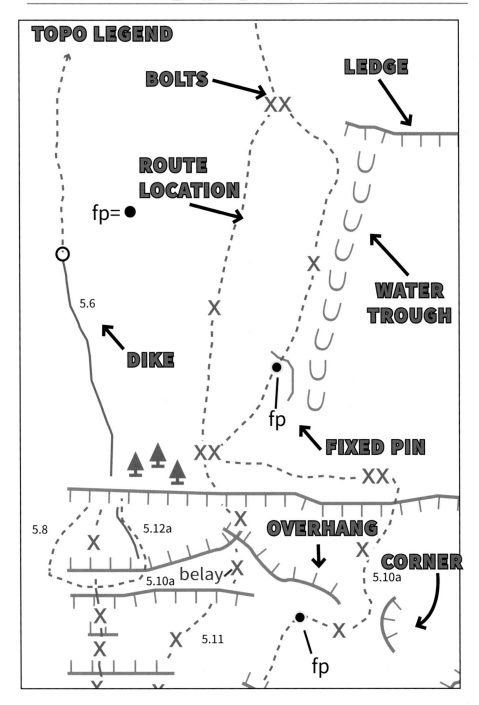

TOPO LEGEND

BOLTS

LEDGE

ROUTE
LOCATION

fp= ●

WATER
TROUGH

5.6

DIKE

fp

FIXED PIN

5.8

5.12a

OVERHANG

CORNER

5.10a

belay

5.10a

5.11

fp

were established in that fashion! Due to the nature of the rock, long leader falls are actually rather uncommon at Stone. However, if you are one of the unfortunate ones, resist the urge to jump out, and instead keep your body close to the rock. You might lose some skin, but you will hopefully save your ankles. Along those lines, long pants are highly recommended when climbing at Stone. More than one climber has been spared a nasty case of rock rash by a good pair of pants. It's also not unheard of to wear kneepads, depending on where you fall on the fashion versus safety convictions spectrum.

"To flow with the granite instead of enforcing your rules on the stone seems to put you in a position for tremendous success! Free your mind and your feet will follow!"

- First Ascensionist Paul "Thor" Pelot

"At Stone, it's all about your head, your heart, and your feet."

- Carl Stearns, in a Stone Mountain feature story in Boulderdash #29,

Climber following the lower start variation on U-SLOT (5.7)

THE SOUTH FACE

The South Face is the hot spot for most of the action at Stone Mountain. Sun drenched rock, stellar routes, lots of moderates, and easy access make this one of the most sought after climbing areas in North Carolina. Routes are characterized mostly by friction climbing that is generally steepest closer to the base of the cliff and gradually backs off towards the summit. Two 60m ropes are necessary to descend from almost all routes.

Parking Area and Restrooms

APPROACH

For all South Face routes, follow the gravel road up to the Hutchinson Homestead then continue along the trail into the large field below the imposing dome. Head across the well-worn trail in the grass to the registration kiosk at the tree line.

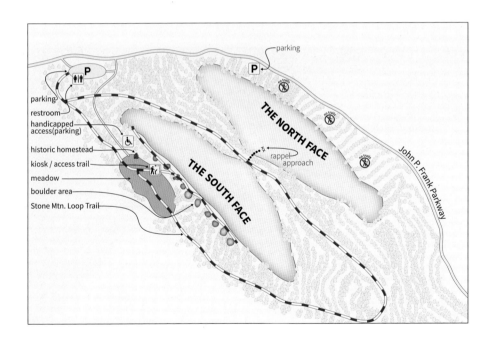

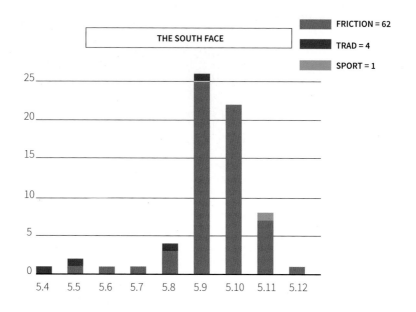

THE SOUTH FACE

FRICTION = 62
TRAD = 4
SPORT = 1

Travis Mabe following on ELECTRIC BOOBS (5.10a)

1 BACK TO SCHOOL 5.9+

P1: This is the left most route on the South Face, beginning left of a large block, below a bolt. Climb up to the first bolt, then traverse right below a lip. At the corner, head up past two more bolts to a bolted belay station. Rap from here or run it out to the top. 3 bolts, bolted anchors. (100 ft.)

2 CAVEMAN 5.10c ★

This route is also the start of the rarely climbed GIRDLE TRAVERSE (aka SPIDERMAN SWINGS SOUTH).

P1: Start on the right side of the cave, on top of a large detached block. Decipher the cruxy start to a bolt, where moderate terrain and another bolt await. Trend up and right to a third bolt, then traverse right over polished rock to belay from a large, sloping ledge known as the First Terrace. 3 bolts, (100 ft.)

P2: Either rappel from the First Terrace, or top out via any of the lines passing that way.

3 REQUIEM TO A DREAM 5.11d

This line should satisfy any hard-core slab addiction. It starts right of the detached CAVEMAN block below a bolt. Two bolts protect delicate 5.11+ climbing. The terrain then backs off somewhat on the way to the third bolt, which is shared with CAVEMAN. Finish traversing right as on CAVEMAN. 3 bolts, (100 ft.)

Variation: An alternate start skips the hard moves right off the deck. From the top of the detached block traverse right to the first bolt.

4 THE DISCIPLINE 5.12a ★

The climbing is unusually steep, the protection is unusually good, but the crux is unusually hard. This aptly named line will require calculated control and willpower.

P1: Start at the diagonal dikes 150 feet left of FANTASTIC. Work your way up the dike past the first bolt and an overlap. Move past 2 more bolts, aiming for the imposing roof up high. Clip a pin and an old bolt, then pull the roof (crux) and follow the dike to a belay on the First Terrace. 4 bolts, 1 pin. (5.12a, 100 ft.)

P2: Follow the dikes up and left to an interesting natural belay utilizing tied off knobs. (5.6, 120 feet)

P3: A casual slab paddle will get you to the top.

Variations: For the less disciplined: Keep following the dike past the third bolt on the first pitch, and pull the roof at another fixed pin left of the original line. (5.11a)

THE INDISCIPLINE – For an unruly 5.8 finish, traverse left along the roof until it ends, then turn the corner and head up to the belay ledge.

Prior to the mid-1990's, climbers shared the cliff with a few rather unlikely mountaineers – a flock of 8-10 feral goats! The herd consisted of one large black male and many white females. A local farmer likely released the goats into the park. These hoofed climbers could easily climb 5.10 and were often seen traversing across the South Face. There were untold numbers of humorous interactions with (human) climbers, until the goats, one by one, passed away from natural causes.

"Let me tell you about the goats! On one weekend, as we topped out, the male walked up to me. With several females watching he suddenly made a little charge and butted me with his horns. The attack was completely unprovoked. The very next weekend he walked up to me again and stood a foot or two away. I was a little pissed about the incident the previous weekend and was determined not to back down; so we had this staring contest that went on for several minutes. Suddenly he reached out his head and bit my thumb. Goat 2, climber 0. It wasn't long after that the goats disappeared. "

Bill Webster (Chapel Hill, NC)

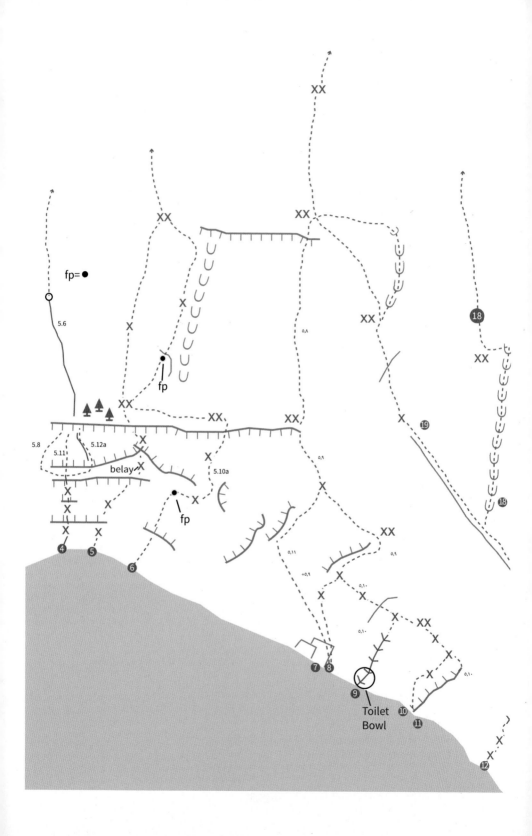

5 HAPPY TRAILS 5.11a ★

(a.k.a. MCGRADY'S ROUTE or DISCO DANCE
OF DEATH)

*Take a light rack for one of the steepest lines at
Stone.*

P1: Just right of THE DISCIPLINE, dance up
the steep face to a bolt just below the right
edge of a small roof. Pull past the roof, clip
another bolt, and make your way to a nice
ledge. Belay from the lone but beefy bolt
drilled into the ledge floor. 2 bolts and a 1
bolt anchor. (5.10a, 60 ft.)

P2: Here comes the tough part…Crank
through the bulge just up from the belay
(5.10) to the base of an intimidating, feature-
less headwall. Take a breath, clip a bolt, and
tackle the crux on your way to the First Terrace and bolted anchors. 1 bolt. (5.11a, 50 ft.)

P3: Continue up, passing one bolt, to a set of
bolted anchors even in height (but left of) the
Second Terrace. 1 bolt. (5.8, 100 ft.)

P4: Scramble up easy terrain or rap from
here.

6 PERMISSION GRANITE 5.10a

Starts 30 feet right of THE DISCIPLINE – this
one needs to be supplemented with gear as
well. This route is seldom done, perhaps due
to its ghetto-like appearance.

P1: Climb a short face, surmount a small
overhang and arrive at a fixed pin. Traverse
right to a bolt, then gain access to the First
Terrace via crux moves in between a pair
of overhangs. Climb past another bolt and
belay at bolted anchors on the First Terrace.
2 bolts, 1 pin. (5.10a, 110 ft.)

P2: Traverse left across the terrace to a bolted
belay station (shared with HAPPY TRAILS).
(5.easy, 120 ft.)

P3: Work your way up the left side of a water
groove, clipping a fixed pin and a bolt along
the way. Unlock the last few tricky moves to
reach the security of the bolted belay (also
shared with HAPPY TRAILS). 2 bolts, 1 pin.
(5.8, 100 ft.)

P4: Scramble up easy terrain or rap from
here.

Left side of the South Face

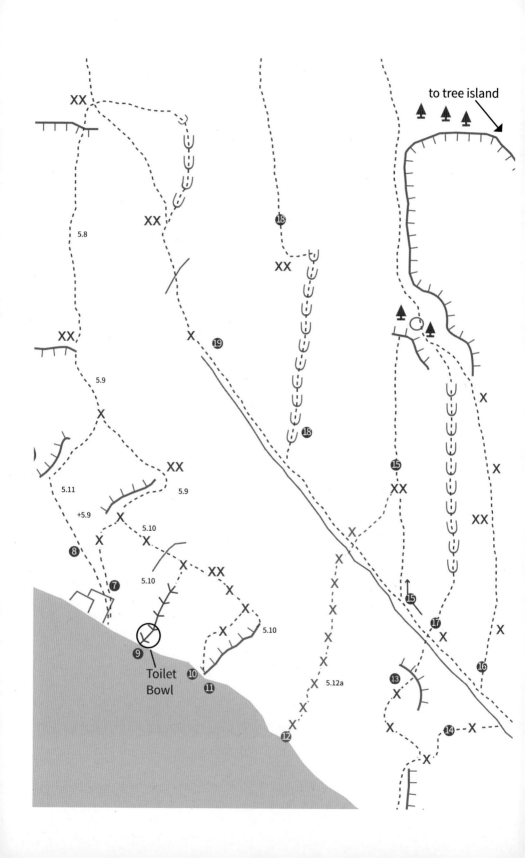

7 FANTASTIC 5.9+ ★★★

This route lives up to its name by offering an amazing array of diversity in just under 500 feet. Definitely a classic, this unique line is filled with hand jams and laybacks, technical face moves, and of course a friction fix. Bring along a medium sized rack – small-medium stoppers and a few cams, as the protection is good, especially where it counts.

P1: Locate the diagonal crack left of FLEET FEET, at two large blocks. Scamper up the block and power up the crack for 30 feet. Bust out onto the sculpted face at the midway point passing 2 bolts and a flexi-flake to a bolted anchor. A fixed stopper once protected the sustained crux, but all that remains now is the head. It's still possible to protect the crux despite the broken stopper. Most parties rap from here. 2 bolts. (5.9+, 90 ft.)

P2: To continue, traverse left and up past one bolt to a bolted belay at the First Terrace. 1 bolt. (5.9, 120 ft.)

P3: Climb past a flake that takes good gear, then up to a bolted belay at the Second Terrace. (5.9, 100 feet).

P4: Follow easier, slabby terrain to a bolted anchor. (5.6, 100 ft.)

P5: Wander off into the woods to finish. (5.easy, 60 ft.)

8 LAST DANCE 5.11c X

Better put on the big boy (or girl) pants for this one. You also better not blow it above the crux on this rarely repeated line.

P1: Start as for FANTASTIC, but don't move onto the face halfway through the crack. Instead stay in the crack for its entirety. Next, move up through the flakes on the left. Tiptoe up the insecure slab to the bolt on the second pitch of FANTASTIC, then head up and left to the anchors on the First Terrace. Very runout above the crux – know your limits. (5.11c, 150 ft.)

P2: Finish on FANTASTIC, or rap here.

View of the Terraces, as seen from FANTASTIC (5.9+)

9 TOILET BOWL 5.10c

Start at a dihedral down the hill (to the right) of FANTASTIC, at a big, green bowl.

P1: Climb the dihedral to a bolt, and traverse left past another bolt, finishing as for FANTASTIC. Alternately, you can move right to the FLEET FEET anchors after the first bolt. 3 bolts. (5.10c, 70 ft.)

P2: Finish on FANTASTIC or rap off.

10 FACE VALUE 5.11d

P1: This is a significantly harder, direct start to FLEET FEET.

Ignore the FLEET FEET flake. Instead opt to climb the face left of the flake. Climb up, and then move right to a bolt. Next, continue on to the bolt just above the end of the FLEET FEET flake. Finish on FLEET FEET. 3 bolts. (5.11d, 70 ft.)

P2: Continue up the FLEET FEET/FANTASTIC combo, or rap off.

11 FLEET FEET 5.10a ★★

This is an excellent route with a well-protected, one move wonder crux – a great option for leaders looking to break into the grade. Most parties just do the first pitch. This line ascends an obvious right-facing flake about 300 feet up and left from BLOCK ROUTE. Take a medium rack.

P1: Follow the flake until it ends at a bolt, then step up and left past another bolt (crux). Traverse along the dike to a bolted belay. 2 bolts. (5.10a, 70 ft.)

P2: Continue angling up and left along the dike toward a bolt. Tiptoe through a smooth section of rock past a bolt, until merging with FANTASTIC at another bolt. 3 bolts. (5.10a, 90 ft.)

P3: Finish on FANTASTIC or rap.

The aptly named TOILET BOWL.

The striking FLEET FEET flake.

13 PEER PRESSURE (5.9+) R/X

Paul "Thor" Pelot and John Barklow atop the North Face, circa 1994

I had always wanted to do LAST DANCE 5.11X, and I decided to give it a go on a Saturday back in 1988. After hiking all the way up there, I realized all of my cams were in the trunk of my car, but rather than hike back down I decided to just go for it.

I climbed the arching crack and placed some stoppers. The climbing was going well, but once the arch became horizontal my stoppers were too small, so I finagled a couple of them up on their side and gave a few tugs, hoping they would hold. After a while the crack disappeared and the climbing got ridiculously hard, so I started to work my way back to my last piece so I could bail. The next thing I knew I was off!

Only wearing a baggy pair of Patagonia shorts, I was rather ill prepared for a fall. I slapped the rock with my arm, which spun me around, disorienting me. I saw my life run through my brain like a movie in a sporadic slide show, and felt the rope get tight for a nano-second as the sideways-placed stoppers put up a weak fight just before they ripped out. I impacted the ledge on my butt; bounced off and tumbled forward, finally coming to a dangling, rag doll stop 50 feet later. Somehow I managed to get my gear back, and after coiling the rope all over my bleeding back and shoulders, we started to hike out. I made it about 30 feet before I got really dizzy and collapsed.

My belayer ran to get help and came back with a farmer, the Ranger, the Mailman, his son and whoever else they could round up, which included a guy with a huge beer belly! I weighed about 200 pounds at the time and knew this was going to be interesting at best. They picked me up and hobbled down the talus field. At one point the big guy sits down to have a smoke, while panting and lamenting how he needs to get in shape in his southern drawl. We finally made it to the ambulance waiting for me in the meadows. Needless to say the ride out was extremely painful!

When we arrived at the hospital, the ER nurse took one look at me and proclaimed, "Those darn crotch rockets get more young guys hurt!" I said, "I fell off Stone Mountain," to which she exclaimned, "So YOU'RE the one…" Amazingly enough, I had gotten out with only a broken tailbone (along with a partially fractured ego, which of course didn't show up on the X-ray!) At least I made the front page on the Winston-Salem Gazette. The headline read, "Virginia Beach Man Falls Off Stone Mountain, and Lives!!!" My days at Stone were classic times to be sure. Though I went on to do almost every other route on the South Face and many of the lines on the North Face, I have yet to return for redemption on LAST DANCE…someday!!

Stonemaster Paul "Thor" Pelot

12 SCIMITAR 5.12a ★★★

This rap-bolted line (cue boo's from the Ethics Police) dares slab aficionados to get their friction on. Though 9 bolts may feel like sport climbing compared to every other route at Stone, don't get lulled into a false sense of security – a badly timed fall before the first 3 bolts will probably end up on the ground.

P1: Locate the bolt line 30 feet right of the FLEET FEET flake. Using faint, vague features and micro-crystals, balance your way past 3 bolts to a small foot rail. Take an opportunity to stretch your calves before embarking on a precarious, insecure journey up to the DREAM WAVES dike. From the dike, angle up and right to bolted anchors. 9 bolts (120 ft.) Descent: Rap down and left to the FLEET FEET anchors, then to the ground (or a 70m will see you down in one rap).

13 PEER PRESSURE 5.9+ R/X

Not the kind of route you hop on because "everybody else is doing it." Although relatively moderate, this route has some pretty serious no-fall zones. Take a light rack and watch out for rope drag.

P1: Start at a low, left-facing corner right of SCIMITAR. Follow the corner to gain a ledge and the first bolt. Angle up and left to the next bolt (don't fall here). Use your friction skills to maneuver up polished rock to another bolt (crux). Continue up and right over an overhang. Follow a water groove to a bolt above the DREAM WAVES dike. Trend up and left along the dike, then tiptoe up to shared bolted anchors at P2 of DREAM WAVES. 4 bolts. (5.9+, 150 ft.)

Descent: Rap from anchors or finish on DREAM WAVES.

Erica Lineberry high-steppin' the ultra-thin SCIMITAR (5.12a)

14 WAHOO START 5.9

This direct start to DREAM WAVES starts the same as PEER PRESSURE. From the small ledge with PEER PRESSURE's first bolt, work up and right, aiming for an overlap/corner with a pine tree. Clip another bolt and traverse right to the anchors atop the first pitch of DREAM WAVES. 2 bolts. Bolted anchors.

> "John Barklow and I did 19 routes in a weekend back in 1992- Two days, Saturday & Sunday until dark. 64 pitches! We would run up a route, down climb THE GREAT ARCH and hit the next one. If our line didn't finish near the Arch we would just run down the trail and head back to the South Face. We started on DIXIE CRYSTALS and worked our way right all the way to GRAND FUNK RAILROAD. I was much younger then, fit as hell, and not to mention VERY comfortable on Stone friction."
>
> – Stonemaster Paul "Thor" Pelot

15 DREAM WAVES 5.9 ★

Start downhill from a large block, just left of a sloping dish. Take a light rack.

P1: Climb straight up to a bolt, then angle up and slightly left to some small flakes. Trend up and right to another bolt, then head up to bolted anchors at a large overlap. 2 bolts. (5.8, 70 ft.)

> "WET DREAMS, ZOO LOVE, and WAHOO START were stout Vince Davis test pieces, all done solo, obviously with dire fall consequences. Dan Hartman and I wanted to bolt them - long after the original "hardmen" had left. Evidently we weren't the only ones, because they eventually were bolted (though not by us). Even with the bolts that were added, these routes are a mental challenge not to be taken lightly! I remember Vince humbly reflecting about those routes atop the South Face summit one day – that was just the way he wanted to climb those routes – for him it was all about the freedom of soloing."
>
> - Stonemaster Paul "Thor" Pelot

P2: Follow the dike that angles up and left past a bolt. Keep following the dike until it is possible to tiptoe up the slab to a set of bolted anchors. You can also clip the first bolt on DIXIE CRYSTALS. This is strongly advised if there is any chance that your second might fall on the initial 5.9 moves. The fall would be enormous. (5.9, 150 ft.)

P3: Climb straight up past a left-facing flake to a ledge with a tree beneath a large left-facing corner. Natural belay. (5.9, 140 ft.)

P4: Climb easy rock just left of the left-facing corner to the top.

16 ZOO LOVE 5.9

This route begins on the DREAM WAVES dike. Take a light rack.

P1: Gain the dike via P1 of DREAM WAVES, or from PEER PRESSURE.

P2: From the first belay of DREAM WAVES, follow the dike up and left, (passing under the first bolt of DIXIE CRYSTALS), until directly beneath a bulge with a bolt. From PEER PRESSURE, climb to the bolt on the dike, then head down and right along the dike until beneath the bulge. Either way, climb up to the bulge, then head up and left to bolted anchors. 1 bolt. (5.9)

P3: Follow the right most water groove to a natural belay just below a large overhang. 2 bolts. (5.9)

P4-5: Finish on DREAM WAVES.

17 WET DREAMS 5.9+ X

A false move in the water groove and your sweet dream ends in a nightmare. Know your limits.

P1: Climb PEER PRESSURE through the third bolt, but instead of following the dike, bust straight up the face to gain a long, unprotected water groove that leads to a ledge with a tree below a large overhang. 3 bolts. (5.9+ X)

P2: Finish on DREAM WAVES.

18 DREAM ON 5.9 R ★★★

P1: Same as DREAM WAVES.

P2: Follow the dike, as for DREAM WAVES. After passing the second bolt on the dike, hang a right at a water groove. Continue to the top of the groove, passing one bolt, then step up to bolted anchors. 3 bolts. (5.9, 150 ft.)

P3: Climb unprotected, low-angled slab to the summit. (5.7, 150 ft.)

19 IMPOSSIBLE DREAM 5.9 ★

Take a light rack.

P1: Same as DREAM WAVES.

P2: Follow the dike until its end. Keep angling left across the slab to bolted anchors. 3 bolts. (5.9, 165 ft.)

P3: From here there are two options. Shimmy up the short water groove, then traverse left to bolted anchors above the Second Terrace, or angle up and left from the belay to the same set of anchors. (5.9, 150 ft.)

20 DIXIE CRYSTALS 5.9 ★★

Sweeter than sugar, this crystallized adventure is one of Stone's finest! Bring a light rack that includes a 4" piece.

P1: Same as DREAM WAVES.

P2: Head up to the obvious hole known as The Navel and finagle some tricky pro. Continue up to a bolt, negotiate a few hard, but well-protected moves, then run it out to a bolted anchor. 1 bolt. (5.9, 100 ft.)

P3: Angle up and slightly left, passing one bolt, some significant runout, and a bit of flaky rock to bolted anchors. 1 bolt. (5.9, 100 ft.)

P4: Continue straight up past one bolt and make for the trees. (5.7, 100 ft.)

P4 Variation: Another option of similar difficulty angles up and left to the base of an overhanging corner. Sling a tree for pro and continue up to the summit.

The following routes are located on the apron below the Tree Ledge and can be used as approach pitches for routes starting from the Tree Ledge. They can also make for a nice day of single-pitching. Descend these routes by rapping from any of the Tree Ledge rap stations (see topo.)

"Depending on which way you go, you may or may not get gear to supplement the bolts. Also, you may find the route harder or easier than 5.9. As for me, I like the path of least resistance and most protection."

- Scott Gilliam (Raleigh, NC), on the right "way" to do WHITE WAY DIRECT

21 WHITE WAY DIRECT 5.9 ★

A lesson in crystal pinching, which will come in handy for those going all the (Great White) Way.

Start at the diagonal dikes uphill (left) from BLOCK ROUTE, in a steep, rocky drainage.

Move up past the dikes to a flake followed by a bolt. Make a heady traverse up and right to another bolt, where easier terrain is waiting to escort you to the leftmost edge of the Tree Ledge. Belay at a tree. 2 bolts. (90 ft.)

22 BLOCK ROUTE 5.8 ★★★

Probably the best protected option for accessing the Tree Ledge. Take a light rack. These days this is one of the most popular routes for reaching the Tree Ledge, so be prepared to wait in line.

Start below a grassy seam/crack on the left edge of the apron. Follow the crack, passing a tree and some bolted anchors 40 feet up. (As long as you have a 60m rope there is no reason to stop here aside from clipping into one of the bolts for pro.) Continue up the face via some funky scoops and dishes to a left-facing corner along the overlap that spans the entire apron. Next comes the one-move wonder crux, which can take as much protection as you want. As gracefully as you can, flop and roll onto the face, and retreat to the trees on the ledge. Natural anchor. (5.8, 140 ft.)

A climber aims for the U-SLOT (5.7)

23 U SLOT 5.7 (5.4 R) ★★★

Now that ENTRANCE CRACK has lost some of its appeal among the masses, this route may take the prize as most popular line to access the Tree Ledge. There are several variations, all featuring good gear at the crux, and a significant runout along easy ground.

Locate a left-facing corner system on the left side of the apron. Either climb up the corner (original line), or right of it on top of the feature (variation), until the crack ends. From here the original line heads up and right along the slab towards a diminishing, scooped-like section in the overlap, then continues straight up to a set of bolted anchors just below the Tree Ledge. A second option traverses up and left from the end of the crack along a dike, aiming for a small notch in the roof. Pull the roof with a couple of eye-opening moves, and finish in the trees. (5.7, 150 ft.)

The following three routes converge at the Tree Ledge to a shared anchor. It is fairly easy to make quick toprope work of these lines, but be sure to clip in to the upper bolts as directionals to protect against unnecessary pendulums, and also be sure that your belayer has experience passing a knot, as these lines are too long to toprope with one rope, even a 70m.

24 CRYSTAL LIZARD 5.8+ R ★★

Significantly more runout than other Tree Ledge approaches of similar difficulty, but fairly featured. Mid-size gear can reduce (but not eliminate) the runout between the first and second bolt.

Start right of U-SLOT below some pods with trees growing out of them. With the trees on your left, climb up to a bolt that seems a little out of the way to get to (but it will keep you out of the trees if you fall). Next, pinch your way up the vertical crystals to reach the overlap, passing another bolt along the way. Once past the overlap, continue up to the Tree Ledge and the RICE KRISPIES anchor. 2 bolts. (140 ft.)

25 RICE KRISPIES 5.10c R/X ★

A false move above the crux and you'll hear your ankle go "snap, crackle, pop" when you hit the ground. Though the tiny granite granules may be reminiscent of the namesake kid's cereal, don't bite off more than you can chew. A very scary lead or a casual toprope – your choice.

Start right of CRYSTAL LIZARD, underneath a small bowl-like feature. Climb directly up to the bowl where you can attempt to build a marginal nest of gear (some swear by a taped hook). Continue up the steep, grainy slab (past evidence of a chopped retro-bolt job) to an overlap. Finish straight up on easier terrain to bolted anchors. Bring small gear. (140 ft.)

"I remember walking up to CAPTAIN CRUNCH and there were three superfit guys roping up, so I stood there and chatted it up. This was their first visit to Stone, but the leader assured me that he was an avid gym climber and led 5.13. I tried to warn them that friciition was a different game, more like imaginary holds, and a lot of smearing. To flow with the granite instead of enforcing your rules on the stone seems to put you in a position for tremendous success! All the parties I rescued over the years had one thing in common, the leader was frozen! I watched him peel about 10 times slapping up the rock and swearing before I offered to rope up and lead it. He said, "Yeah I gotta see this," and handed me the sharp end. I led through without slipping and tried to give instruction along the way. He was livid, but also a lot more humble after seeing an old man with a beer gut power through the crux without any problems." Paul "Thor" Pelot

26 CAPTAIN CRUNCH 5.11a R/X ★

So named for the ground fall taken when the first ascensionist accidentally stepped on his hammer while drilling the second bolt. Another heady friction challenge that is set up well for a headpoint. If leading, use a running belay; it will hopefully keep you off the ground in the event that you blow the crux.

Start 30 feet right of CRYSTAL LIZARD, at a black water streak. Follow the water streak on a steep slab past three bolts. A tricky bulge move is waiting for you before the more moderate bit to the shared anchor with RICE KRISPIES. Bring a few cams for the overlap at the top. 3 bolts. (140 ft.)

27 FUDDY MUCKER 5.9+ (a.k.a. DECEPTION CRACK)

This route has become so vegetated that it may not be possible to climb it anymore without gardening tools. The crack appears to be completely closed off with dirt and vegetation. With acres of stellar clean granite everywhere it might be best to simply let Mother Nature reclaim this one.

Locate the crack 40 feet right of CAPTAIN CRUNCH. Climb the obvious, vegetated crack that trends up and left, stepping over the large tree limb about a third of the way up the route. Once you hit the group of pine trees, head up and right to a small clearing. Try to

Bill Webster eyes down the big runout on CAPTAIN CRUNCH (5.11a)

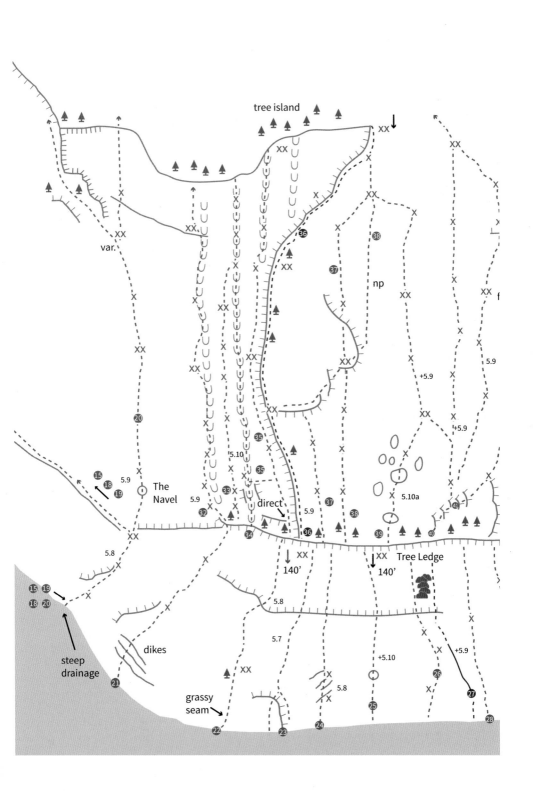

tree island

var.

The Navel

20

15 18 19   5.9

5.10

35

35

33

32

direct

34

36

36

37

38

np

+5.9

+5.9

5.10a

41

5.9

f

39   40

Tree Ledge

XX 140'   XX 140'

5.8

15 19
18 20

steep drainage

dikes

21

grassy seam

22   23   24   25

5.8

5.7

5.8

+5.10

26

27   28

+5.9

keep the copious amounts of plant debris out of your belayer's eyes. Belay at a large pine adjacent to the clearing. Double-rope rappel from RICE KRISPIES anchor. (140 ft.)

28 WOSL 5.9 R

Start just right of the FUDDY MUCKER at a dark water stain. Head directly up to the Tree Ledge passing one bolt along the way. A few small cams can provide some protection before the lone bolt, but a fall near the top is groundfall guaranteed. Another good candidate for the running belay. 1 bolt (140 ft.)

Variation: A slightly more protected start begins at FATHER KNOWS BEST and traverses left at the top of the crack.

29 FATHER KNOWS BEST 5.9

This is the bolted line just left of ENTRANCE CRACK. If toproping, be aware that this is a popular descent route. Please rig your toprope so that other parties can still rappel down. Start in the small crack just left of the bolt line, and then romp your way up past two bolts to bolted anchors. 2 bolts (130 ft.)

ENTRANCE CRACK

30 ENTRANCE CRACK 5.4 R/X

This was once the most popular way to gain the Tree Ledge. Though many new climbers at Stone still make their grand entrance via this route, these days it seems more climbers prefer U SLOT or BLOCK ROUTE. Start at the obvious hand crack on the far right side of the apron below the Tree Ledge. Follow the crack to a pine tree, then head up the offwidth crack to the Tree Ledge. Take a light rack for the hand crack, but unless you're packin' big bros be prepared for quite the runout in the offwidth section. (130 ft.)

We had "toprope trained" at Crowder's and thought we were ready. We roped up with one rack of cow bells and nuts, a 120 foot army no-stretch kernmantal and one 150 foot climbing rope. After leading ENTRANCE CRACK with chimney technique that can only be described as awful, our party of 3 proceeded to securely wedge our rucksack deep inside the ENTRANCE CRACK when we tried to haul it up. Now back in 1979 Stone was not a huge attraction, but even then we made a scene shutting down the main entryway to the Tree Ledge. Bound and determined, we managed to free the bag and make our way successfully to the top of Stone Mountain via THE GREAT ARCH, but not without creating a spectacle. Total epic time: 6 hours.

– Frank Orthel, on his first experience at Stone

FATHER KNOWS BEST - *This route's name came partially from FA Paul "Thor" Pelot's father, who was a firm believer in the Bosch Bulldog that he kept in his basement. During Pelot's first FA attempt to equip this line, he spent three hours on a small eyebrow with a Star masonry bit, eventually cramping his calf so badly that he now has permanent scarring. He later returned on his 27th birthday with 5.10 drills and made quick work of the bolts by hand. At one point he was advised by "a preppy-looking guy" to leave it without the last bolt, because "Who needs bolts?!?" When Pelot returned to the line a few hours later after grabbing lunch, he just smiled and shook his head as he saw the preppy trash-talker bailing over on ENTRANCE CRACK.*

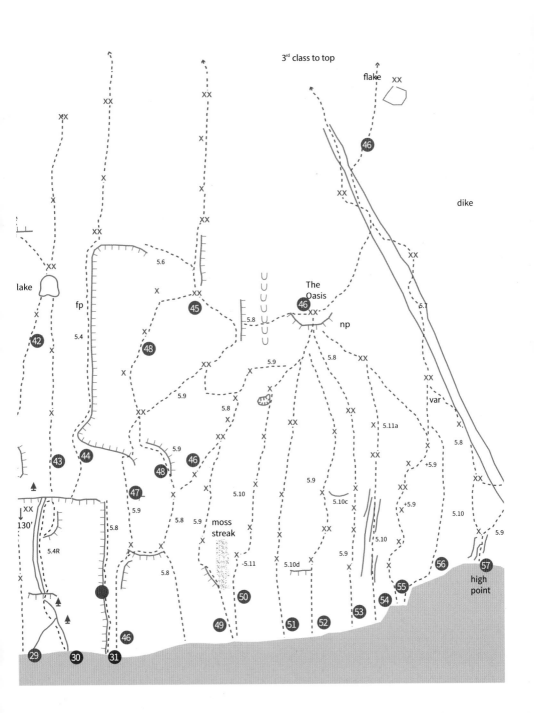

3rd class to top

flake

dike

The Oasis

lake

fp

5.6

5.4

5.8

np

5.7

var

5.9

5.8

5.11a

5.8

+5.9

5.8

5.9

5.9

5.10c

+5.9

5.10

5.10

5.9

5.9

5.10

5.9

moss streak

5.8

5.9

5.8

-5.11

5.10d

5.9

130'

5.4R

5.8

5.8

high point

42

43 44

48

45

46

48

46

47

46

29 30 31

49

50

51 52

53

54

55

56 57

Luke Howard cruising the upper section of BOMBAY GROOVE (5.10a)

Stephanie Gilliam cruising BOMBAY GROOVE (5.10a)

31 DIRTY CRACK 5.8+ ★

Climbs a lot better than it sounds, the first ascensionist even called it "Squeaky Clean" for a while! This line follows the obvious corner system past a couple of well-timed trees to the Tree Ledge. Take a variety of gear for the well-protected crack that thins out towards the top. (130 ft.)

The next dozen routes begin atop the Tree Ledge, which is the very large ledge riddled with (you guessed it) trees in the center of the South Face. It can easily be identified from the field at the base of the cliff. All routes in this section top out, though many parties choose to climb only the first pitches. Please be considerate of other parties on busy weekends and don't create traffic jams – if you're not headed to the top, let other climbers play through.

32 GREAT WHITE WAY 5.9 ★★★

They say groove is in the heart – and this one will surely get yours pumping! Locate the leftmost of two water grooves left of The Great Arch.

P1: Slab up the face near the left side of the left hand water groove past two bolts. Next, get into the groove for another two bolts. 4 bolts to bolted anchors. (5.9, 110 ft.)

P2: Keep following the water groove past one bolt, then run it out to a bolted station. 1 bolt. (5.9, 110 ft.)

P3: Continue to get your groove on along easier terrain all the way to the trees. (5.6, 50 ft.)

33 BETWEEN THE WAYS 5.10c ★★

This aptly named squeeze job lies sandwiched between "the ways." This route and SCIMITAR are the only two rap bolted lines at Stone.

P1: Start beneath the obvious bolt line between the two water grooves left of the GREAT ARCH. Smear and pinch your way up microcrystals on the steep wall for three bolts, then relax a bit as the angle backs off for the last

three bolts. 6 bolts. Bolted anchors. (5.10c, 165 feet).

P2: Move up and right to the first bolt on P2 of GREAT BROWN WAY, and follow the water groove to the top. 1 bolt. (5.9, 130 feet)

34 GREAT BROWN WAY 5.10c ★★★

After numerous failed attempts by locals, this route was one of a handful of routes nabbed by visiting climbers in the late 1970's. This route climbs the dark water groove just left of the Great Arch. Bring a light rack.

P1: Climb past some flakes to the first bolt. Finesse your way up surprisingly steep rock to the second bolt. Next, breathe a sigh of relief as you cruise the groove to the bolted anchors just right of the groove. 2 bolts (5.10c, 120 ft.)

"When I first started to climb at Stone in the 1970s the only climbing shoe available were EBs. I worked my way through the grades until I got to BROWN WAY. I took maybe 30 falls on the bulge until finally the shoes held and the right crystals were properly massaged. As soon as sticky rubber climbing shoes came on the scene I returned to BROWN WAY and easily walked it. The change in boot technology with the introduction of sticky rubber was nothing short of revolutionary; especially in friction climbing areas such as Stone. This example should make modern climbers pause and think about all of those first ascents that were put up on the lead with pre-sticky rubber shoes and hand drilled bolts, usually from tiny stances."

Bill Webster (Chapel Hill, NC)

"I saw Jess Tucker solo BROWN WAY once. Now you got your ass on the line on that one!!! One slip and its 'lights out!' I soloed all the routes above the Tree Ledge, but if you slip on those you just slide down and break both your ankles – slide off BROWN WAY and you're gone!"

Paul "Thor" Pelot

> *"My son Henry and I had our own adventure on THE GREAT ARCH when he was only 10, and I have to admit that it scared the crap out of me. I was leading the first pitch, with a pack on and a 10 year old belaying me. The crack was wet, full of leaves, and at one point I really thought I was going to pitch off. This was pretty ironic considering my climbing partners and I used to routinely downclimb solo the Arch to get off of the top, and here I was thinking I was going to fall on lead. I got it together and we had a great climb. And I will never forget how good that post-climb Coca-Cola tasted out of the parking lot vending machine!"*
>
> *- Mike Grimm (Boone, NC), co-owner of Misty Mountain Threadworks*

P2: Keep groovin' past three generously spaced bolts all the way to the trees. Keep an eye out for crumbly rock in a few sections. 3 bolts (5.9, 150 ft.)

㉟ BOMBAY GROOVE 5.10a ★★★ (a.k.a. YANKEE GO HOME)

Ascending the arête above the Great Arch, this line offers a very unique and exposure-filled vantage point of the South Face – it's especially wild if there is another party on the GREAT ARCH. The second name shows how well the visiting first ascensionists were received by some of the locals. Bring a light rack.

P1: Start the same as GREAT BROWN WAY. Maneuver up through the flakes to the shared first bolt. Instead of slabbing up, make a heady traverse out right towards the arête. Layback the arête past an additional bolt, then step left to the shared bolted anchors on GREAT BROWN WAY. (5.10a, 120 ft.)

P2: Move up and right to a bolt at the base of a water groove. Get into the groove and head directly up, passing one more bolt along the way. Belay at the first set of bolted anchors, or clip it for pro and keep climbing to another set at the top. (5.9+, 150 ft.)

Note: A 70m rope can make it from the top back down to the Tree Ledge in 3 raps.

A party on the classic GREAT ARCH (5.5)

Brian Payst starting out on the classic GREAT WHITE WAY (5.9)

36 THE GREAT ARCH 5.5 ★★★

This enormous, clean dihedral is perhaps the most striking line in all of North Carolina climbing; reminiscent of features found in the high Sierra. Superb laybacking at a friendly angle and gear options galore make this mega-popular route worth ticking for new and experienced leaders alike. This route will usually have a constant line during the Stone season. Bring a full rack if you want to sew it up, or a light one if you're comfortable at the grade.

Start at the obvious, enormous, right-facing dihedral on the left side of the Tree Ledge.

P1: Make your way to the corner (crux), and follow the crack to a bolted belay. (5.5, 130 ft.)

P2: Keep moving up the corner (thinner this time) to a bolted belay station on the face. (5.5, 100 ft.)

P3: Keep on arching up the dihedral as it leads to the Tree Island (5.4, 150 ft.)

Double-rope rap, or scramble to the summit and hike off to the left.

> *"On my first trip to Stone, Jess Tucker was soloing MERCURY'S LEAD with nothing but some Hawaiian print shorts and a chalkbag with some old flip flops clipped to the side. He took one look at me over on THE GREAT ARCH with my Yosemite rack and said "Hey you got any 'sticker shoes'?" I nodded and lifted up my brand new Fires. Jess responded, "Throw all that gear in your trunk, get some draws and go to WHITE WAY!" Watching him solo was like nothing I can explain, like a dance more than a climb, so fluid and purposeful, every movement planned in advance. If it weren't for Jess I may have never made Stone my home for years. From that point on I was hooked on Stone friction and I never looked back. I drove down from VA Beach every weekend I could, and put over 100,000 miles on an old Hyundai Excel."* -
>
> *Paul "Thor" Pelot, on meeting Stone Mountain legend Jess Tucker*

37 MERCURY'S LEAD 5.9 ★★

So named because the first ascensionist wished he had wings on his feet at certain points along this sustained, heady line. This is the first bolted line encountered right of

A busy day on the South Face – climbers on THE GREAT ARCH (5.5), and MERCURY'S LEAD (5.9)

THE GREAT ARCH, and a great way to whip your mental muscles into shape.

P1: Follow the pattern of small, but consistent sloping mini-edges past two bolts. Keep your head together during the runout to the anchors as you high-step through the crux to easier terrain. Upon reaching the foot rail and left-facing flake, breathe a sigh of relief and either continue up and right to the STORM IN A TEACUP anchors, or traverse directly left to the anchors atop Pitch 1 of THE GREAT ARCH. 2 bolts. (5.9, 120 ft.)

P2: Work your way across the slab past STORM IN A TEACUP, then past a leftward-leaning diagonal feature (J hook) to a bolt. Balance up to one more bolt and anchors on the right. (5.7, 150 ft.)

P3: Finish along easy terrain to the Tree Island (5.4, 60 feet).

38 STORM IN A TEACUP 5.10a ★★★

This line climbs to the left of the large circular white spots easily visible from the field below. Bring a light rack if you decide to venture into the crack at the top of P1.

P1: Climb straight up past three bolts to a belay at the base of the J hook. 3 bolts. (5.10a, 150 ft.)

P2. Continue and finish at anchors to the right of THE GREAT ARCH. (5.8, 90 ft.)

The landmark white circular spots of RAINY DAY WOMEN

P3. Follow easy rock to the tree island. 1 bolt. (5.4, 60 ft.)

39 RAINY DAY WOMEN 5.10a ★★★

Stone's first 5.10 is a worthy opponent for the Stone leader looking to break into the grade.

P1: Start directly below the right-most of the white circular spots in the middle of the Tree Ledge. High step your way up the slab past one bolt, then trend up and right past another bolt to a bolted anchor. 2 bolts. (5.10a, 90 ft.)

P2: Head straight up to a single bolt, then angle up and slightly left to another bolted anchor. 1 bolt. (5.9, 100 ft.).

P3: Climb up to a lone bolt, then make a sharp turn left and slightly up to the bolted anchors shared with MERCURY'S LEAD and STORM IN A TEACUP. 1 bolt. (5.7, 110 ft.)

P4: Keep on scrambling to the tree island (5.4, 60 ft.)

40 BANANA BREATH 5.10a ★★

This bold line starts 20 feet right of RAINY DAY WOMEN. The long first pitch makes for a sustained mental game.

P1: Start at the flakes at the center of the Tree Ledge, and climb up to a high first bolt. Tip-toe up and slightly left past two more bolts. Belay off of a single bolt (fourth bolt). 3 bolts, 1 bolt anchor. (5.10a, 120 ft.)

P2: Continue straight up past two more bolts to the P2 belay of YARDARM. (5.9, 150 ft.)

P3: Scramble left to the Tree Island, or romp up to the South Face summit.

41 ADRIFT 5.9 ★

Another fun slab climb, similar in style and difficulty to MERCURY'S LEAD.

P1: Start the same as for BANANA BREATH, but at the first bolt angle up and right past two more bolts to a bolted anchor just left of the YARDARM flake. 3 bolts. (5.9, 150 ft.)

P2: Head up towards the overlap and the first

bolt on P2 of YARDARM. Follow YARDARM to its anchors. (5.8, 150 ft.)

42 YARDARM 5.8- ★★

An exciting introduction to friction climbing, this route often has a queue of eager slab-sters-in-training. Small cams can reduce the runout to the very high first bolt. Take care that your shoes remain clean, as there are sections of flakey crystals that can interfere with good traction on the rock.

P1: Start 20 feet right of BANANA BREATH at some low flakes. High-step it up and right to the first bolt about 30 feet off the deck. Then steel yourself for quite a runout on easier, featured terrain up and right along a water drainage to a bolted belay atop a flake. 2 bolts. (5.8, 150 ft.)

P2: Continue up and left passing a few overlaps and a bolt. The difficulty backs off a good deal on the way past a second bolt to another bolted belay shared with BANANA BREATH. 2 bolts. (5.8, 150 ft.)

P3: A casual romp leads to the South Face summit. Alternately, if you'd like to get back down to the Tree Ledge for a different route, you can traverse to rap stations on either the left or the right.

43 CLOSER TO THE HEART 5.9 ★

This line provides stellar position right in the heart of the South Face, although the runout to the first bolt may find you closer to a break-down than anything else!

P1: This is the bolted line just left of the NO ALTERNATIVE flake. Climb directly up, aiming for the high bolt on the face. Continue up to another bolt a long way off, and make your way straight up to the bolted anchors atop YARDARM. 2 bolts. (5.9, 150 ft.)

P2: Trend slightly right and up to a single bolt above some small overlaps, then head straight up to bolted anchors. Be mindful of a few sections of flaky rock. 1 bolt. (5.8, 150 ft.)

P3: Keep slabbin' your way up to the summit.

44 NO ALTERNATIVE 5.5 ★★★

This line is a great alternative to THE GREAT ARCH. The first pitch is a mirror image (though much smaller) of its neighbor on the other side of the Tree Ledge. Bring a light rack with gear to 3 inches.

P1: Start at the obvious left-facing corner on the right side of the Tree Ledge, and follow the flakes and corner system to a bolted belay atop the flake. (5.4, 175 ft.)

P2: Proceed straight up to a bolt 75 feet up from the belay, passing a few small overlaps that will accept small gear along the way. After the bolt, the angle lessens, along with the difficulty. 1 bolt, bolted anchors. (5.5, 150 ft.)

P3: Exit to the trees on easy, low-angle terrain.

There's NO ALTERNATIVE (5.5) but to enjoy this classic!

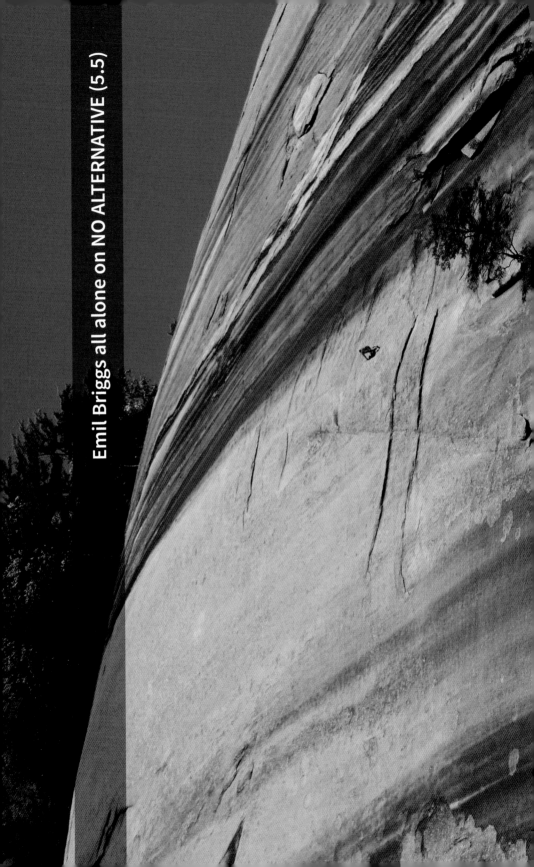

Emil Briggs all alone on NO ALTERNATIVE (5.5)

Is it possible to get hurt at Stone Mountain?

A cautionary tale.

Despite the sometimes terrifying runouts at Stone, how many people have you actually met that have been seriously injured in a fall? The answer is most likely - zero. It can happen, though usually not like the following, somewhat bizarre double-header. Sometime back in the 1990's I met two friends at Stone. The man, (let's call him "Joe") was working in Georgia. And the woman (we'll lend the name "Mary") was in Philadelphia. During his one week off they decided to meet in North Carolina for climbing and hiking. We all met in the parking lot and after a brief round of hugs and kisses took off for the cliff. Joe wanted to start with MERCURY'S LEAD. I was talking to Mary as Joe took off up the route. At some point I looked up and saw that for some reason he had started to go off route after the first bolt. At that time the bolts on STORM IN A TEACUP were only a dream. I warned him that he was off route with no hope of protection. He started to traverse back to the route, but suddenly he was off! As he started the long slide toward the Tree Ledge I yelled at Mary to run. This was meant to be the old Stone Mountain running belay, which, if done properly, can shave many feet off of an otherwise huge slide. Note the condition "if done properly". For some reason Joe had tied Mary directly into a tree, with a very long bit of slack between the tree and his girlfriend. Just enough it turns out for her to get up a good head of steam running before she hit the end of the sling. She suddenly jerked to a halt and swung down off the narrow ledge, crashing into a tree. Meanwhile Joe slid for about 50 feet with the palms of both hands firmly pressed against the wall. The fall was surrealistic - as he went down, the slide actually slowed until he came to a complete stop a few feet above the ledge. At first all seemed well until the casualty reports started to come in. Mary, it turns out, broke two ribs hitting the tree. The palms of both of Joe's hands looked like they had been scalped. The skin had separated near the wrist and had rolled up into two neat little tubes of flesh near the base of the fingers. I thought at the time that they looked like the neatly rolled up lids of two freshly opened sardine tins. The next day we met in the parking lot for a second time. She was in pain just breathing and he had both hands swaddled in huge bundles of bandages like hand mummies. Misery abounded. So folks it is possible to hurt yourself at Stone. It's rare but can be done. Just because it's Stone don't lose your focus. Be careful out there.

–Bill Webster (Chapel Hill, NC)

45 ANCHOR RODE 5.6

This non-descript traversing route serves as a connector between The Oasis and the belay station on the first pitch of NO ALTERNATIVE. Can be combined into one pitch, but be mindful of rope drag.

P1: Make your way to The Oasis however you see fit.

P2: Traverse left across the water groove to the anchors below the left-facing corner on pitch 2 of AUTUMN SPEAKS. (5.6)

P3: This short pitch angles up and left over lower-angle terrain to the bolted anchors atop the NO ALTERNATIVE flake (5.6)

Descent: Rap from NO ALTERNATIVE anchors.

All of the routes on the right side of the South Face either top out or funnel together at a large, sloping dish referred to as The Oasis. Bring your approach shoes if you're planning to hike off the summit. If you want to squeeze in a few more pitches after topping out, walk left to the anchors atop NO ALTERNATIVE to rappel down to the Tree Ledge. For routes ending at The Oasis, the most direct rap lane is STRAWBERRY PRESERVES.

46 THE PULPIT 5.8 ★★★

Protected better than most routes at Stone, this moderate classic should not be missed! This line offers more variety and interesting terrain than the typical Stone slab route. Bring a light rack with mostly small pieces.

P1: Start at the obvious, left-facing flake that angles up and slightly right. Follow the flake, then venture onto the slab and head right onto a large, sloping ramp with a bolt. Traverse right along the ramp (passing another bolt). Next, climb up a shallow but fairly featured groove to another bolt. Angle up and right past a fourth bolt to bolted anchors. 4 bolts, bolted anchors (5.8, 160 ft.)

P2: Smear up for about 60 feet, passing two bolts. Hang a left at the second bolt and start traversing until you are directly below the anchors (remnants of an old fixed pin can serve as a waypoint). Featured climbing in rolling scoops will deposit you at bolted anchors. 2 bolts, bolted anchors. (5.8, 120ft.)

P3: Climb diagonally up and right along easy terrain passing a shallow left-facing corner that will take gear. Step right over a water

groove (which can be rather exciting when wet), and traverse over to a large dish-like feature known as The Oasis. (5.8, 150 ft.)

P4: Climb up and right to join up with the "tracks" of GRAND FUNK RAILROAD. Follow the large parallel dike system to GRAND FUNK's anchors, but then continue straight up to the large flake for which THE PULPIT was named. Finish at bolted anchors above the flake (5.8-, 180 ft.)

P5: Meander up low-angle rock to the summit. (180 ft.)

47 HOOK AND BLADDER 5.9

Climb up to the first bolt on THE PULPIT, but instead of traversing right, head straight up, keeping left of the brown water streak. Keep climbing past a narrow black dike, ending at the shared bolted anchors with AUTUMN SPEAKS. 1 bolt, bolted anchors. (5.9, 160 ft.)

48 AUTUMN SPEAKS 5.9 ★

Named after the park ranger's daughter back in the 1980's. A diverse line that offers spicy runout friction as well as gear-laden crack climbing. Bring a light rack with small to mid-size gear.

P1: Start the same as for THE PULPIT, but instead of moving right at the third bolt, angle up and left, following a curving flake. Next, continue straight up to bolted anchors. 3 bolts. (5.9, 120 ft.)

P2: Zig up and left to a bolt, then zag back right past two more bolts. At the third bolt, traverse right to a set of bolted anchors below a left-facing corner. 3 bolts. (5.9, 140 feet).

P3: Follow the corner up slabby terrain to a bolted anchor (5.5, 80 ft.)

P4: Climb a direct line above the belay past two bolts to bolted anchors. 2 bolts. (5.9, 100 ft.)

Scramble up to the summit or rap off.

This route engulfs a route that was called BOTANY 10, which was a 5.8 pitch that originally linked P1 of THE PULPIT with the base of the Tree Ledge and NO ALTERNATIVE. Once AUTUMN SPEAKS was established, a few more variations became possible.

49 THE SERMON 5.9

This line is a direct start to THE PULPIT. Begin immediately left of a wet, mossy streak.

P1: Travel up and left along a short ramp, then up past 2 bolts to a shared bolted belay with THE PULPIT. 2 bolts. (5.9, 140 ft.)

50 PURPLE DAZE 5.11b ★

A sustained test-piece – prepare your calves for the inevitable screaming about to ensue!

P1: Start just right of the wet, mossy streak. Balance your way up the thin face, passing four bolts to either a gear belay in some flakes, or a single bolt belay slightly higher. 4 bolts. (5.11b, 150 ft.)

P2: Either traverse left to join up with THE PULPIT, or continue up unprotected, albeit more moderate (5.9) terrain to the Oasis. (100 ft.)

51 STRAWBERRY 5.10d ★★★ PRESERVES

For many years parties protected the initial moves by slinging a tree branch that grew close to the rock. The tree branch is long gone, but the CCC added a bolt during the re-bolting initiative in 1997. At 25 feet this new bolt makes the route reasonably safe, but still exciting.

P1: Carefully balance your way up to the high first bolt, then continue directly up past two more bolts to a bolted belay. 3 bolts. (5.10d, 120 ft.)

P2: Continue up unprotected rock to The Oasis, where you can then link up with any number of options. (5.8, 100 ft.)

52 PANDORA'S WAY 5.9 ★

Though the evil runout on the second pitch may be reminiscent of something you'd find in her box, the rest of PANDORA'S WAY is a nice moderate slabfest.

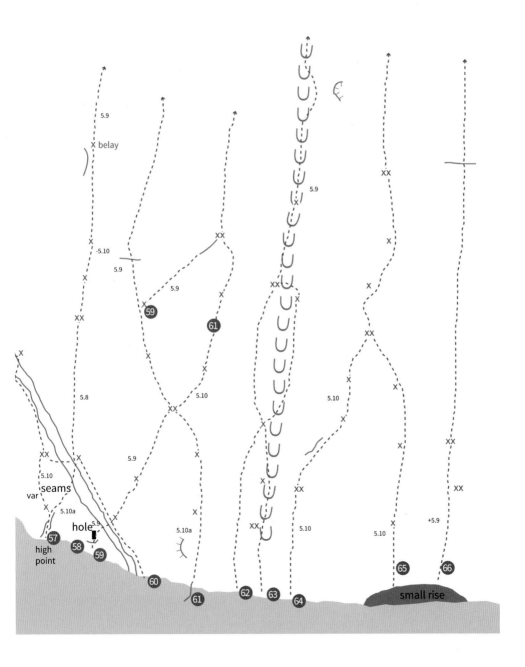

5.9

x belay

x -5.10

5.9

x

xx

5.9

5.9

xx

59

61

x

5.8

x

xx

5.10

5.9

5.9

x

xx

5.10

5.10a

var

seams

5.10

x

5.10a

x

hole 5.9

57

high
point

58

59

60

5.10a

61

62

63

64

5.9

x

x

xx

x

xx

5.10

x

xx

x

x

xx

5.10

5.10

65

+5.9

xx

x

xx

66

small rise

ORANGE BLOSSOM SPECIAL - *The FA of the first pitch of this route was "protected" by a lone tree branch that hovered against the cliff. This natural protection was bent time and time again until it finally broke – under the weight of Joe Harvey sometime in the 1980's. Harvey fell just below the anchors and grounded out at 60 feet, taking the tree limb down with him. In a moment of determination (or insanity, depending on how you look at it!), he got up, dusted himself off and soloed his way back up the first pitch. He then proceeded to send the next pitch (which in the opinion of many is even scarier).*

ELECTRIC BOOBS was one of three routes established by Bob Rotert and Tom McMillan during their high school spring break in 1973. The name was inspired by the popular Elton John song "Bennie and the Jets." Bob Rotert remembers fondly, "Of course the lyrics actually say 'She's got Electric BOOTS,' but we added our own chauvinistic twist." The other routes established as a result of that three day weekend were PANDORA'S WAY and MERCURY'S LEAD.

P1: This pitch is fairly short. Climb straight up to a bolt just right of an overhang. Continue to bolted anchors. 1 bolt. (5.9, 60 ft.)

P2: Move up a short distance to a bowl-like feature containing a bolt. Step left out of the bowl and endure 50 feet of sustained friction climbing to the second bolt. At this point you're on easy street – enjoy flakes and jugs (that will take gear) for another 120 feet or so. Beware of loose rock in the flakes. 2 bolts. (5.9, 160 ft.)

A 60m will not make it all the way to The Oasis on the second pitch. Unless you want to simul-climb or have a 70m rope, bring some gear to build a natural belay in the flakes by the pine tree, then continue to The Oasis via a low-angle third pitch.

53 **THE PURRING 5.10c** ★★★

Hard but reasonably protected climbing on the first pitch leads to a scary but moderate runout on the second. Take a light rack and long runners.

P1: Focus on good footwork as you move up the steepening slab, culminating in a tricky crux between the third and fourth bolt. The climbing above eases off and ends at a set of bolted anchors. 4 bolts. (5.10c, 120 ft.)

P2: Angle up and left toward The Oasis, staying right of the small pine tree. There are a few spots for gear as well as knobs that can be slung and tied off towards the end of the pitch. Beware of flaky rock towards to top. (5.9, 100 ft.) Finish on THE PULPIT or rappel.

54 **ORANGE BLOSSOM 5.11a R/X** ★★ **SPECIAL**

The first pitch of this serious line is an unprotected solo with nasty repercussions in the event of a fall – Make sure you've got your head together before you tie into the sharp end .

P1: Start at the brown water streak and make for the anchors. (5.10, 70 ft.)

P2: With the mental crux down, tackle a short section of steep slab (the physical crux) and one bolt before running it out again (this time on easy ground) to bolted anchors. 1 bolt. (5.11a, 100 ft.)

P3: Tiptoe unprotected to The Oasis (5.8, 80 ft.)

55 **ELECTRIC BOOBS 5.10a** ★★★

A beautifully sculpted line away from the crowds that boasts far more bolts than the typical Stone climb.

P1: Locate a low bolt below undulating waves of rock right of THE PURRING, and just downhill from GRAND FUNK RAILROAD. A low crux with a weird bulge move paves the way to a lovely romp over more of the namesake protuberances. How one tackles the crux is dependent on height, but there are solid options for everyone. 3 bolts. (5.10a, 90 ft.)

P2: Move up and right to a faint ramp-like weakness. Follow it up and slightly left to a bolt. Traverse right across a holdless sea of friction, aiming for another bolt. With a sigh of relief, angle up and left to the anchors for ORANGE BLOSSOM SPECIAL. 2 bolts. (5.9+, 150 ft.)

P3: Rap from here, or continue on to The Oasis.

Variation: It is possible to combine both pitches into one classic line by climbing straight up from the last bolt to finish at the shared bolted anchors with GRAND FUNK. (5.9+, 100 ft.)

56 AMTRAK 5.10 X

This is strictly a solo route with no protection. It starts just right of ELECTRIC BOOBS and runs straight up to the bolted anchors at the top of pitch 2 of GRAND FUNK RAILROAD.

Climber getting started on GRAND FUNK RAILROAD (5.9-)

Climber enjoying the sculpted features of ELECTRIC BOOBS (5.10a)

A fall day high atop GRAND FUNK RAILROAD (5.9-)

57 GRAND FUNK RAILROAD 5.9- ★★★

One of the best long routes at Stone. This climb follows unusual and consistent "track-like" features for about 600 feet. Smaller pieces can be useful to supplement the bolts, especially if you are continuing past the second pitch. P2 is short. Don't be tempted to pass the anchor unless you want to simul-climb or end up stranded in the middle of nowhere.

P1: Start at a high point along the cliff base, a few feet uphill from ELECTRIC BOOBS, below a series of obvious thin dikes. Climb up to the first bolt, then traverse right to the larger dike system for which the route is named. Stay on the tracks up and left past a bolt to bolted anchors. 2 bolts. (5.9, 100 ft.)

P2: Keep chugging along the tracks past one bolt, then step over a water groove and continue up to bolted anchors. 1 bolt. (5.8, 80 ft.)

P3: Make for a pocket beside the tracks about 20 feet up from the belay, then continue up the tracks to bolted anchors. (5.7, 150 ft.)

P4: The angle lessens, but the song remains the same. Toot, toot! Keep chugging…eventually intersecting with shared anchors for THE PULPIT. (5.6, 150 ft.)

P5: Keep moving along the dike until it peeters out, then scamper up to the summit.

Variation: A direct, 5.10 R/X variation on P1 climbs straight up from the first bolt along sustained rock to the bolted anchors atop P1.

58 P.F. FLYERS 5.10a ★

This route starts between GRAND FUNK and TAKEN FOR GRANITE, beneath an obvious black streak that runs over the headwall.

P1: Climb straight up, clipping the bolt above the dikes, then continue along easier terrain to bolted anchors. 1 bolt. (5.10a, 125 ft.)

P2: Maneuver up the steep slab, passing 2 bolts and a flake that will take gear. Continue up to a single bolt belay. In the event that you are using a 50m rope, you'll have to belay at the flake. 2 bolts, single bolt belay. (5.10a, 170 ft.)

P3: Finish up and slightly right on progressively easier terrain. (5.4).

59 TAKEN FOR GRANITE 5.9 ★★

This route starts right of GRAND FUNK beneath an overlap with a hole that will take gear.

P1: Climb up to the hole, then angle up and right to shared bolted anchors with SATURDAY NIGHT LIVE, passing two bolts along the way. 2 bolts. (5.9, 90 ft.)

P2: Trend up and left past two bolts. At the second bolt start heading right to the shared bolted anchors of SATURDAY NIGHT LIVE. 2 bolts. (5.9, 140 ft.)

60 BLOOD ON THE TRACKS 5.9+ R

This first pitch variation to GRAND FUNK starts right of the original GRAND FUNK start, where the railroad track feature begins. Take a skyhook.

61 SATURDAY NIGHT LIVE 5.10a ★

Begin left of a large, brown water streak, just right of a vague right-facing corner.

P1: Climb past two bolts, then trend up and left to the bolted anchors shared with P1 of TAKEN FOR GRANITE. 2 bolts. (5.10a, 110 ft.)

P2: Angle up and right past two bolts on increasingly easier terrain to another bolted anchor station. 2 bolts. (5.10a, 130 ft.)

"My first lead at Stone was with pioneer Vince Davis. In 1981 we met in the parking lot and he asked if I wanted to do GRAND FUNK RAILROAD. I jumped at the chance, as 5.9 was way over my head at the time. Also before sticky rubber, Stone had a reputation for being even more serious than it is now. Vince led the first pitch and I led the second. As I was about to leave the belay, he held out a bag and asked "Would you like some cocaine?" He meant chalk of course, but I stuck my hand in Pandora's box and I have been hooked for life!"

- Mike Grimm

P3: Scamper up to the summit.

62 MAMA'S GOIN' CRAZY 5.10 X

Start just left of the obvious brown water streak.

P1: Climb up the slab, past a lone bolt beside the water streak. End at bolted anchors shared with BROWN SUGAR. 1 bolt. (5.10, 180 ft.)

P2: Continue up the water streak to a natural belay in a left-facing flake (5.9, 130 ft.)

P3: Stroll up low-angle terrain to the top.

63 BROWN SUGAR 5.10

Locate the large brown water streak with a set of low double bolts. Take a light rack for the P2 belay.

P1: Follow the path of bolts up the water streak to a set of bolted anchors shared with MAMA'S GOIN CRAZY. 4 bolts. (5.10, 180, ft.)

P2 and P3: Same as MAMA'S GOIN' CRAZY

64 PYROMANIA 5.10a ★

Locate another low set of double bolts to the right of the BROWN SUGAR water streak. Take a light rack and a 1-1.5" piece.

P1: Starting right of the brown water streak, climb up to the set of double bolts, then angle up and right past two more bolts to a bolted anchor shared with TEFLON TRIP. 3 bolts. (5.10a, 120 ft.)

P2: Finish on TEFLON TRIP (5.10a, 150 ft.)

65 TEFLON TRIP 5.10c ★

Those ready for a friction challenge will enjoy the polished rock on this smooth, non-stick line. Start right of PYROMANIA, on the left side of a small rise along the base of the cliff.

P1: Delicately tiptoe up a shallow groove to a high first bolt. Slab your way past two more bolts to a shared bolted anchor with PYRO-MANIA. 3 bolts. (5.10c, 120 ft.)

P2: Climb directly up to a bolt 25 feet up, then trend up and right past a second bolt.

Make for a set of double bolt anchors. 2 bolts. (5.10a, 150 ft.)

"SUFFICIENTLY BREATHLESS was established with very little protection. The first pitch was about 100 feet long and had only a single bolt some 40 feet up. During the first ascent I was low on bolts, so I only placed a single bolt for the belay, intending to come back another time to add a second one. On the second ascent of the route, I climbed up past the first bolt, and on to the single bolt belay rather uneventfully. I clipped in to the bolt and shouted, "Off Belay!" to my partner. I then leaned back onto the bolt to get ready to bring my partner up…and the bolt promptly snapped off! I somehow (read: Guardian Angel) managed to not fall complete-ly backwards, and I instinctively thrust myself face forward into the rock. I slipped down the face, and knowing what was happening I turned my feet on edge.

Somehow my right foot managed to catch a crystal – stopping me from plummeting almost 100 feet to the ground! I was completely unrav-eled at what had happened, high off the deck without a bolt kit, and the only bolt on the route some 60 feet below me. After a moment to try and collect myself a bit, I tried down climbing for a spell, but I wasn't feeling too good about it, as everyone knows it is much easier to climb up than it is to down. After a while I realized it might actually be easier for me to free solo the rest of the route to the top rather than trying to down climb. So I dropped the rope and free soloed the remaining 300 or so feet to the top – hence the name SUFFICIENTLY BREATHLESS!

-From First Ascensionist Bob Rotert

66 SUFFICIENTLY BREATHLESS 5.9+ R/X

Despite the moderate grade, this is a very serious route with deadly fall consequences in multiple sections.

Start on the right side of the small rise along the cliff base, beneath a set of very high double bolts. Bring a light rack.

P1: Pray your slab skills are sufficient enough to get you to a set of double bolts at 40 feet, then another 30 or so to bolted anchors. 1 set double bolts. (5.9+, 80 ft.)

P2: Keep climbing straight up (with zero protection), with a dike on your left, until reaching a natural belay at a horizontal crack. (5.9+, 120 ft.)

P3: Continue up for a full rope length to a giant quartz block. Belay here without the safety of anchors – make sure both you are your partner are on the same page. (5.9, 150 ft.)

P4: Breathe a sigh of relief and scurry up to the top of the summit.

67 SPIDERMAN SWINGS SOUTH 5.10d

This route starts on the low-angled rock right of SUFFICIENTLY BREATHLESS and tours the entire South Face, ending on the far left-hand side of the wall. Simul-climb until the leader reaches 300 feet, then begin traversing to the left. Any bolts and belay stations are fair game; just follow the path of least resistance. Be sure to cross over THE GREAT ARCH in the middle of P3, and clip the bolt just over the lip. Climb over the arch and onto the upper face (crux), then continue traversing left until reaching more low-angle terrain on the left side of the South Face. Downclimb easy rock to the base on the extreme left side. Alternately, you can make the traverse from the opposite direction, by beginning on CAVE-MAN. Same rules apply, only in reverse. End by downclimbing the low-angled face right of SUFFICIENTLY BREATHLESS.

Old hardware meets new hardware on the North Face

NORTH FACE

Ah, the North Face. The terrain is steeper, the grades stiffer, and the rock more polished. Despite its proximity to good parking, just getting there is an accomplishment in itself, as all approaches involve either a hefty amount of bushwhacking or treading across large volumes of low-angled slab. Because of the sometimes flaky rock and large sections of lichen, a wire brush will probably come in handy. But don't let any of that deter you – there are numerous stellar routes to be found on this section of rock. If you are of the adventurous sort that thrives on tunneling through rhododendrons and playing "Where's Waldo" with bolts glistening in the sun on an impeccable sea of granite, the North Face is for you!

One thing you can guarantee about the North Face - you won't find yourself waiting in line for your route. On a typical fair weather winter day the South Face can easily be a mob scene, while the North face will usually be completely empty. Many of the routes will take a couple of pieces of small to mid-size gear in between bolts, and as with the South Face routes, many of the routes require double ropes to get down. In 2009 the Carolina Climbers Coalition sponsored a re-bolting effort that replaced many (but not all) of the North Face bolts. However, the hardware not replaced during the initiative is original (about 30 years old), so carefully inspect any bolts before entrusting your life to them. Additionally, some bolts may be missing their hangers, so it is a good idea to bring nuts that can converted to rivet hangers.

WARNING!

The North Face can be an intimidating place. It is not well-travelled, therefore help from other parties will be harder to come by. While the author has personally confirmed the route descriptions for much of the wall, every single inch was not covered. So bring an adventurous spirit and more gear than you think you need, as it is entirely likely that a few bolt counts might be inaccurate. Use common sense and don't venture out onto some huge blank slab unless you're sure you can handle it.

APPROACH

First the good news. The North Face is actually far closer to the road than the vastly more popular South Face. The bad news is that at the time of this writing there was not so much as a hint of a trail.

The best approach for the left side of the North Face (INDIAN LOOKOUT and STAINLESS STEEL AREAS) is from the pull-off by the Wilkes County sign. If you cross the creek and make a straight line away from the pull-off, you will arrive along the base of the lower apron (and routes on the left side of the North Face) in about 20 minutes. (It is also possible to access the rest of the North

The blanket of shade that shrouds the North Face

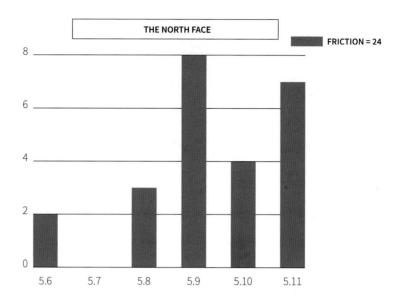

THE NORTH FACE

FRICTION = 24

Face from this parking option, but unless you already have your bearings, you will likely spend a lot of time thrashing in the woods.) Be considerate of other cars when you park, as this pull-off also provides easy access to a swimming hole in the summer. If there is no more room to park, keep driving to the main parking lot and hike back along the road for about 8 minutes.

You can also access the STAINLESS STEEL area from the top via the summit trail. From the parking lot hike the loop trail clockwise for about 15 minutes until the top of the North Face is to your left. Not long after passing the bolted railings, look for an unmarkedside trail that leads through a short band of trees over to the slabs. Walk across the slabs, angling down, until you can spot a bolted anchor just before the angle steepens. A short, low angle rappel will take you to another set of anchors, which mark the top of QUINN THE ESKIMO. From here there are a couple of options, the most obvious being to rap

To North face summit- At this point go straight to reach top of the North Face.

down and right to the 3 bolted anchor (2 new ones, one archaic) atop TEARDROP. If you have two 70m ropes you will have exactly enough rope to make it from the STAINLESS STEEL Area Rap (SSAR) anchors to TEARDROP in one double-rope rappel. Two more raps will reach the bottom.

1 INDIAN LOOKOUT 5.8 ★★★

This loooong pitch offers a unique vantage point on the North Face. Supplement with some small pro. This route starts on the left side of the apron, to the right of a large, left-facing arch, and beneath an overlap/roof feature. Scramble up the 5.easy slab to reach a set of bolted hangers (no rap rings) from which to belay.

P1: Traverse right to a bolt just above the right side of the overlap, then trend up and left to a bolt below a flake system. Make your way left, out towards the edge of the arch. Clip a bolt, and run it out on gradually-easing terrain to the finish. 3 bolts. (165 ft.)

Variation #1: A direct start can be done by climbing straight up above the overlap and joining forces with the original version at the edge of the arch. Due to the unprotected lower section, a fall here could be serious, so be confident at the grade (5.10a R)

Variation #2: A direct finish clips the first bolt of the original line, then climbs directly up past two more bolts, trending slightly left towards the top. (5.10a)

Descent: Double-rope rap to the base of the route, then either scramble back down the slabs, or traverse right to rap from the RAIN DANCE belay anchors.

The next four routes mostly consist of one good pitch sandwiched in between a scrambly approach pitch to belay anchors (5.easy) and a long (and unprotected) top out pitch on slab that decreases in angle the higher you go. The bolted anchors at the top of the first pitches all have rap rings, so if logging mileage is more important than getting high off the ground, you can skip the last pitches and rap back down the way you came (a 70m will just

reach with stretch). **If you've been stricken with a case of summit fever, scramble up the low-angled terrain to the top (there are no anchors, but a few well-placed tree islands can be used to bring up your second) and walk off right to link up with the summit trail to get back down.**

2 RAIN DANCE 5.10d ★

No rain dances allowed until all members of your party are on the ground. Scamper up the low-angle slab to a set of bolted belay anchors 40 feet right of the INDIAN LOOKOUT overlap.

P1: Take a fairly straight path over a few sloping bulges and some lichenous rock. 3 bolts. (5.10d, 130 ft.)

P2: Get slab-happy all the way to the top. (5.5)

3 REBEL YELL 5.11a ★★

Fans of steep friction climbing will cry "More,

more, more" after getting a taste of this North Face classic.

Start same as for RAIN DANCE.

P1: Follow the line of three bolts to the right of RAIN DANCE. 3 bolts. Bolted anchors. (5.11a, 120 ft.)

P2: Progressively moderate terrain leads to the top. (5.5)

4 DAMNED YANKEES 5.10b

Slab up to a set of bolted belay anchors 60 feet right of the INDIAN LOOKOUT overlap, and about 20 feet right of RAIN DANCE. A wire brush might come in handy in some sections.

P1: Balance your way up featured, but lichen-covered terrain right of REBEL YELL, passing three bolts to a bolted anchor. 3 bolts. (5.10b, 115 ft.)

P2: Run it out, slab it out, and top it out. (5.5)

⑤ PAW PAW 5.9 ★

This line shares a start with DAMNED YAN-KEES. Tackle the thin water groove in between DAMNED YANKEES and STAINLESS STEEL.

P1: Ascend the thin water groove, passing three bolts along the way to a bolted anchor. 3 bolts. (5.9, 115 ft.)

P2: Stay in the groove until it gradually fades away into low-angle rock. No protection on this one either.

I was fortunate enough to have the opportunity to climb on the North Face several times back in the day. The routes are stellar, but can often feel extremely dicey due to the decomposing granite chips. It makes you feel like you're climbing on slick gravel – extremely insecure! There's also a lot of lichen…I used to put a large wire brush on a sling around my neck and employ a "swipe and step" method. Also due to the lack of sun in the winter it can be very cold – I've often seen ice chutes forming in the water grooves! - Paul "Thor" Pelot

Descent information is provided for each individual climb, however all of the routes in the STAINLESS STEEL Area can be topped out via a final pitch, aiming for the SSAR anchors. Scramble up to the summit and link up with the summit trail heading down and right.

⑥ STAINLESS STEEL 5.9+ R ★★

You'd better have nerves of steel for the long, sustained runouts on this line. A 5.easy approach scramble follows a thin, featured white water groove up from the apron, then angles up and left to a set of belay anchors with rap rings.

P1: This short pitch angles up and left past one bolt to a set of bolted anchors. 1 bolt. (5.8, 50 ft.)

P2: Make for a lone bolt at 25 feet and head up the black streak for a looooong way to a large tree in the middle of the North Face. 1 bolt. (5.9+, 100 ft.)

Descent: Double-rope rappel from the tree, or continue up and right to finish on QUINN..

⑦ QUINN THE ESKIMO 5.11a R ★

This route shares a start with STAINLESS STEEL.

P1: Same as STAINLESS.

P2: Tackle the faint streak angling up and right. Clip two bolts, and then endure a long runout to a third bolt before reaching bolted anchors. (5.11a, 180 ft.)

Descent: Double-rope rap from anchors.

The next three routes begin in a giant pothole feature littered with flakes that will accept gear. The pothole also has a little bit of vegetation (as well as some standing, stagnant water…in warmer weather don't forget the bug spray!). Reach the pothole by climbing the same featured water groove as for STAINLESS STEEL, then follow the vegetation up and right. Climbing out of the pothole is steep, even overhanging in some places – be sure to bring a few small to mid-sized pieces to protect these moves off the deck.

⑧ DEFEET 5.11a

P1: Climb out of the pothole on its left side, and balance your way past three bolts to bolted anchors. 3 bolts. (5.11a, 80ft.)

P2: Aim for a single bolt and when the angle kicks back, either finish up and left on the QUINN anchors.(150 ft, 5.11a)

⑨ CHAPPED GREEN 5.11a ★

P1: Surmount the giant pothole on the right side and Climb more or less straight up. Belay on the 4th bolt. 4 bolts. (170 ft.) (230 ft.)

P2. From the 4th bolt, continue up until the angle lessens, then traverse over to the TEARDROP belay, housed in a small depression. (75 ft.)

10 ROAD SHOW 5.9 ★

P1: Traverse right and up out of the pothole along a dike to a bolt, then continue climbing straight up past another bolt to bolted anchors. 2 bolts. (5.9, 115 ft.)

P2: Keep climbing past another couple of bolts until you reach another set of bolted anchors, up and slightly to the right. 2 bolts. (5.9, 115 ft.)

11 TEARDROP 5.9- ★

Start at the base of the apron below a left-facing flake system. Bring a light rack with nuts.

P1: Work your way up the thin face to gain the corner system. Ascend the corner, then follow the dike up and right, then angle back left to finish in a large teardrop-shaped bowl feature. 2 bolts, bolted anchors. (5.9-, 100 ft.)

P2: Escape the teardrop up and right via a dike, then aim for a bolt high up on the face, then bolted anchors. (5.9-, 70 ft.)

P3: Keep climbing straight up past a 2 bolts to shared anchors with ROAD SHOW. 2 bolts. (5.9-, 100 ft.)

12 BOWL GAME 5.9 ★★

This line is a variation of P2 on TEARDROP, and connects the teardrop bowl to a smaller bowl high on the face. Bring a light rack.

P1: Same as P1 on TEARDROP.

P2: Same as TEARDROP.

P2: Exit the teardrop stage right, and climb up to a bolt. Then continue straight up past one more bolt to a set of bolted anchors. 2 bolts. (5.9, 100 ft.).

P3: Follow a thin water groove past another small bowl feature to a set of anchors in a small depression. (5.8, 100 ft.)

13 DIRTY DOZEN 5.10d ★

Though not quite a dozen, this route boasts more bolts than the average North Face line, although you'll still need a light rack. Begin at the base slightly uphill and to the right of TEARDROP.

P1: Zig zag your way past three wandering bolts to a set of bolted anchors. (5.10d, 100 ft.)

P2: Climb past three bolts, then continue up past a group of trees on the right. Bear right above the trees and keep climbing up past three more bolts to a set of bolted anchors. (5.10d, 180 ft.)

P3: Step right a bit and make for a single bolt, then angle back left to shared anchors with BOWL GAME. (5.9, 150 ft.)

There is a large crop of trees that extends partway up the base of the North Face, so approaching routes on the right side of the face from the pull-off will require some additional adventures in bushwhacking, but as long as you hug the base, you should be able to get your bearings pretty easily. A decidedly less thrashy, but less obvious approach is to hike to the summit trail for about 15 minutes and then break off the trail to the left onto the slabs. Make your way down the slabs until you near the tree line. Depending on the path you choose, these slabs can sometimes be fairly steep, so it is recommended to don your climbing shoes at this point. Hug the base of the cliff or cross the slabs to reach your route of choice. All routes descend by either rapping down from a lower pitch, or topping out and walking off right to merge with the summit trail.

The next three routes begin atop the North Face Terrace, above the highest point of the tree line along the base. The easiest way to access the Terrace routes is to climb P1 and most of P2 of DIRTY DOZEN. When the Terrace comes into view towards the end of P2, traverse right for 30 feet to reach belay bolts on the sloping platform just above the trees. The traverse is relatively easy, but not well-protected, and a swing would be unpleasant, so be careful. All three routes utilize the same belay anchors.

14 MERK-N-MAN 5.9 ★

This is the leftmost route on the platform. Bring a light rack.

P1: From the left side of the platform, ascend the progressively deepening white water groove past two bolts to bolted anchors. 2 bolts. (5.9, 80 ft.)

P2: Keep groovin' all the way to bolted anchors at the top. (5.9, 170 ft.)

15 SURFER JOE AND MOE 5.11b ★ THE SLEEZE

This test of technical prowess follows a water groove directly up from the belay bolts to the top.

P1: Climb straight up past two bolts. Then cross over the groove and climb past three more bolts to bolted anchors. 5 bolts. (5.11b, 120 ft.)

P2: Scramble to the summit, then traverse left to MERK-N-Man anchors. (5.9, 100 ft.)

16 SIDE SHOW 5.10d ★ (aka LAWSLAND)

P1: Clip a bolt up and right from the belay, then follow the obvious dike that diagonals up and right to bolted anchors near a horizontal crack system. 4 bolts. (5.10d, 100 ft.)

P2: Pull the bulge via the horizontal and make for the summit. (5.8)

The next three routes are probably the least accessible of the North Face, but are all distinctive and worth the extra effort to get there. Two approaches are described, each coming in from a different direction.

From the belay bolts on the North Face Terrace: Depending on your comfort level you can either walk right across the terrace and then angle down, or rappel down and right, ending up in the trees for both options. Battle the briars as you walk to the right for about 100 feet. You will pass a steep wall with an abandoned project (2 bolts and a sling that appears to be from the Jurassic period), and end up below the obvious HIGH ANXIETY dihedral. The other option is to approach from the very bottom of the ZIN SLIDE slab. Follow the base as it cuts up and left to a high point, where you will then see the HIGH ANXIETY dihedral.

17 HIGH ANXIETY 5.9 ★★★

The features on this route are out of character for the North Face, providing a diversion from the typical slab paddle. To keep the stress levels low(er), bring a rack with small cams and nuts.

P1: Find the large, right-facing corner that leads to a slab roof/overlap. Follow the corner as it angles up and right and turns into an overlap. Bolted anchors. (5.9, 100 ft.)

P2: A few cruxy moves and a bolt or two leads to a belay at a giant crater-like feature. (5.9, 100 ft.)

P3: Ascend the crater on its right side and romp up to the summit.

18 POPSICKLE TOES 5.11a ★

Take a light rack.

P1: Start slightly downhill and 75 feet right of HIGH ANXIETY, beneath a diagonal overlap. Climb straight up past two bolts to bolted anchors at an arching overlap feature beneath a bulge. 2 bolts. (5.11a, 120 ft.)

P2: Pull over the bulge and climb up the water groove past three more bolts and (eventually) easing terrain towards the top. (5.11a, 100 ft.)

19 DARK STAR 5.11a ★

This line shares a start with POPSICKLE TOES.

P1: Clip the first bolt on POPSICKLE, then hang a hard right, aiming for a left-facing flake. Then tiptoe up the black water streak past one bolt to a set of bolted anchors. (5.11a, 100 ft.)

P2: Get into the groove and make for the top. (5.10, 100 ft.)

The right side of the wall (ZIN SLIDE area) is ironically home to some of the oldest as well as the newest routes on the North Face. The best way to access this area is via the summit loop trail. Hike toward the summit (hanging a left onto the trail from the gravel road). In about 10 minutes you will see a staircase that curves up and right. Walk straight past the

stairs aiming for the slabs. Either down-climb the slabs near the tree line or bush-whack along indistinct game trails down

lower in the trees. The first route you will encounter is INLAND WATERWAY #2. To reach ZIN SLIDE, keep moving left across the base. Keep your eyes peeled for a set of shiny belay bolts 200 feet off the deck – these mark the start of ZIN SLIDE.

You can also reach this area from DARK STAR. Walk right and scramble down the edge of slab along the tree line for about 100 feet, where you should be able to spot the shiny belay anchors for ZIN SLIDE directly across from you, about 100 feet away. At the time of this writing there was a tattered sling on a tree that was at the same height as the anchors – if you see it and are wanting to climb ZIN SLIDE, start traversing there. If you are done for the day and ready to hike out, or wanting to get on the lines on the extreme right side of the North Face, continue scrambling down the slab to reach the base. If down climbing slab is not your thing, there is a beefy chain (on a single bolt) about 40 feet

below the sling that you can use to rappel to the base.

20 ZIN SLIDE 5.9+ ★★★ (a.k.a. ZEN SLAB)

Over the years this seems to have become the token "first route" on the North Face for many climbers. Scurry up the low angle slab from the base to reach the belay bolts 200 feet off the deck.

P1: Climb up a wide, dark streak, passing three bolts and finishing at bolted anchors. 3 bolts. (5.9, 160 feet.)

P2: Climb up and right past one bolt, negotiate a bulge (crux), and continue past one more bolt to bolted anchors. (5.9+, 75 ft.)

P3: Scramble up to the top.

21 INLAND WATERWAY 5.6 X

There is a lone bolt down and right from the belay bolts on ZIN SLIDE. Other than that, this route is an unprotected solo to the top of the North Face. Wander up the path of least resistance, trending up and left along a water groove towards the summit.(750 ft.)

The next 3 routes were established in January of 2005 by Mike Fischesser. These long romps to the North Face summit offer a good introduction to this side of the dome at moderate grades. Take a light rack.

SHARK

22 GRITTY CITY 5.8+ ★★

With the new age of sticky rubber, I'm sure this route was a lot "grittier" than some of Fischesser's previous ascents.Approximately 150 feet right of ZIN SLIDE, scan the upper section of the cliff for a feature that somewhat resembles a shark (swimming east). Start below this feature.

P1. Climb 5.easy slab to a set of bolted anchors. (150 ft.)

P2. Slab straight up the sea of granite to a set of bolted anchors a long way away. 2 bolts. (5.6, 180 ft.)

P3. Climb up increasingly steeper rock to a set of bolted anchors down and right from the shark feature. (5.8+, 180 ft.)

P4. Climb up and left above the shark, clip a bolt, then keep slabbin' all the way to the top, on gradually easing terrain. 1 bolt. (5.8+, 200 ft.)

23 32 YEARS LATER 5.6 ★★

More than three decades later, and Mike Fischesser is still a Stonemaster – pretty impressive!

Start 20 feet right of GRITTY CITY.

P1: Climb straight up past one bolt and make for bolted anchors. (5.6, 150 ft.)

P2. Head straight up from the belay to another set of bolted anchors on the right side of a water groove. (5.6, 180 ft.)

P3. Bounce back and forth along the water groove, passing at least one bolt and ending at anchors on the right side of the groove. 1 bolt. (5.6, 180 ft.)

P4. Scramble up the slab to the summit.

24 INLAND WATERWAY #2 5.8+ ★★

Start beneath a series of overlaps, approximately 50 feet right of 32 YEARS LATER.

P1: Follow a faint white streak to a bolt below an overlap. Continue straight up, passing another bolt to a set of bolted anchors. 2 bolts. (5.6, 150 ft.)

P2: Climb straight up to bolted anchors. ? bolts. (5.8, 180 ft.)

P3: Aim for a water groove with a bolt just before the angle steepens. Continue up to bolted anchors. 1 bolt. (5.8+, 180 ft.)

ALPHABETICAL ORDER ROUTE INDEX

CROWDER'S MOUNTAIN

PILOT MOUNTAIN

MOORE'S WALL

STONE MOUNTAIN

ROUTE INDEX BY GRADE

CROWDER'S MOUNTAIN

SPORT

5.6
Razor's Edge ★, 76

5.8
Holy Guacamole ★★★, 83

5.9
Opinionated ★★★, 72
Overlooked and Underrated ★★, 82

5.10A
Dewey Used to Love It ★, 83
Path to Extinction, 33
Plane Above Your Head ★, 80

5.10B
No Added Weight ★★, 70
Rawlhide ★★, 84
Tom Waits for No One ★★, 70
Top That Direct ★, 28

5.10C
Bolter Problem, 27
Burn Signals ★★★, 66
Electra ★★★, 48
Gimp ★★, 76
Master Beta ★★, 74
Rocky and Bullwinkle, 83

5.10D
Energy Czar ★★★, 51
New Policy ★★, 79
Plane Truth, 80
Proselytizer ★, 82

5.11A
Freuhlein, 33
Pteranodon, 33
Waspafarian, 27

5.11B
Buschman, 80
Desperately Seeking Juggage ★, 71
Not See, 33
Orange Prickadilly, 79
Red Red Wine , 74

5.11C
Perplexus , 27
Toxic Shock ★, 33

5.11D
Butcher of Baghdad, 51
Disgustipated ★★, 84
Koma's Arete ★★, 28
Stark Whining ★★, 29
Whining ★★★, 29

5.12
Mudbone , 29

5.12A
Anthrax ★★★, 28
Slabster's Lament ★★★, 29
T.k.o. ★★, 74
Welcome to Crowder's ★★★, 74

5.12B
Fashion ★★, 75
Fashion Super Direct ★★★, 75
Silence the Critics ★, 70
Snag ★★, 32
Spitter, 34

5.12C
Slabster's Direct ★★, 32

5.12D
Carnivore, 34

5.13A
Terrorist ★★, 32
Thratcher, 34

CROWDER'S MOUNTAIN

TRAD

5.3
Red Wall Chimney, 73

5.4
Four Play , 53
Gastonia Crack ★★★, 41
Two-Pitch ★, 62

5.5
Balcony ★★, 59
Big Crack, 57
Connect the Cracks, 59
Ditch Two Pitch, 62
Eat a Pitch, 62
Escaping Right, 61
In This Corner, 44
Orange Corner ★★, 55

Trash Compactor, 63
Whale of aTale, 55

5.6
Big Dihedral, 60
Cro-Magnon Crack ★★, 83
Dirt-Hedral, 55
Handle with Care, 53
Mike's Crack ★, 42
No Experience Necessary, 82
Nose ★, 46
Nuke the Whales ★, 55
Two Peach, 63

5.7
A Fine Line, 55
Bear, 61

Caterpillar ★★★, 48
Eat a Peach ★, 62
I'm Lichen the Climb, 55
Iron Curtain, 60
Lake View Slab, 35
Loyal Order of the Toad, 55
Middle Finger ★★, 59
Pocket of Like'n , 59
Save the Wails ★, 55
Spring Fever, 73
This Ain't No Place for You
    Algebra, 79
What Else is There to Do ★, 52

5.8
911, 74
Air View Slab, 35

PILOT MOUNTAIN

SPORT

PILOT MOUNTAIN

TRAD

MOORES WALL

SPORT

MOORES WALL

TRAD

STONE MOUNTAIN
SPORT

STONE MOUNTAIN
TRAD

STONE MOUNTAIN

SLAB/FRICTION

FIRST ASCENT INDEX
CROWDER'S MOUNTAIN

60 Seconds Over Tokyo (5.10a): Eddie N. Pain
911 (5.8): Doug Reed, Freddie Young

A Fine Line (5.7): Eddy Ramirez (2012)
Absent from the Body (5.9+): Eddie N. Pain, Chris Little (12/1989)
Aerial Act (5.10D): Shane Cobourn, Free Solo Late 1980's
Air View Slab (5.8): Bruce Blatchley
Another Brick In the Wall (5.10A): Doug Reed, Wes Love (1985)
Anthrax (5.12A): Diab Rabie, Gus Glitch
Anthrax Whine (5.12): Gus Glitch (1993)
Arborcide (5.9): Sean Cobourn
Arborist (5.10B): Wade Parker
Ask Mr. Science (5.9+): Doug Reed, Chip Self
Axis (Bold As Love) (5.11C/D): Doug Reed (1986), Ffa Bob Rotert, Wes Love (1986)

Balcony (5.5): Unknown
Bear (5.7): Unknown
Beer Wolf (5.9+): Wes Love, Rodney Lanier
Belly Crawl (5.9): Doug Reed, Wes Love
Between the Betwixt (5.10B): Wes Love, Doug Reed
Big Crack (5.5): Unknown
Big Dihedral (5.6): Unknown
Black Flag (5.10D): Doug Reed (1986)
Black Flag Direct (5.13A): Doug Reed
Black Sand Beaches (5:11B): Gus Glitch (1989)
Black Sand Bitches (5.11D R/X): Gus Glitch (1989)
Bolter Problem (5.10C): Gus Glitch
Brick In the Wall (5.10D): Doug Reed
Buddha Bulge (5.10A): Eddie N. Pain, Rodney Lanier (1989)
Burn Crack (5.10C/D): Cal Swoager, Wes Love (1982)
Burn Signals (5.10C): Wade Parker
Buschman (5.11B): Gus Glitch (1993)
Butcher of Baghdad (5.11D): Diab Rabie

Cambodian Holiday (5.9): Rob Fuquay, Doug Reed
Carnivore (5.12D): Gus Glitch (1991)
Caterpillar (5.7): Unknown
Championship Wrestling (5.9): Doug Reed, Wes Love, Thomas Kelley
Christmas Present (5.8): Rodney Lanier
Connect the Cracks (5.5): Eddy Ramirez
Cro-Magnon Crack (5.6): Sean Cobourn

Desperately Seeking Juggage (5.11B): Gus Glitch, Monica Browne
Destination (5.8+): Thomas Kelley, Jim Hutton
Dewey Used to Love It (5.10A): Sean Cobourn, Ffa Rodney Lanier, Mark Pell
Diesel (5.11A): Eddy Ramirez (2012)
Direct (5.9+ X): Unknown
Dirt-Hedral (5.6): Eddy Ramirez (2012)
Disgustipated (5.11D): Gus Glitch (1995)

Dish (5.9 R): Unknown
Dixie Fury (5.12A): Doug Reed
Double Naught Spy (5.9 R): Sean Coburn, Bruce Blatchley
Doug's Dihedral (5.11C R): Doug Reed
Dr. Jeckyl's Hide (5.9): Bruce Blatchley
Dr. Jeckyl's Ride (5.10A): Bruce Blatchley
Drive On (5.8): Wes Love, Doug Reed

Eat A Peach (5.7): Wes Love, David Huntley
Eat A Pitch (5.5): Eddy Ramirez
Elastic Rebound Theory (5.11D): Doug Reed, Eddie N. Pain, Alvino Pon
Elastic Shaman (5.13): Gus Glitch (1993)
Electra (5.10C): Doug Reed, Ben Fowler, Wes Love (1986)
Energy Czar (5.10D): Wes Love, Doug Reed
Entertainment For Men (5.9): Sean Cobourn, Joey Griffin (1993)
Escape From the Gumbies (5.9+): Unknown
Escaping Left (5.8): Unknown
Escaping Right (5.5): Unknown
Eye Sockets (5.10B): Shane Cobourn, Doug Reed, Sean Cobourn

Fashion (5.12B): Doug Reed
Fashion Direct (5.12C): Diab Rabie
Fashion Super Direct (5.12): Gus Glitch
Felon (5.13A): Gus Glitch (1993)
Finger Crack (5.8): Unknown
Firestone (5.10): Doug Reed, Wes Love
Flat Tire (5.10): Doug Reed, Wes Love
Flexible Flyer (5.9+ R): Doug Reed, Wes Love
Four Play (5.4): Sean Cobourn, Shane Cobourn
Fortress Fingers (5.10A/B): Wes Love, Rodney Lanier (1983)
Freuhlein (5.11A): Monica Browne, Sharon Rabie
Fugusi (5.11D): Gus Glitch (1993)

Gastonia Crack (5.4): Unknown
Gimp (5.10C): Diab Rabie
Golden Shower (5.9+): Cal Swoager, Wes Love
Gumbies Go Home (5.10D): Shane Cobourn, Doug Reed, Sean Cobourn (1985)

Handle With Care (5.6): Doug Reed (Solo)
Heady Areteddy (5.9): Eddy Ramirez
Holy Guacamole (5.8): Monica Browne, Gus Glitch

I'm Lichen the Climb (5.7): Eddy Ramirez
In This Corner (5.5): Sean Cobourn, Jim Hutton
Instant Karma (5.10B): Cal Swoager, Wes Love
Instant Karma Direct (5.10D): Fa Gil Harder, Kip Connor, FFA Rodney Lanier, Wes Love
Intimidator (5.8): Doug Reed, Sean Cobourn
Iron Curtain (5.7): Gary Mims, Tom Shropshire

PILOT MOUNTAIN

MOORE'S WALL

Too Much Chalk (5.8): Tim Fisher, Wes Love (May 1981)
Too Much Fun (5.9): Bruce Meneghin, Tom Howard 1976
Tri-Sockets (5.7) – Scott Gilliam 2008
Turdslinger (5.6): Unknown

U-Haul (5.10A): Unknown
Unbroken Chain (5.10B/C): Eric Zchiesche, Tom McMillan
Undercover Lover (5.9+): Tom Calicutt, J. Fisher (1994)
Underdog (5.12B/C R): Porter Jarrard (1989)

Vascular Disaster (5.11B/C): Tim Fisher, Jim Overby (1985)
Visual Splendor (5.10D): Seth Tart, Dennis Buice, Joy Cox
Voodoo Chile (5.10D R): Jeff Lauschey, Bruce Burgess (1986)

Wailing Wall (5.6): Unknown
Walk Don't Run (5.7): Unknown
Walk In the Light (5.10B/C): Unknown

Walking the Gerbil (5.10D): Tim Fisher, Jim Overby (May 1988)
War Games (5.12B): Seth Tart
Washboard (5.6): Unknown
Welcome to Moore's (5.10D R): Tim Fisher, David Petree, Tim Schneider 1985 Var: Tim Fisher
Whipping Post (5.10A): Frank Orthel, Steve Orthel
Wild-Eyed Southern Boys (5.12A): John Black
Wild Kingdom (5.11D R): Tom Howard, Bob Rotert, 1978 (One Point of Aid) FFA Rob Robinson, Tom McMillan 1979
Wild Kingdom (5.11D R): 2 Variations: Tim Fisher
Wildlife (5.12B R/X): Doug Reed
Windigo (5.11C): Tim Fisher, Jim Williamson (June 1988)

Yosemite Sam (5.12B): Seth Tart
Your Cheatin' Start (5.8) Unknown

Zeus (5.13B): Harrison Dekker 1989
Zombie Woof (5.10C): Carlton Ramm (1978)
Zoo View (5.7+): Tom Howard, Bruce Meneghin (1976)

STONE MOUNTAIN

32 Years Later (5.6): Mike Fishchesser (January 2005)

Adrift (5.9): Bill Webster, Emily Hull-Ryde
Amtrak (5.10 X): Vince Davis (Solo)
Anchor Rode (5.6): Fess Green, W. Wyland (1969)
Autumn Speaks (5.9): Dan Hartman (Solo)

Back to School (5.9+): Jess Tucker (1985)
Banana Breath (5.10A): Chris Rowins, Chris Kulczycki (1978)
Between the Ways (5.10C): Mike Fischesser (1994)
Block Route (5.8): Unknown
Blood on the Tracks (5.9+ R): Sandy Fleming, Steve Pachman, Ron Shehee
Bombay Groove (5.10A): Chris Rowins, Chris Kulczycki (1978)
Botany 10 (5.8) : Unknown
Bowl Game (5.9): Jess Tucker, Vince Davis
Brown Sugar (5.10): Sandy Fleming, Steve Pachman (1984)

Captain Crunch (5.11A): Paul "Thor" Pelot (April 1991)
Caveman (5.10C): Tom McMillan, Jim Mcever
Chapped Green (5.11A): Jess Tucker, Vince Davis
Closer to the Heart (5.9): Paul "Thor" Pelot, Rick Poedtke (2/1992)
Crystal Lizard (5.8+): Unknown

Damned Yankees (5.10B): Unknown
Dark Star (5.11A): Jeff White (Rope Solo)
Defeet (5.11A): Vince Davis, Jess Tucker
Dirty Crack (5.8): Paul "Thor" Pelot, Mike Flood (June 1988)

Dirty Dozen (5.10D): Gary Slate, Dave Black, Alan Bartlett
Discipline (5.12A): Sandy Fleming, Steve Pachman (1983)
Dixie Crystals (5.9): Gerald Laws, Kenny Hibbits (1978)
Dream On (5.9): Kelvin Sparks, Tommy Croitz
Dream Waves (5.9): Chris Rowins, T. Meager (1976)

Electric Boobs (5.10A): Bob Rotert, Tom McMillan (1973)
Entrance Crack (5.4 R): George Dewolfe, John Thorne (1965)

Face Value (5.11D): Jeff Lauschey, Monty Reagan
Fantastic (5.9+): Gerald Laws, Buddy Price (1974)
Father Knows Best (5.9): Paul "Thor" Pelot, Rick Poedtke (March 1991)
Fleet Feet (5.10A): Zeb Gray
Fuddy Mucker (5.9+): Unknown

Grand Funk Railroad (5.9-): Bob Mitchell, Will Fulton (1971)
Great Arch (5.5): Bill Chatfield, Fess Green (1965)
Great Brown Way (5.10C): Chris Rowins, Chris Kulczycki (1978)
Great White Way (5.9): Gerald Laws, Buddy Price (1974)
Gritty City (5.8+): Mike Fishchesser (January 2005)

Happy Trails (5.11A): Jeff White, Gary Slate, FFA Jeff White, Fred Bauer (1980)
High Anxiety (5.9): Gary Slate, Jeff White
Hook And Bladder (5.9): Unknown

Impossible Dream (5.9): Sandy Fleming, Steve Pachman (1982)

CREDITS

COVER PHOTO CREDITS

FRONT COVER: Stephanie Gilliam cruising BOMBAY GROOVE (5.10a), Stone Mountain. Photo by Scott Eney
BACK COVER: (Upper left) Climbers on GREAT ARCH (5.5) and MERCURYS LEAD (5.9), Stone Mountain. Photo by Bill Webster
Upper Right: Robert Fogle on MR. HENAR (5.12b), Pilot Mountain. Photo by Bill Webster (**Lower Right)** Katie Hughes on the ultra-classic ZOO VIEW (5.7+), Moore's Wall. Photo by Jeff Dunbar (**Lower Left)** Erica Lineberry leading SLABSTERS LAMENT (5.12a), Crowder's Mountain. Photo by Manuela Eilert